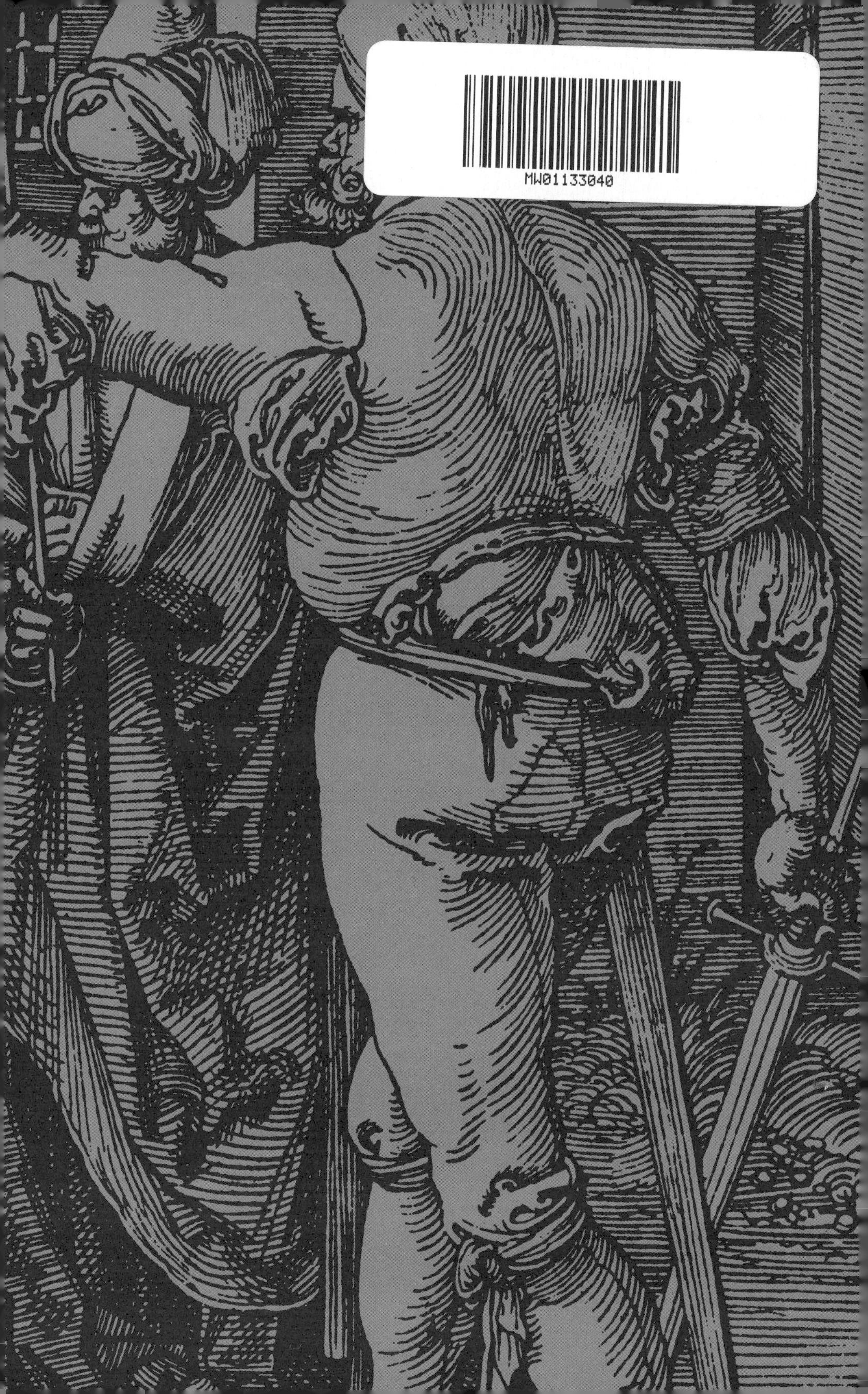

The Dark Horse Book of
The Dead

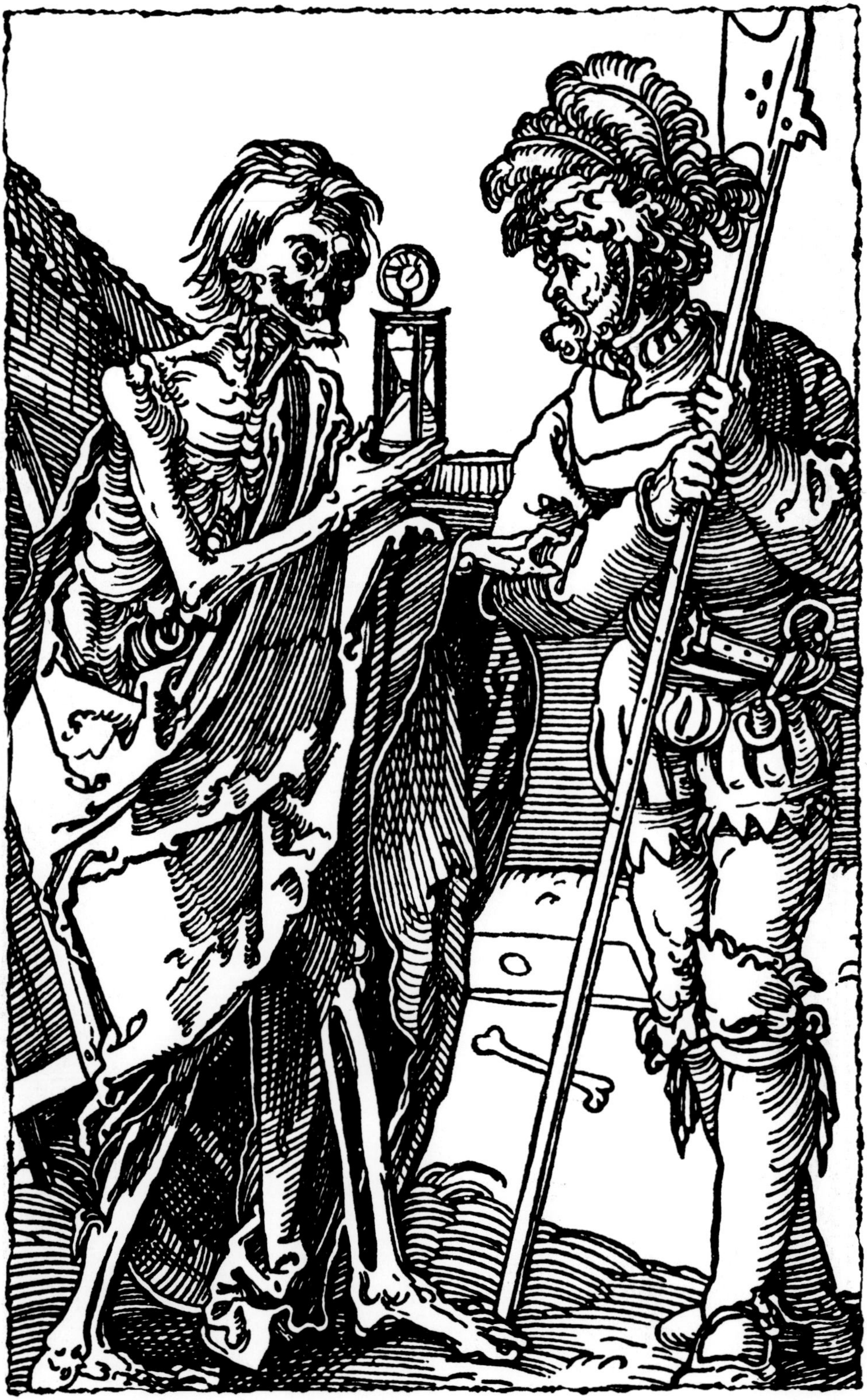

The
Dark Horse
Book of

The Dead

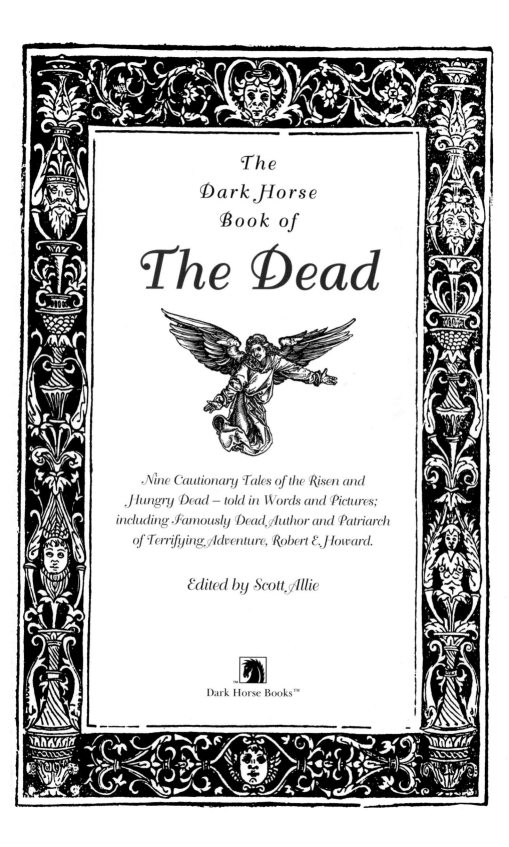

Nine Cautionary Tales of the Risen and
Hungry Dead – told in Words and Pictures;
including Famously Dead Author and Patriarch
of Terrifying Adventure, Robert E. Howard.

Edited by Scott Allie

Dark Horse Books™

Cover Illustration
Gary Gianni

Cover Design and Colors
Jim Keegan

Assistant Editor
Matt Dryer

Designer
Joshua Elliott

Art Director
Lia Ribacchi

Publisher
Mike Richardson

Special thanks to
Jason Hvam, Mark Cox, Jim Keegan, and Steve Tompkins.

Special thanks also to Barbara Baum at Robert E. Howard Properties and Gary Dunham at Bison Books for permission to use "Old Garfield's Heart." For other tales by Robert E. Howard, check out Bison Books at http://unp.unl.edu/books/bisonBooks.jsp.

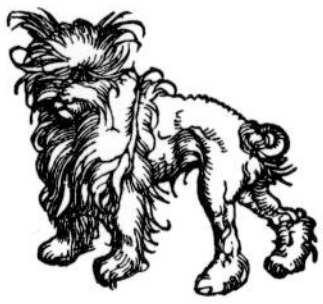

Published by Dark Horse Books
A division of Dark Horse Comics, Inc.
10956 SE Main Street
Milwaukie, OR 97222

First edition
June 2005
ISBN: 1-59307-281-3

1 3 5 7 9 10 8 6 4 2
Printed in China

Table of Contents

The Hungry Ghosts 7
Story and Art *Kelley Jones*   Colors *Michelle Madsen*   Letters *Nate Piekos*

The Ghoul 13
A Hellboy Adventure
Story and Art *Mike Mignola*   Colors *Dave Stewart*   Letters *Clem Robins*

Old Garfield's Heart 24
Story *Robert E. Howard*   Art *Gary Gianni*

The Ditch 35
Story *David Crouse*   Art *Todd Herman*
Colors *Dave Stewart*   Letters *Richard Starkings & Comicraft*

Death Boy 41
Story *Bob Fingerman*   Art *Roger Langridge*

The Wallace Expedition 49
Story and Art *Eric Powell*   Letters *Comicraft's JG Roshell*

Queen of Darkness 57
Story and Art *Pat McEown*   Colors and Letters *Michelle Madsen*

Kago No Tori 66
Story *Jamie S. Rich*   Art *Guy Davis*
Colors *Dave Stewart*   Letters *Lois Buhalis & Tom Orzechowski*

The Magicians 76
A Devil's Footprints Story
Story *Scott Allie*   Art *Paul Lee & Brian Horton*
Colors *Dave Stewart*   Letters *Michelle Madsen*

Let Sleeping Dogs Lie 85
Story *Evan Dorkin*   Art *Jill Thompson*

Introduction

I won't bore you with an unlikely anecdote this time. Actually, I have a couple, but I won't try to build a story around my childhood hallucinations of President Kennedy's limo rolling through my neighborhood with a bloodstained Jackie looking calmly ahead. And I shouldn't go too deeply into that first funeral I attended. I'd never laid eyes on that dead woman during her life, had never even seen a picture, but she'd been my own personal boogeyman, a threatening voice calling my house to tell seven-year-old me that it was *her* house. But it shows dubious taste to draw skeletons from the family closet in a book essentially about zombies.

This was supposed to be the last of this series, but cooler (and greedier) heads won out, and we'll be doing another next year. I'd thought that three volumes was pushing my luck enough as it was. I gave in mainly for my love of working with Gianni, Keegan, Mignola, Stewart, Thompson, Dorkin, Lee, Horton, and Madsen, the artists who've been with us every volume so far, and who seem willing to keep coming back. I've known most of the others joining us this time since I walked in the door at Dark Horse, and I'm grateful to be able to fill up books with work that genuinely excites me. I've been on this job for ten years, and have watched other people lucky enough to work in comics grow bored with it. Everybody in this book has contributed in some way to keeping the art form new for me, and I hope this book, or any one of the books I've made, has the same effect on you.

These days zombies are upbeat, fun, even celebratory, so hopefully this foreword has been a not-too-clichéd expression of gratitude, with its sentiment about hoping that you enjoy this job that we enjoy doing for you. On behalf of Matt Dryer and our boss, Mike Richardson, thanks for supporting us as we host these parties.

R.I.P.,

Scott Allie

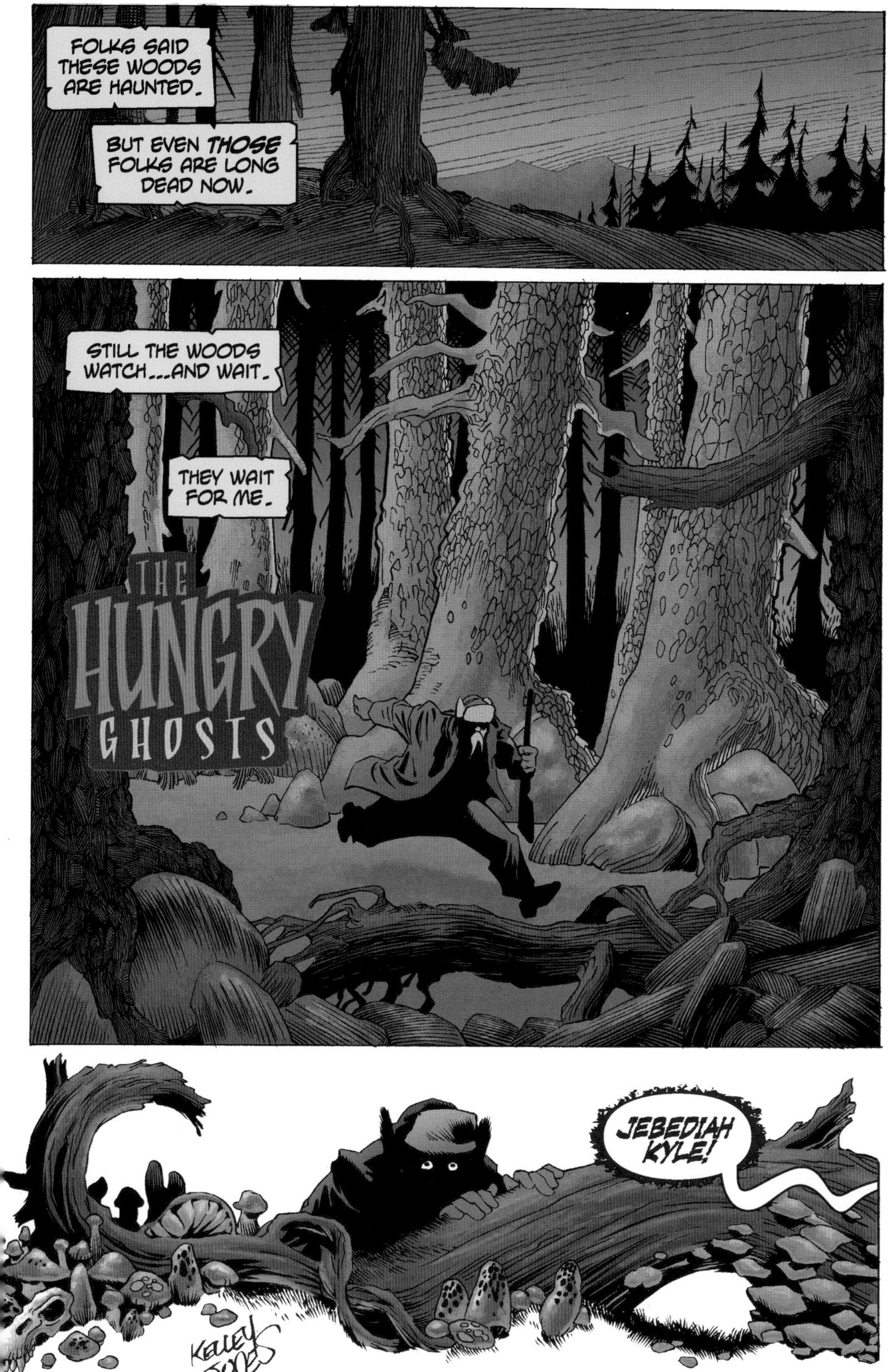
FOLKS SAID THESE WOODS ARE HAUNTED.
BUT EVEN THOSE FOLKS ARE LONG DEAD NOW.
STILL THE WOODS WATCH...AND WAIT.
THEY WAIT FOR ME.
THE HUNGRY GHOSTS
JEBEDIAH KYLE!
KELLEY JONES '04

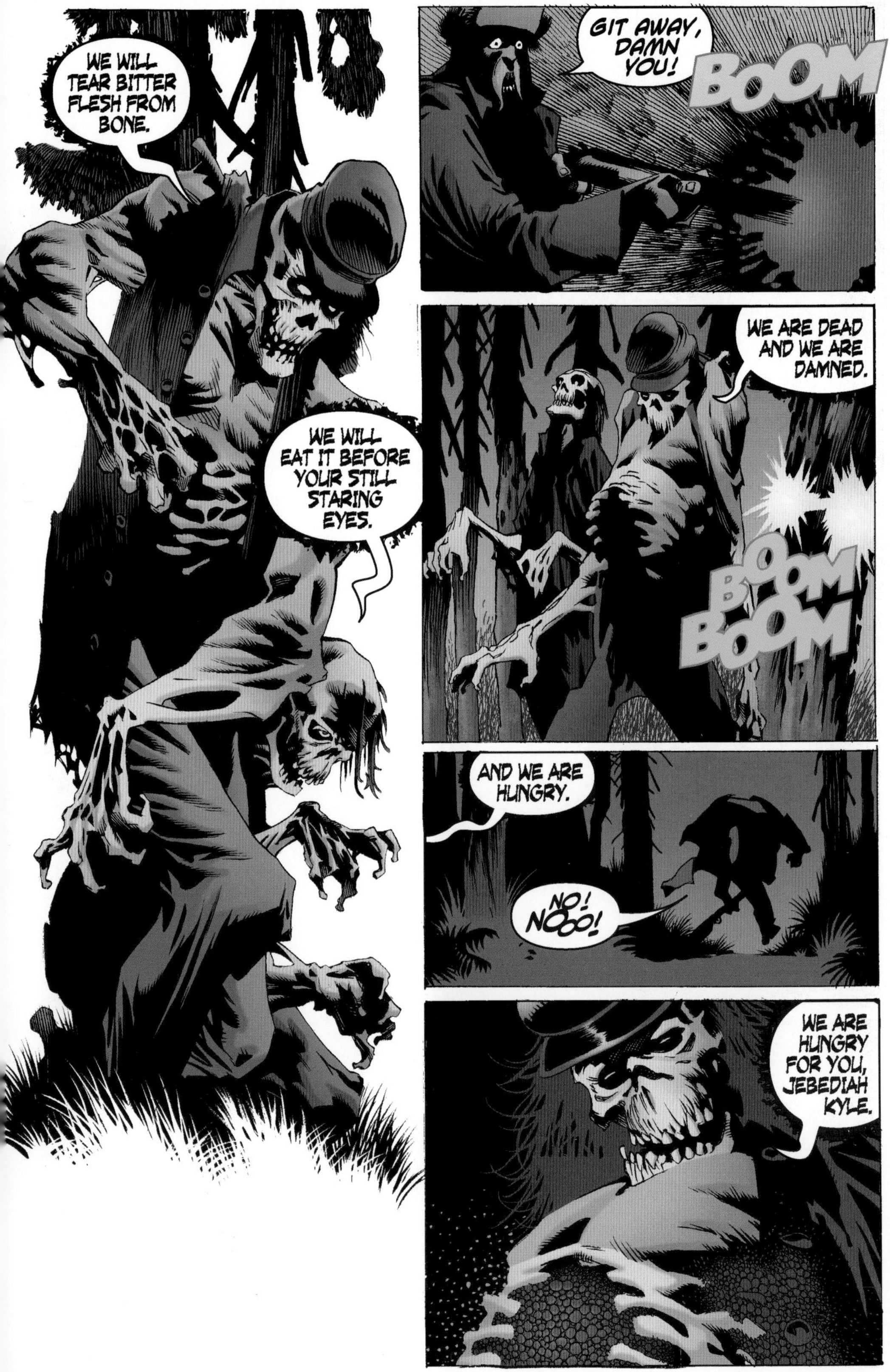
WE WILL TEAR BITTER FLESH FROM BONE.
WE WILL EAT IT BEFORE YOUR STILL STARING EYES.
GIT AWAY, DAMN YOU!
BOOM
WE ARE DEAD AND WE ARE DAMNED.
BOOM BOOM BOOM
AND WE ARE HUNGRY.
NO! NOOO!
WE ARE HUNGRY FOR YOU, JEBEDIAH KYLE.

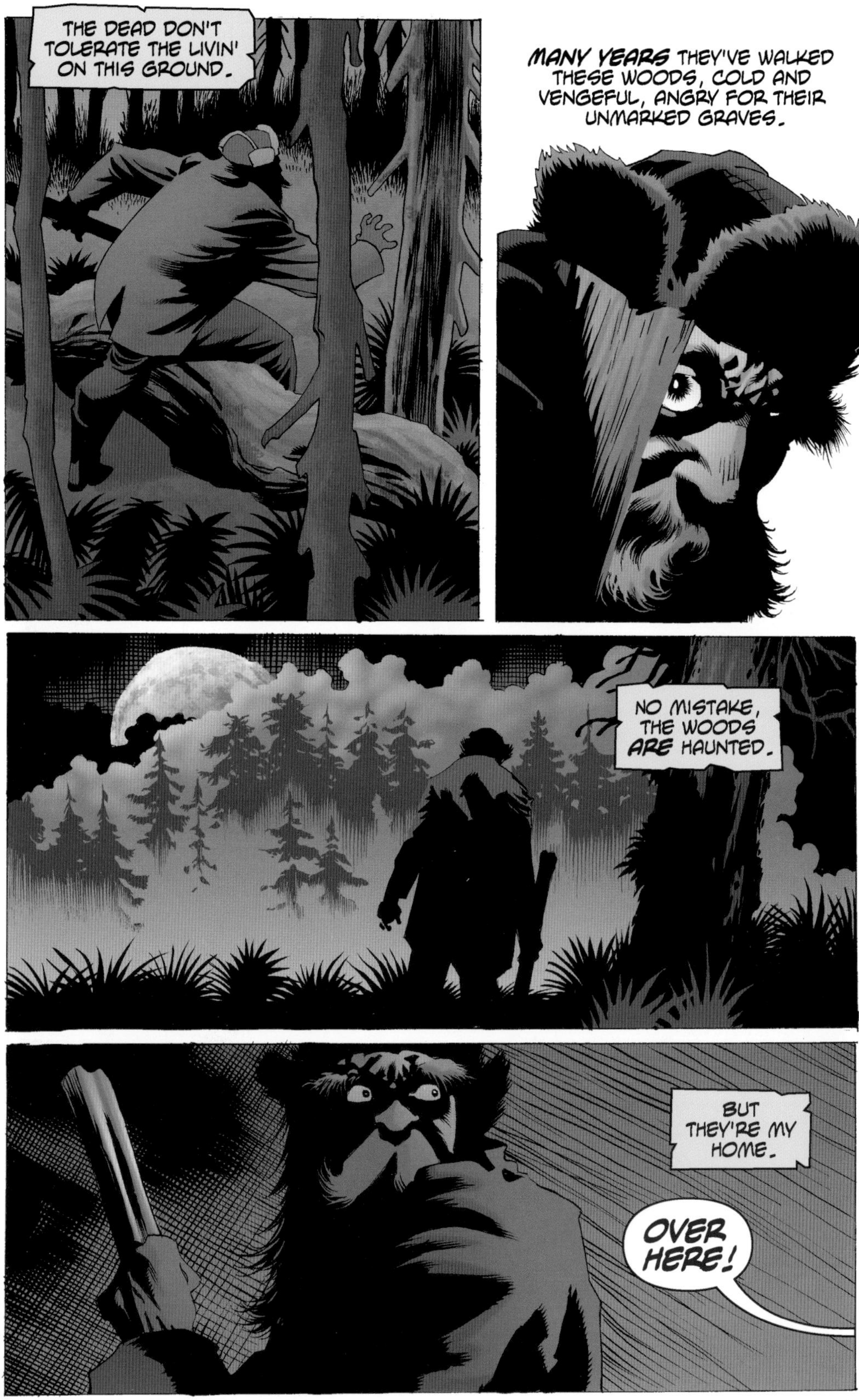
THE DEAD DON'T TOLERATE THE LIVIN' ON THIS GROUND.
MANY YEARS THEY'VE WALKED THESE WOODS, COLD AND VENGEFUL, ANGRY FOR THEIR UNMARKED GRAVES.
NO MISTAKE, THE WOODS ARE HAUNTED.
BUT THEY'RE MY HOME.
OVER HERE!

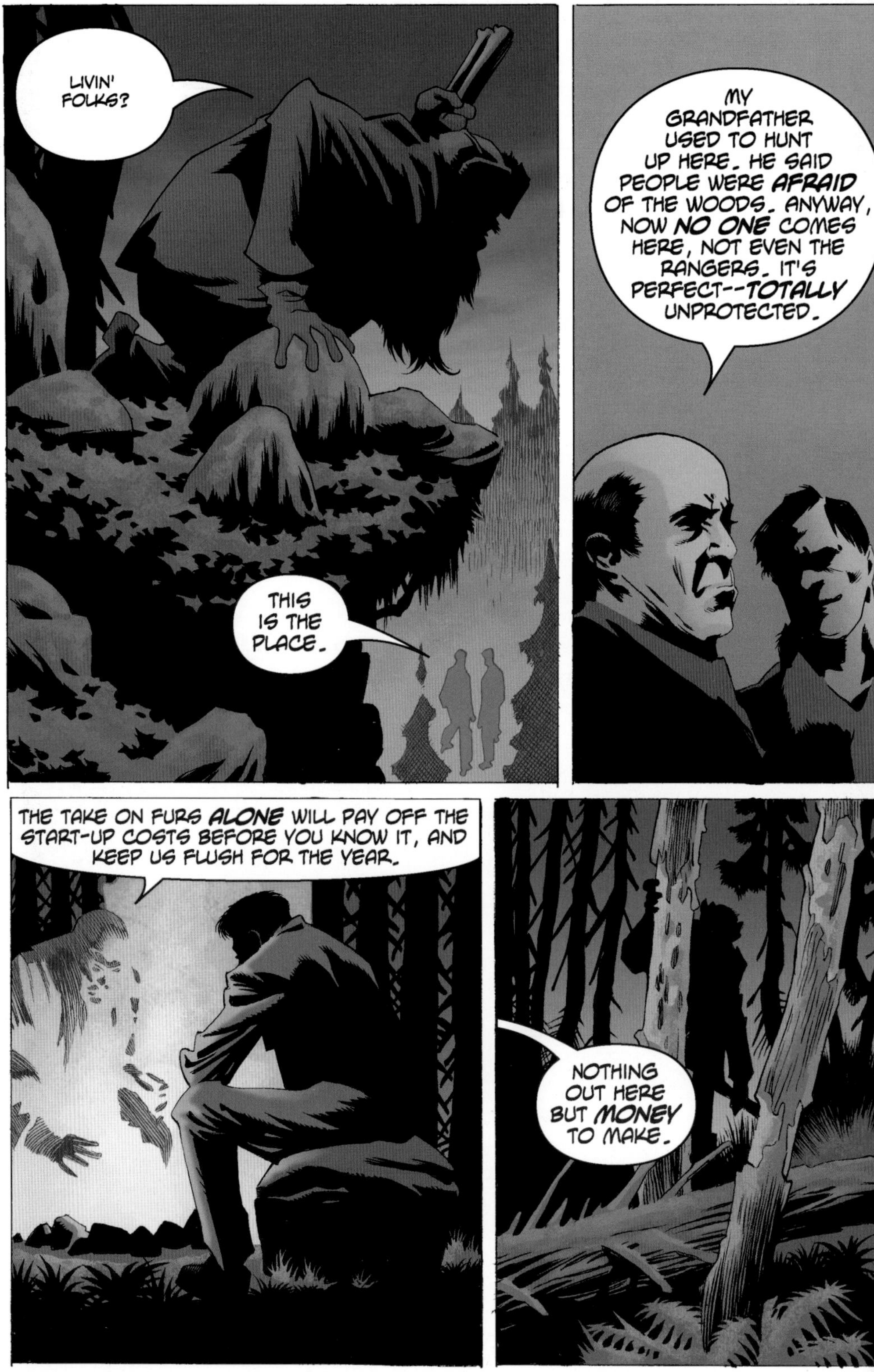
LIVIN' FOLKS?
THIS IS THE PLACE.
MY GRANDFATHER USED TO HUNT UP HERE. HE SAID PEOPLE WERE AFRAID OF THE WOODS. ANYWAY, NOW NO ONE COMES HERE, NOT EVEN THE RANGERS. IT'S PERFECT--TOTALLY UNPROTECTED.
THE TAKE ON FURS ALONE WILL PAY OFF THE START-UP COSTS BEFORE YOU KNOW IT, AND KEEP US FLUSH FOR THE YEAR.
NOTHING OUT HERE BUT MONEY TO MAKE.

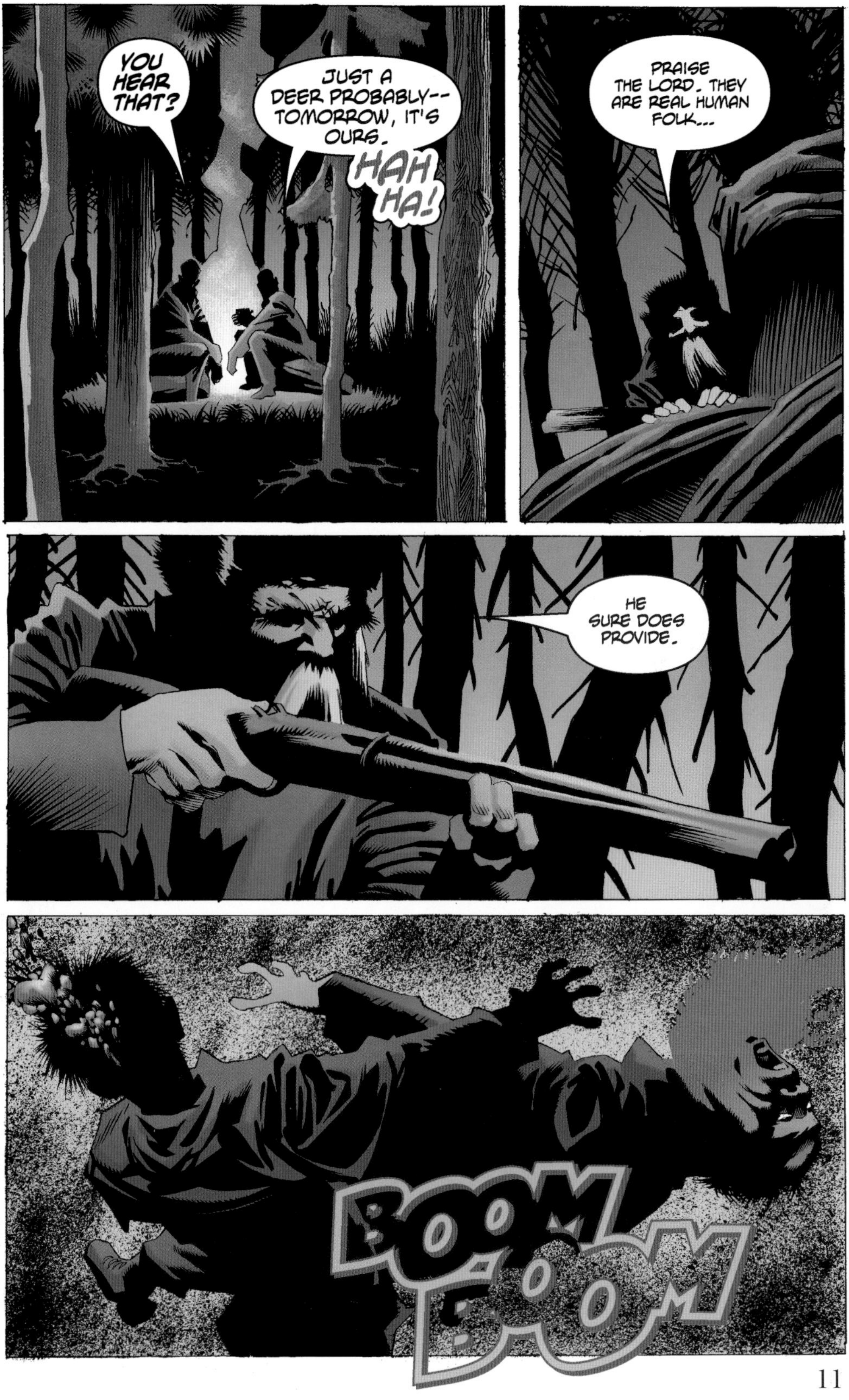
YOU HEAR THAT?
JUST A DEER PROBABLY-- TOMORROW, IT'S OURS.
HAH HA!
PRAISE THE LORD. THEY ARE REAL HUMAN FOLK...
HE SURE DOES PROVIDE.
BOOM
BOOM

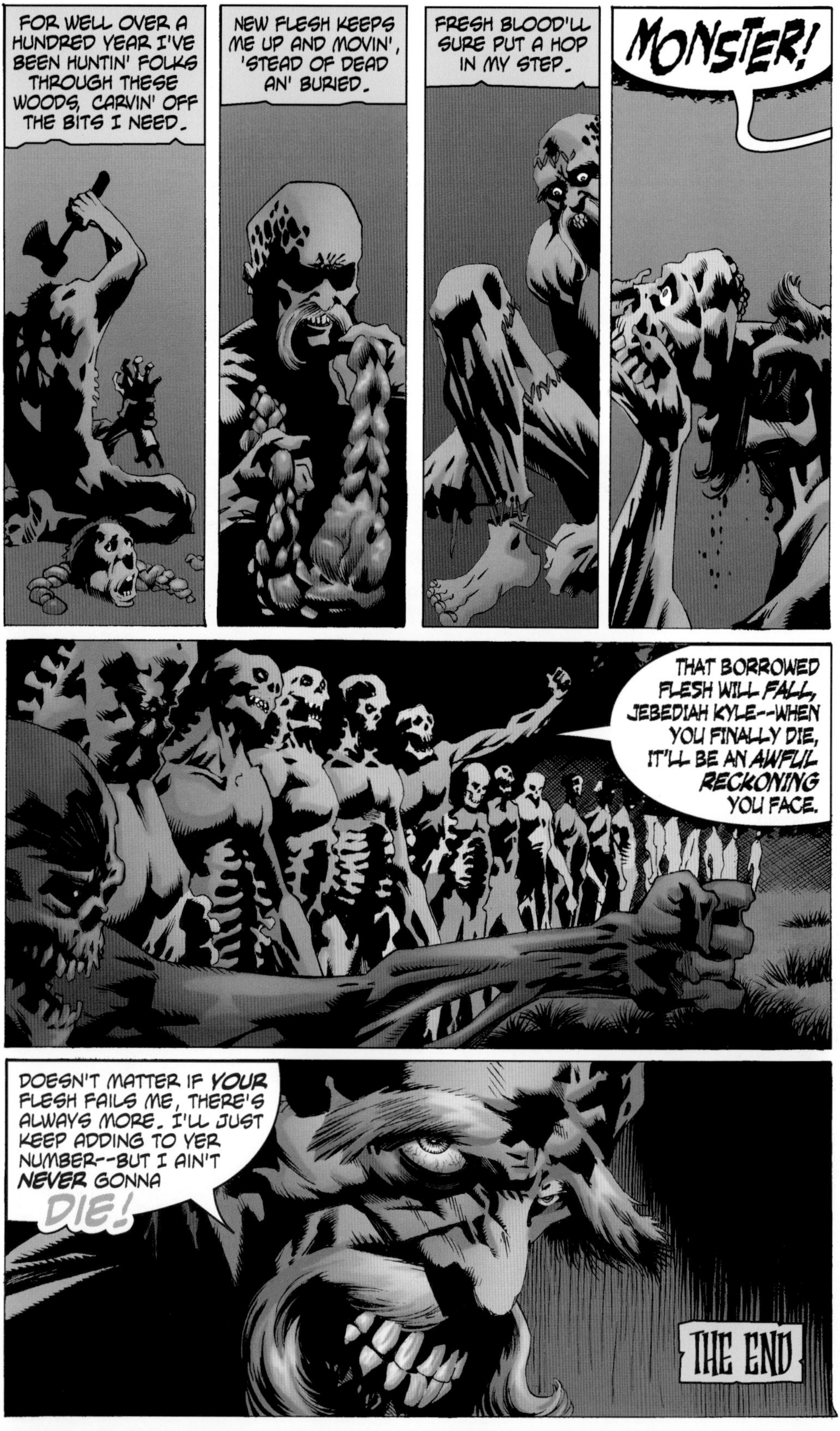
FOR WELL OVER A HUNDRED YEAR I'VE BEEN HUNTIN' FOLKS THROUGH THESE WOODS, CARVIN' OFF THE BITS I NEED.
NEW FLESH KEEPS ME UP AND MOVIN', 'STEAD OF DEAD AN' BURIED.
FRESH BLOOD'LL SURE PUT A HOP IN MY STEP.
MONSTER!
THAT BORROWED FLESH WILL FALL, JEBEDIAH KYLE--WHEN YOU FINALLY DIE, IT'LL BE AN AWFUL RECKONING YOU FACE.
DOESN'T MATTER IF YOUR FLESH FAILS ME, THERE'S ALWAYS MORE. I'LL JUST KEEP ADDING TO YER NUMBER--BUT I AIN'T NEVER GONNA DIE!
THE END

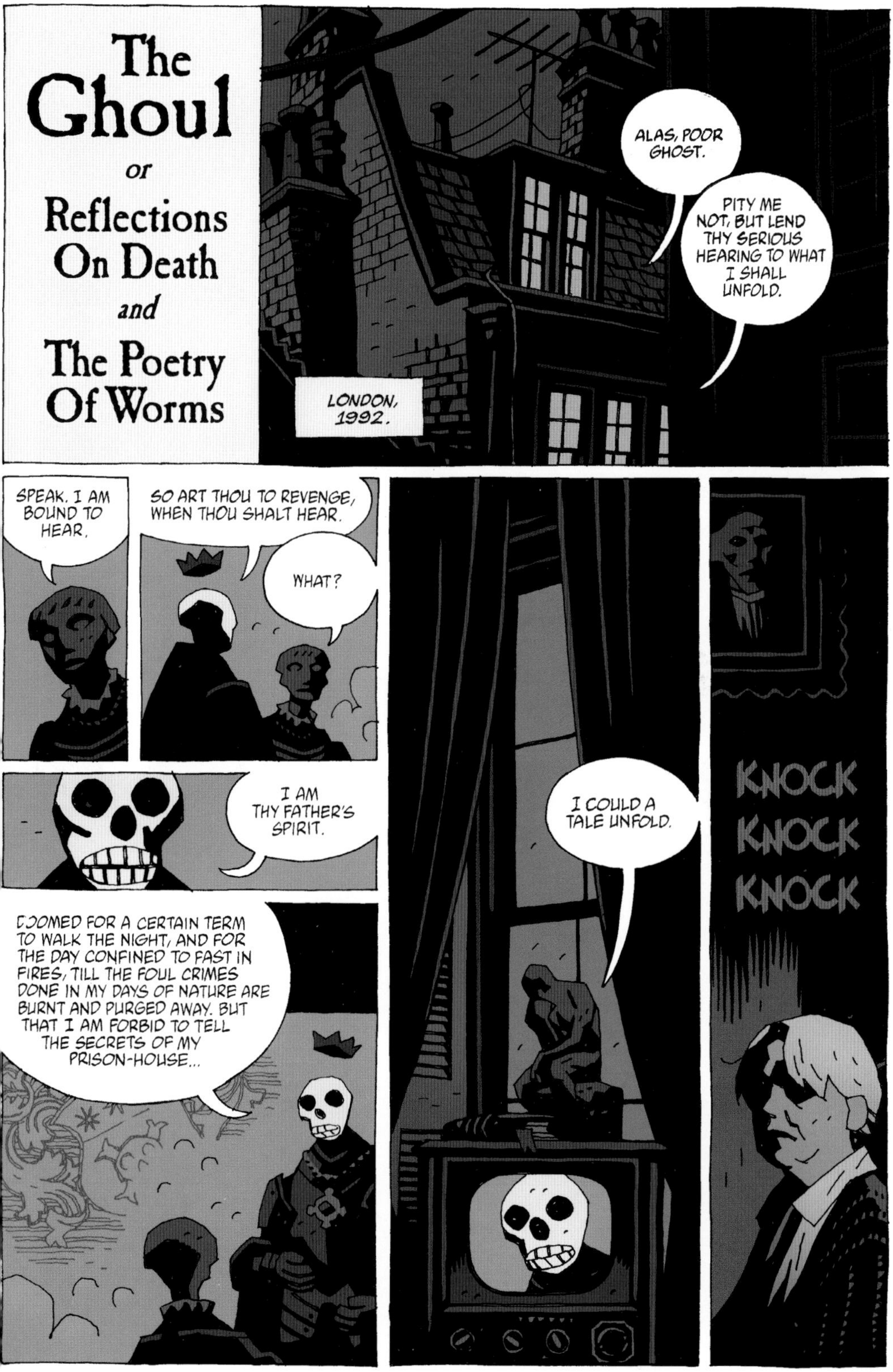
The Ghoul or Reflections On Death and The Poetry Of Worms
LONDON, 1992.
ALAS, POOR GHOST.
PITY ME NOT, BUT LEND THY SERIOUS HEARING TO WHAT I SHALL UNFOLD.
SPEAK. I AM BOUND TO HEAR.
SO ART THOU TO REVENGE, WHEN THOU SHALT HEAR.
WHAT?
I AM THY FATHER'S SPIRIT.
DOOMED FOR A CERTAIN TERM TO WALK THE NIGHT, AND FOR THE DAY CONFINED TO FAST IN FIRES, TILL THE FOUL CRIMES DONE IN MY DAYS OF NATURE ARE BURNT AND PURGED AWAY. BUT THAT I AM FORBID TO TELL THE SECRETS OF MY PRISON-HOUSE...
I COULD A TALE UNFOLD.
KNOCK
KNOCK
KNOCK

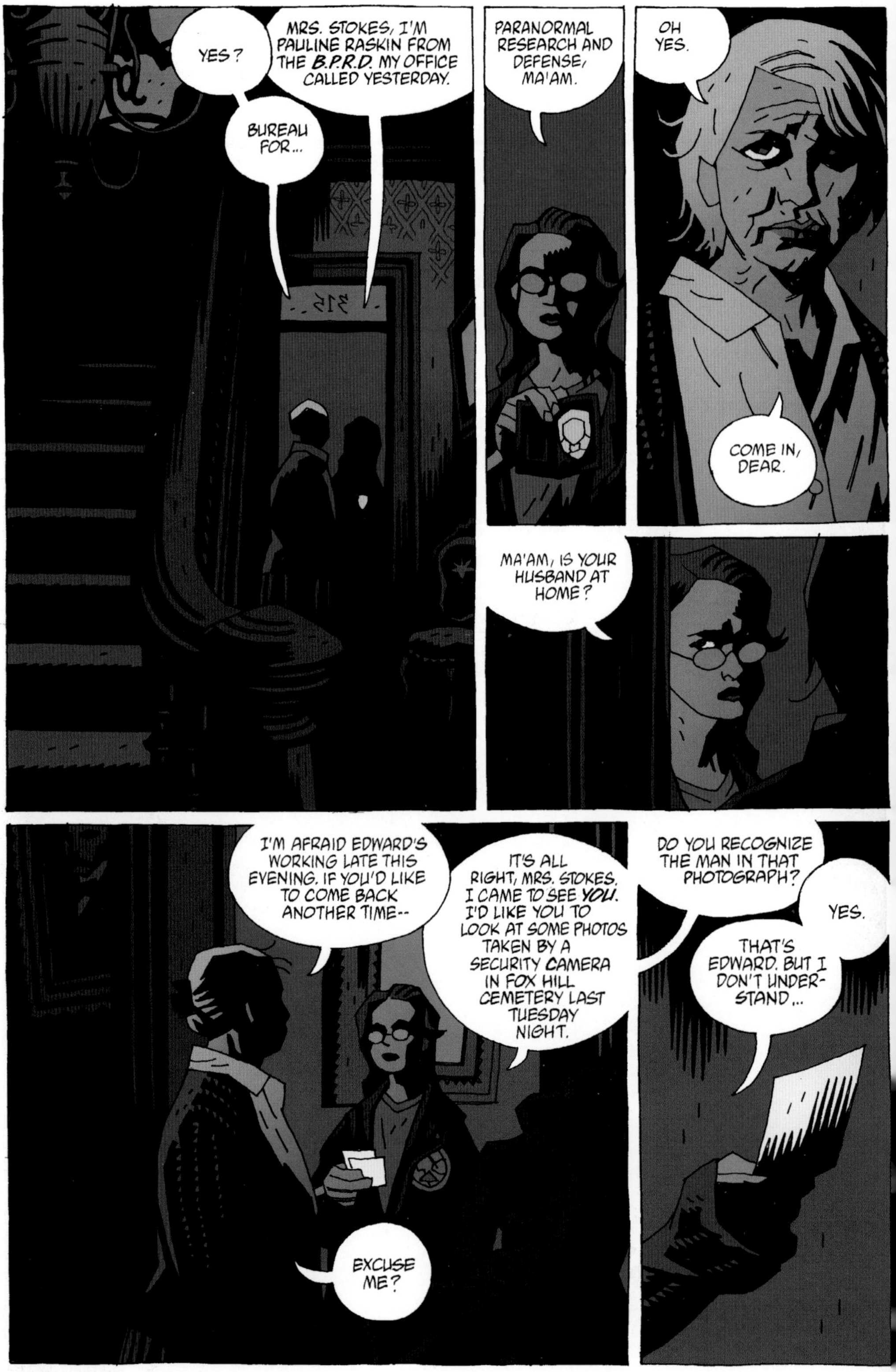
YES?
MRS. STOKES, I'M PAULINE RASKIN FROM THE B.P.R.D. MY OFFICE CALLED YESTERDAY.
BUREAU FOR...
315
PARANORMAL RESEARCH AND DEFENSE, MA'AM.
OH YES.
COME IN, DEAR.
MA'AM, IS YOUR HUSBAND AT HOME?
I'M AFRAID EDWARD'S WORKING LATE THIS EVENING. IF YOU'D LIKE TO COME BACK ANOTHER TIME--
IT'S ALL RIGHT, MRS. STOKES. I CAME TO SEE YOU. I'D LIKE YOU TO LOOK AT SOME PHOTOS TAKEN BY A SECURITY CAMERA IN FOX HILL CEMETERY LAST TUESDAY NIGHT.
EXCUSE ME?
DO YOU RECOGNIZE THE MAN IN THAT PHOTOGRAPH?
YES.
THAT'S EDWARD. BUT I DON'T UNDERSTAND...

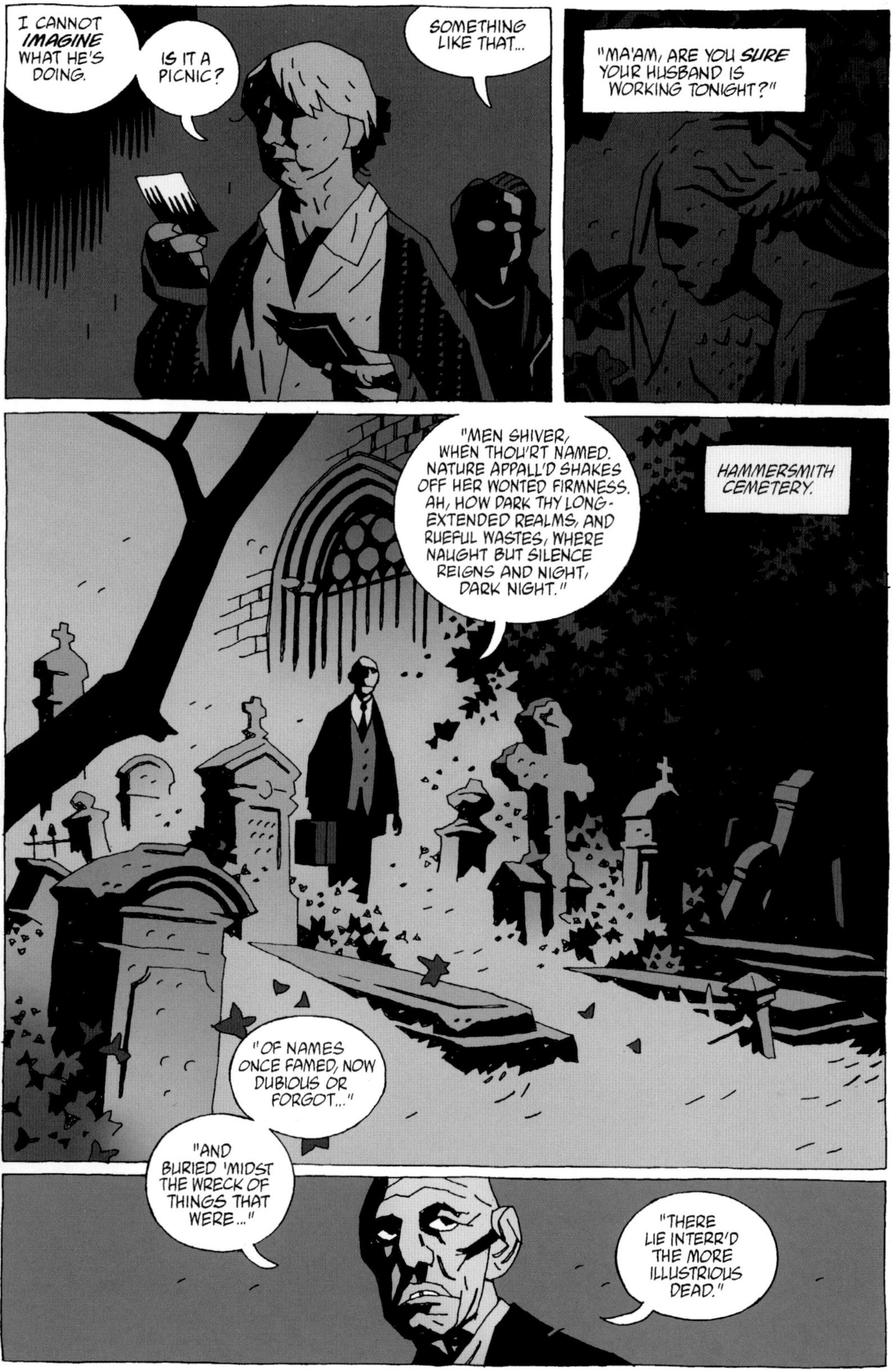
I CANNOT IMAGINE WHAT HE'S DOING.
IS IT A PICNIC?
SOMETHING LIKE THAT...
"MA'AM, ARE YOU SURE YOUR HUSBAND IS WORKING TONIGHT?"
"MEN SHIVER, WHEN THOU'RT NAMED. NATURE APPALL'D SHAKES OFF HER WONTED FIRMNESS. AH, HOW DARK THY LONG-EXTENDED REALMS, AND RUEFUL WASTES, WHERE NAUGHT BUT SILENCE REIGNS AND NIGHT, DARK NIGHT."
HAMMERSMITH CEMETERY.
"OF NAMES ONCE FAMED, NOW DUBIOUS OR FORGOT..."
"AND BURIED 'MIDST THE WRECK OF THINGS THAT WERE..."
"THERE LIE INTERR'D THE MORE ILLUSTRIOUS DEAD."

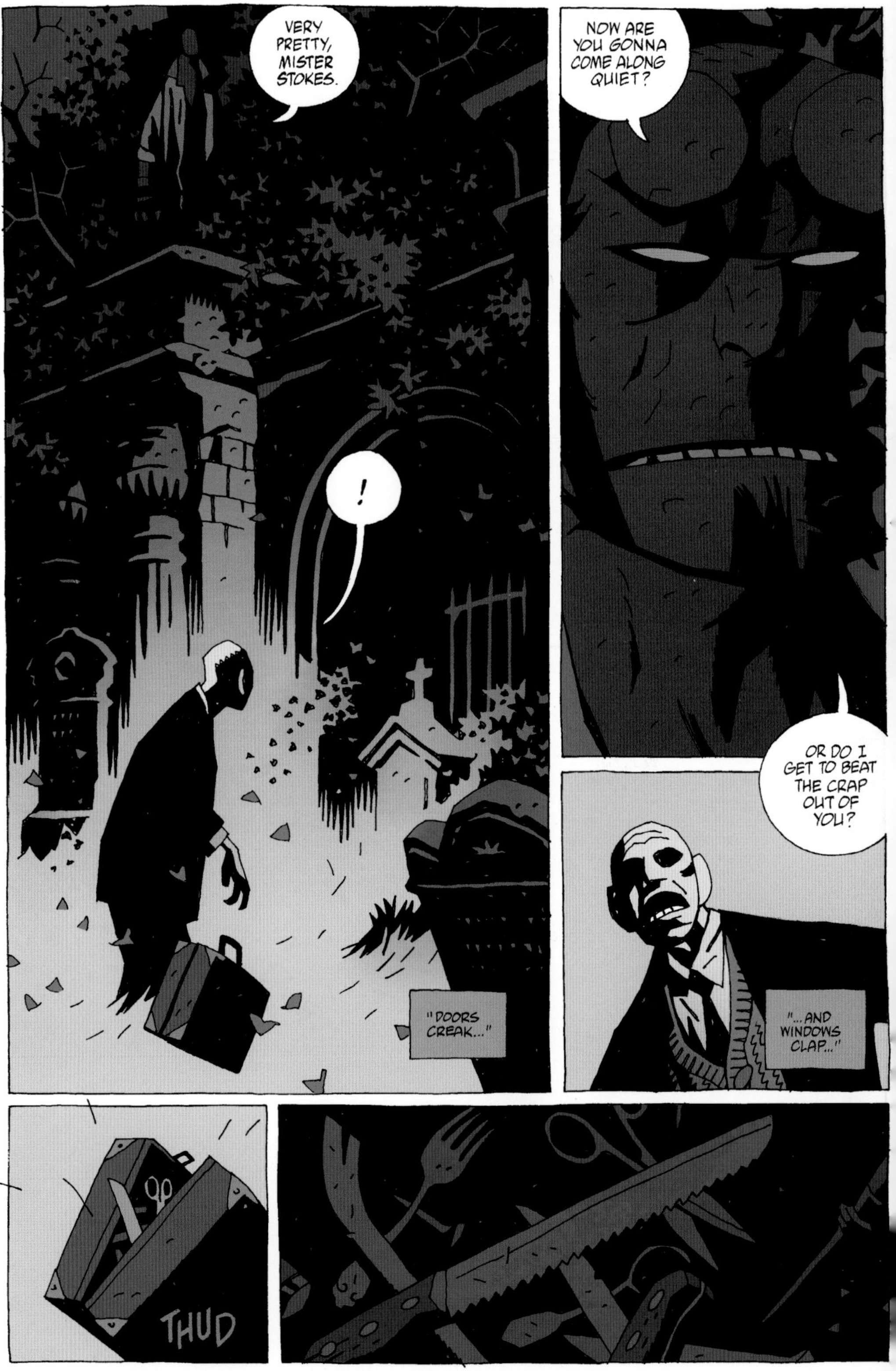
VERY PRETTY, MISTER STOKES.
!
"DOORS CREAK..."
NOW ARE YOU GONNA COME ALONG QUIET?
OR DO I GET TO BEAT THE CRAP OUT OF YOU?
"...AND WINDOWS CLAP..."
THUD

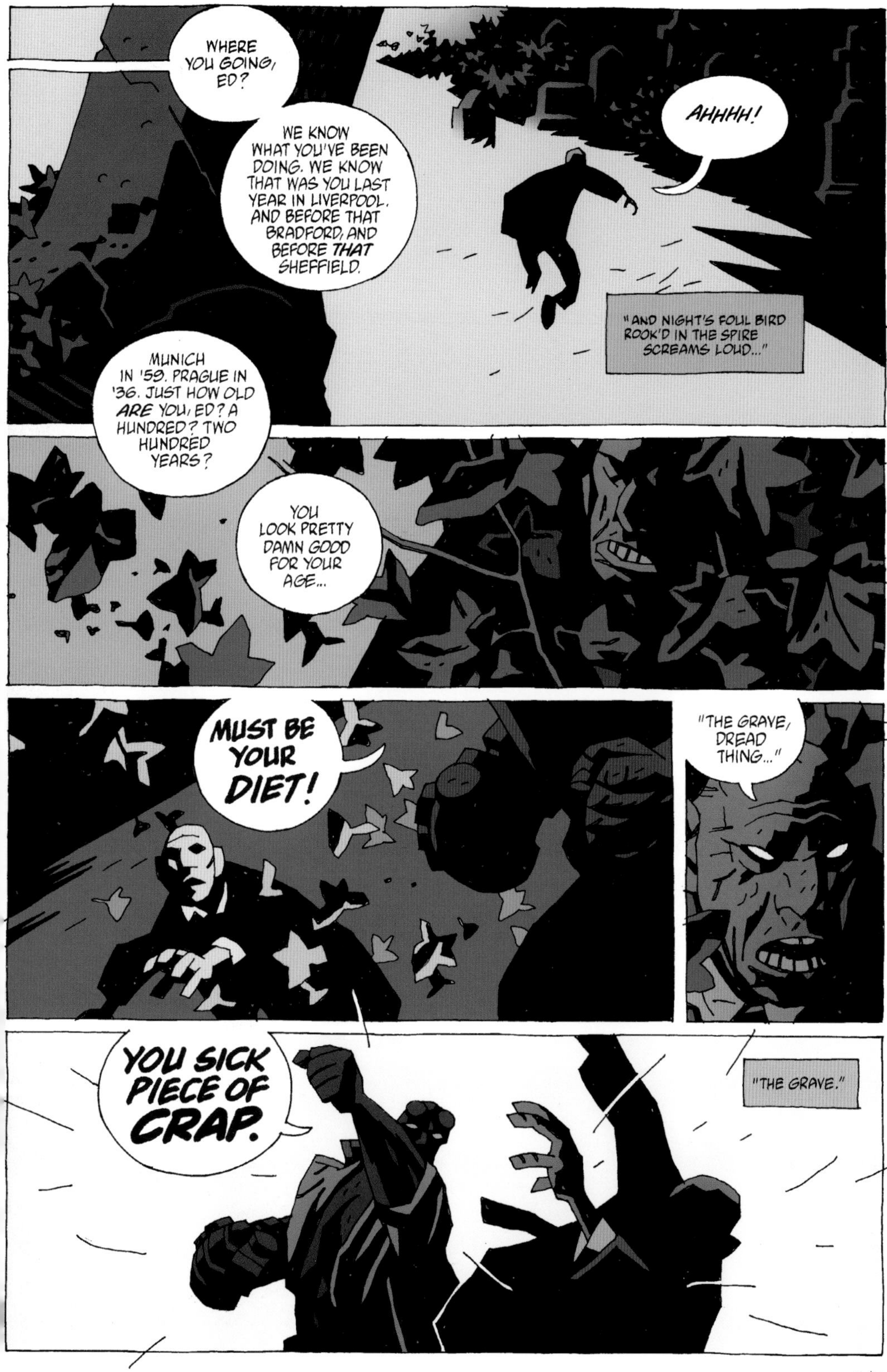
WHERE YOU GOING, ED?
WE KNOW WHAT YOU'VE BEEN DOING. WE KNOW THAT WAS YOU LAST YEAR IN LIVERPOOL, AND BEFORE THAT BRADFORD, AND BEFORE THAT SHEFFIELD.
AHHHH!
"AND NIGHT'S FOUL BIRD ROOK'D IN THE SPIRE SCREAMS LOUD..."
MUNICH IN '59. PRAGUE IN '36. JUST HOW OLD ARE YOU, ED? A HUNDRED? TWO HUNDRED YEARS?
YOU LOOK PRETTY DAMN GOOD FOR YOUR AGE...
MUST BE YOUR DIET!
"THE GRAVE, DREAD THING..."
YOU SICK PIECE OF CRAP.
"THE GRAVE."

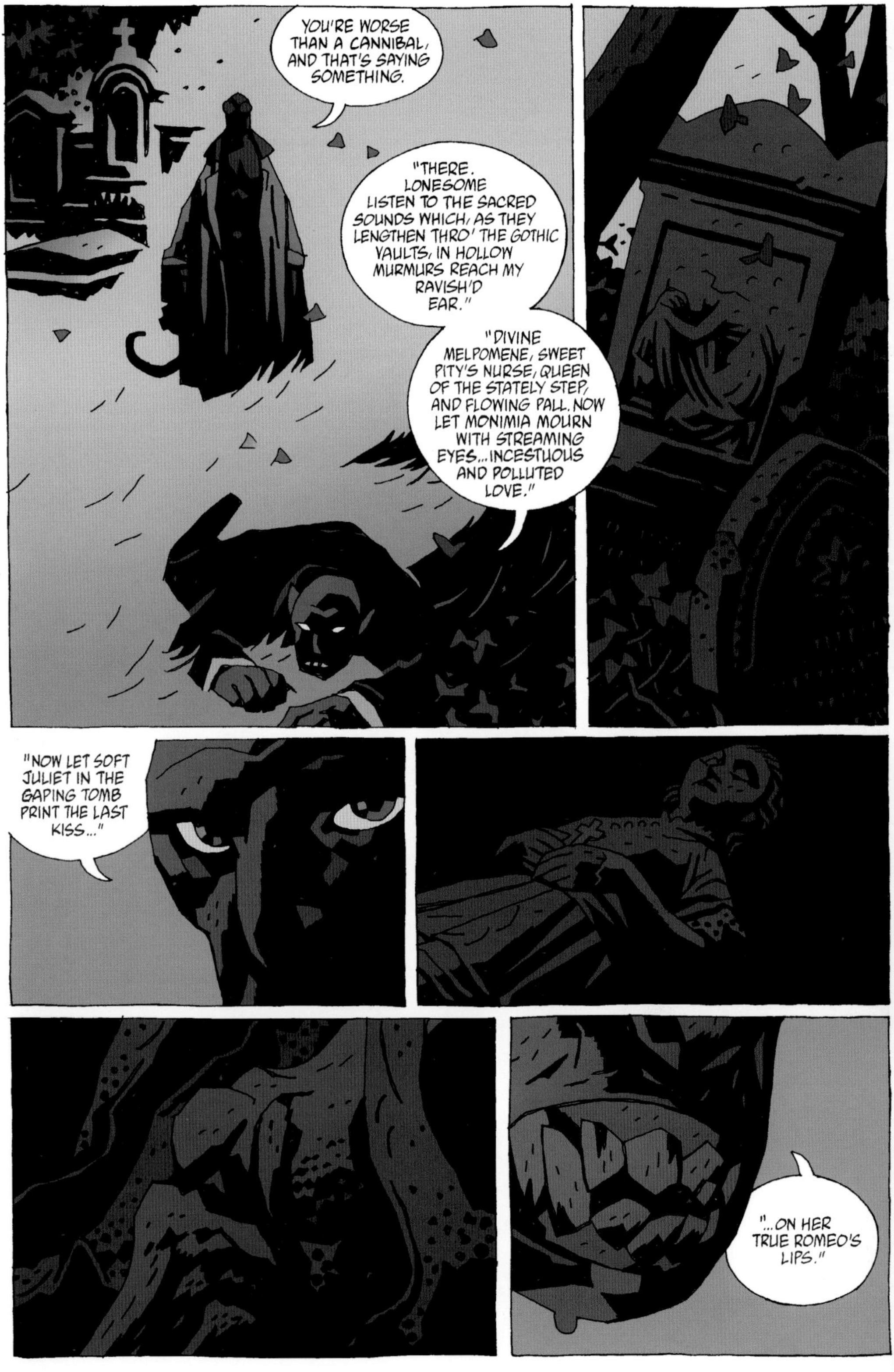
YOU'RE WORSE THAN A CANNIBAL, AND THAT'S SAYING SOMETHING.
"THERE. LONESOME LISTEN TO THE SACRED SOUNDS WHICH, AS THEY LENGTHEN THRO' THE GOTHIC VAULTS, IN HOLLOW MURMURS REACH MY RAVISH'D EAR."
"DIVINE MELPOMENE, SWEET PITY'S NURSE, QUEEN OF THE STATELY STEP, AND FLOWING PALL. NOW LET MONIMIA MOURN WITH STREAMING EYES... INCESTUOUS AND POLLUTED LOVE."
"NOW LET SOFT JULIET IN THE GAPING TOMB PRINT THE LAST KISS..."
"...ON HER TRUE ROMEO'S LIPS."

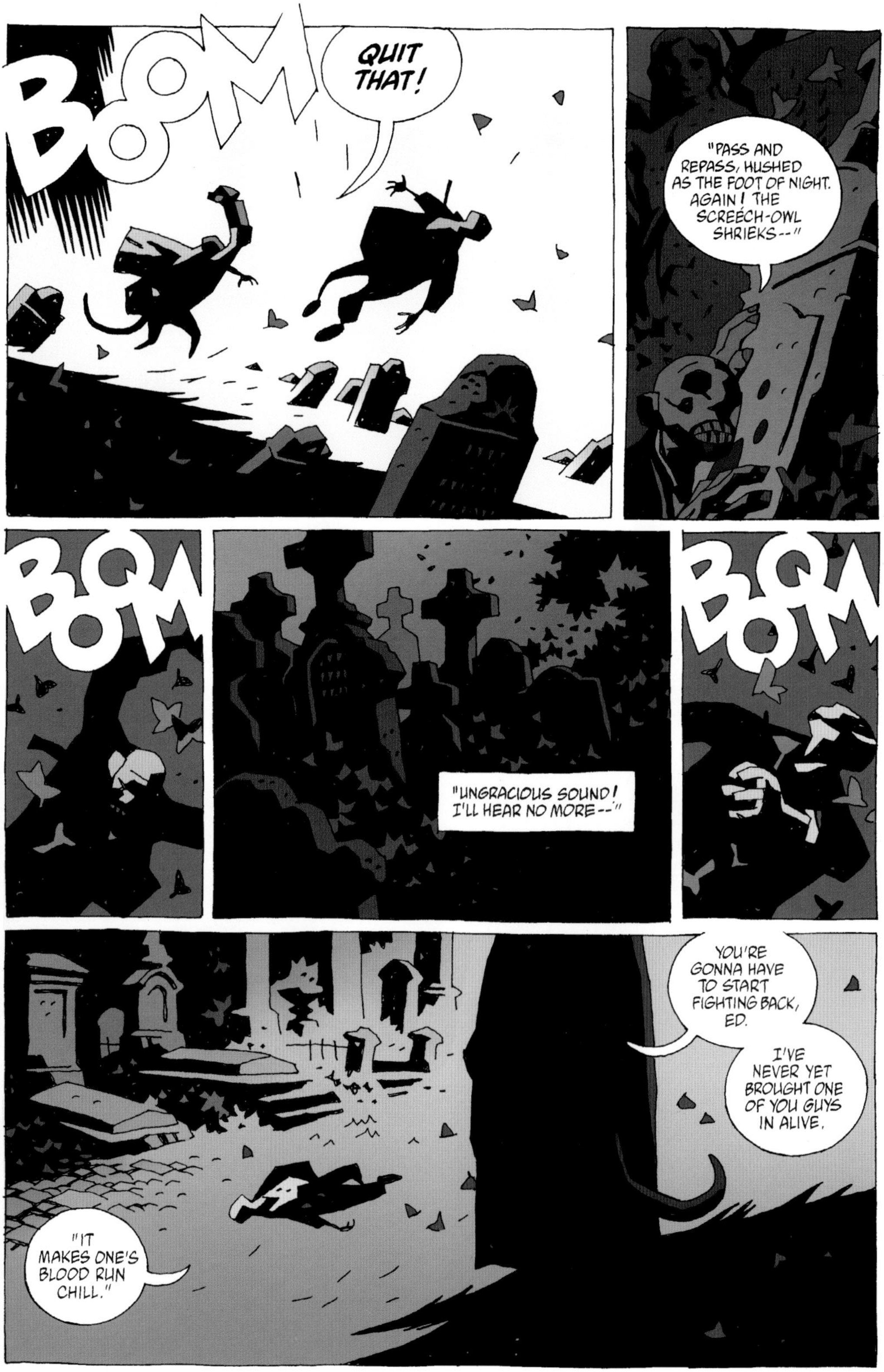
BOOM
QUIT THAT!
"PASS AND REPASS, HUSHED AS THE FOOT OF NIGHT. AGAIN! THE SCREECH-OWL SHRIEKS--"
BOOM
"UNGRACIOUS SOUND! I'LL HEAR NO MORE--"
BOOM
YOU'RE GONNA HAVE TO START FIGHTING BACK, ED.
I'VE NEVER YET BROUGHT ONE OF YOU GUYS IN ALIVE.
"IT MAKES ONE'S BLOOD RUN CHILL."

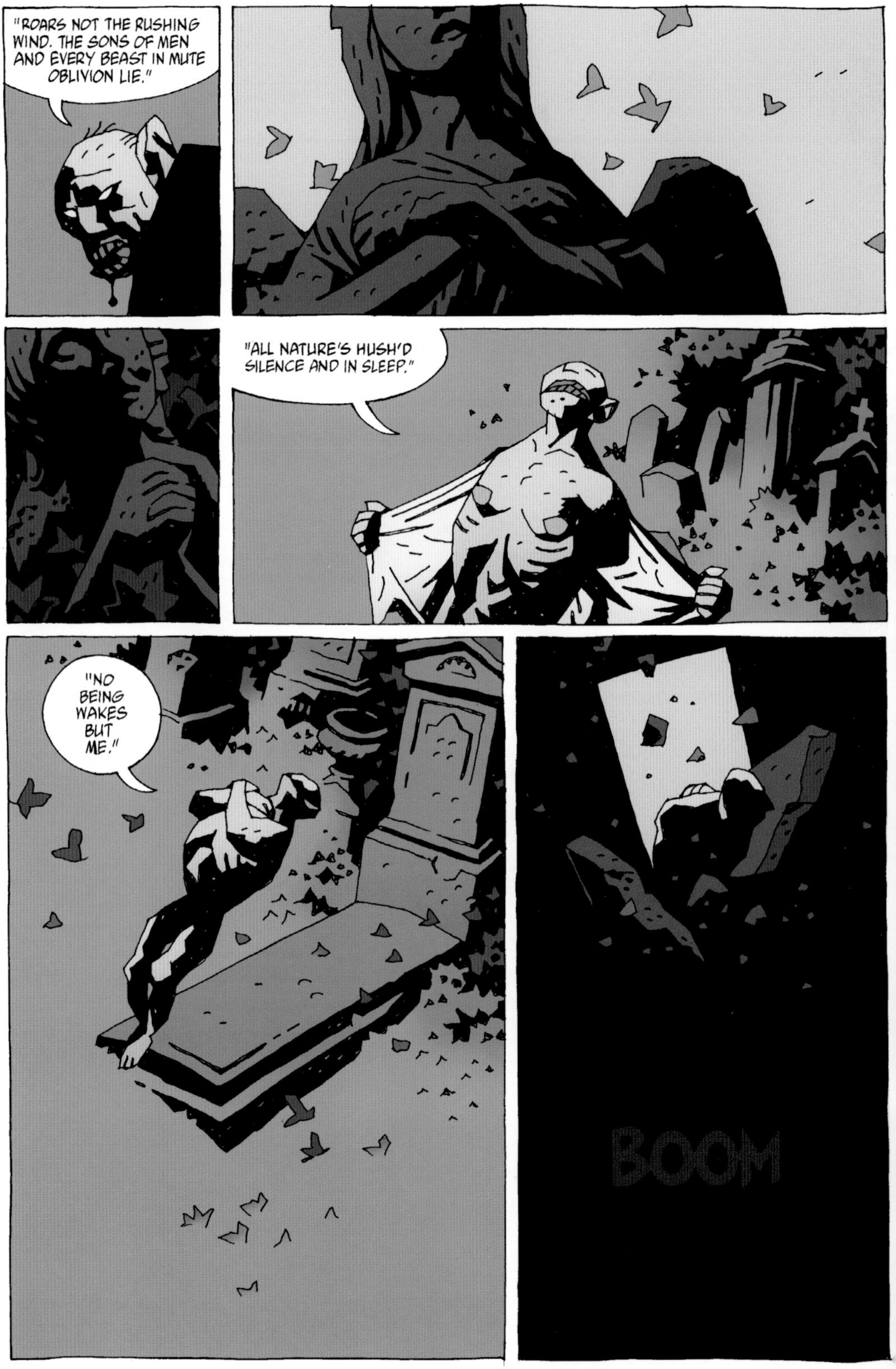
"ROARS NOT THE RUSHING WIND. THE SONS OF MEN AND EVERY BEAST IN MUTE OBLIVION LIE."
"ALL NATURE'S HUSH'D SILENCE AND IN SLEEP."
"NO BEING WAKES BUT ME."
BOOM

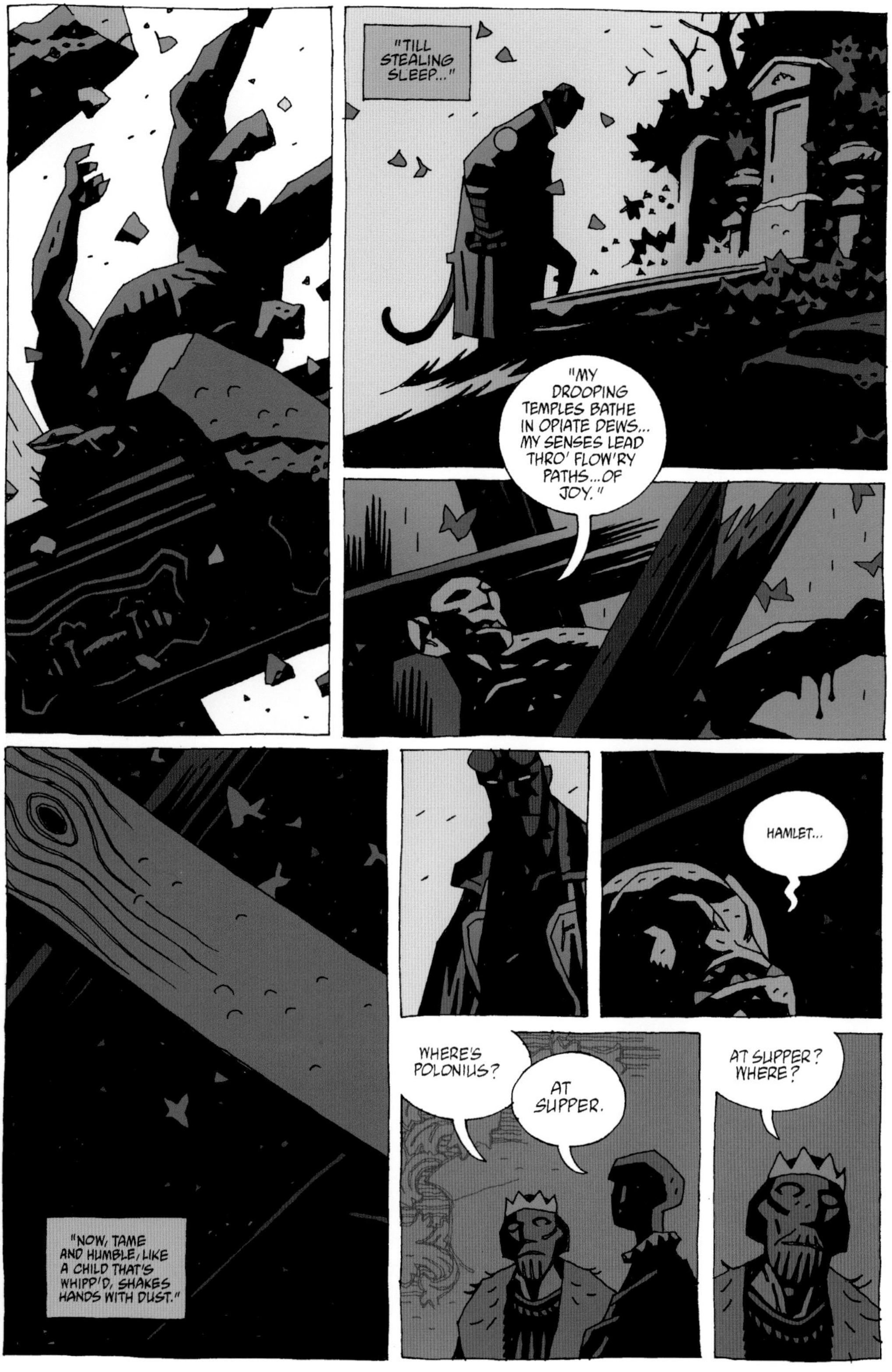
"TILL STEALING SLEEP..."
"MY DROOPING TEMPLES BATHE IN OPIATE DEWS... MY SENSES LEAD THRO' FLOW'RY PATHS...OF JOY."
"NOW, TAME AND HUMBLE, LIKE A CHILD THAT'S WHIPP'D, SHAKES HANDS WITH DUST."
HAMLET...
WHERE'S POLONIUS?
AT SUPPER.
AT SUPPER? WHERE?

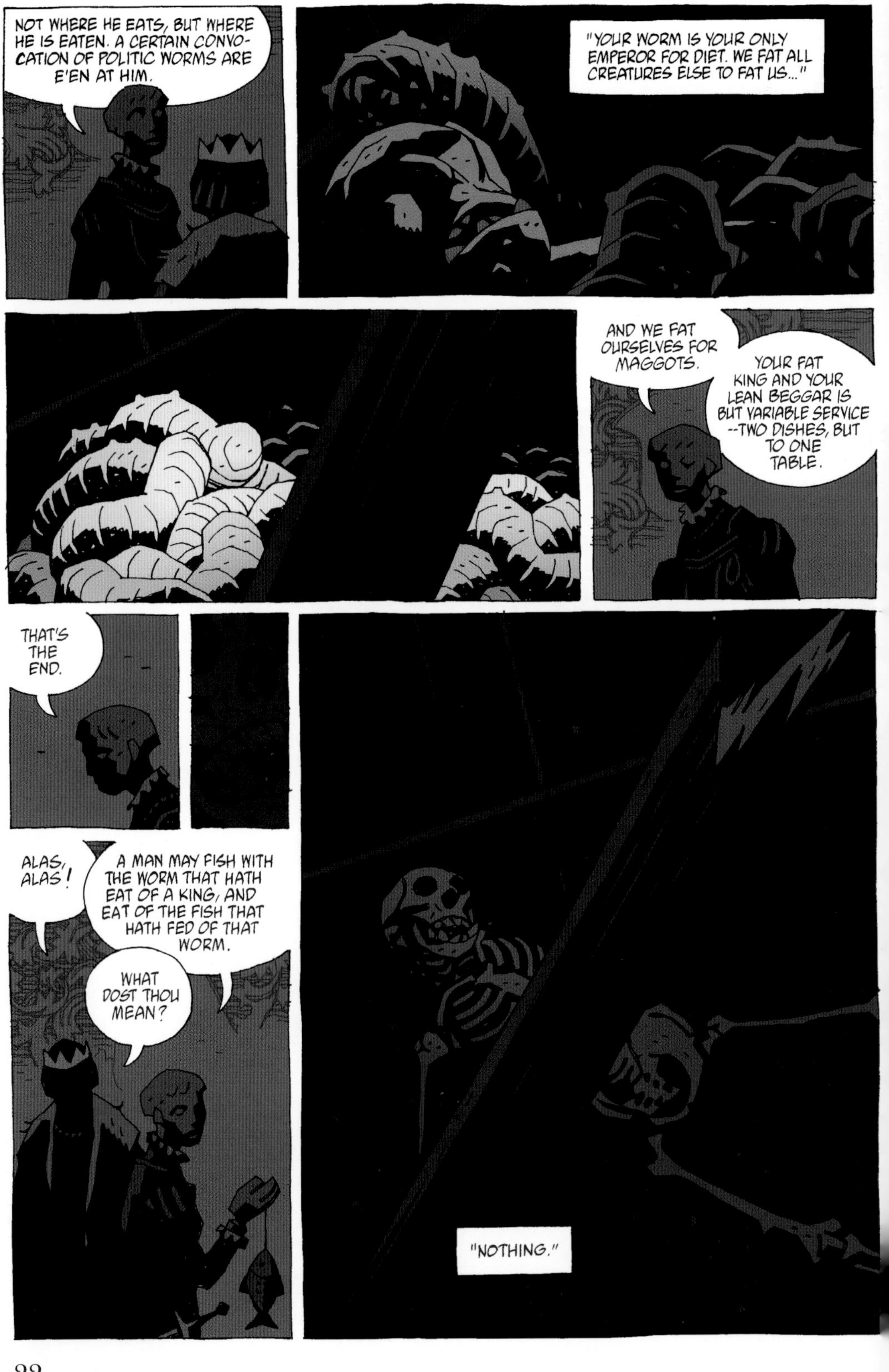
NOT WHERE HE EATS, BUT WHERE HE IS EATEN. A CERTAIN CONVOCATION OF POLITIC WORMS ARE E'EN AT HIM.
"YOUR WORM IS YOUR ONLY EMPEROR FOR DIET. WE FAT ALL CREATURES ELSE TO FAT US..."
AND WE FAT OURSELVES FOR MAGGOTS.
YOUR FAT KING AND YOUR LEAN BEGGAR IS BUT VARIABLE SERVICE --TWO DISHES, BUT TO ONE TABLE.
THAT'S THE END.
ALAS, ALAS!
A MAN MAY FISH WITH THE WORM THAT HATH EAT OF A KING, AND EAT OF THE FISH THAT HATH FED OF THAT WORM.
WHAT DOST THOU MEAN?
"NOTHING."

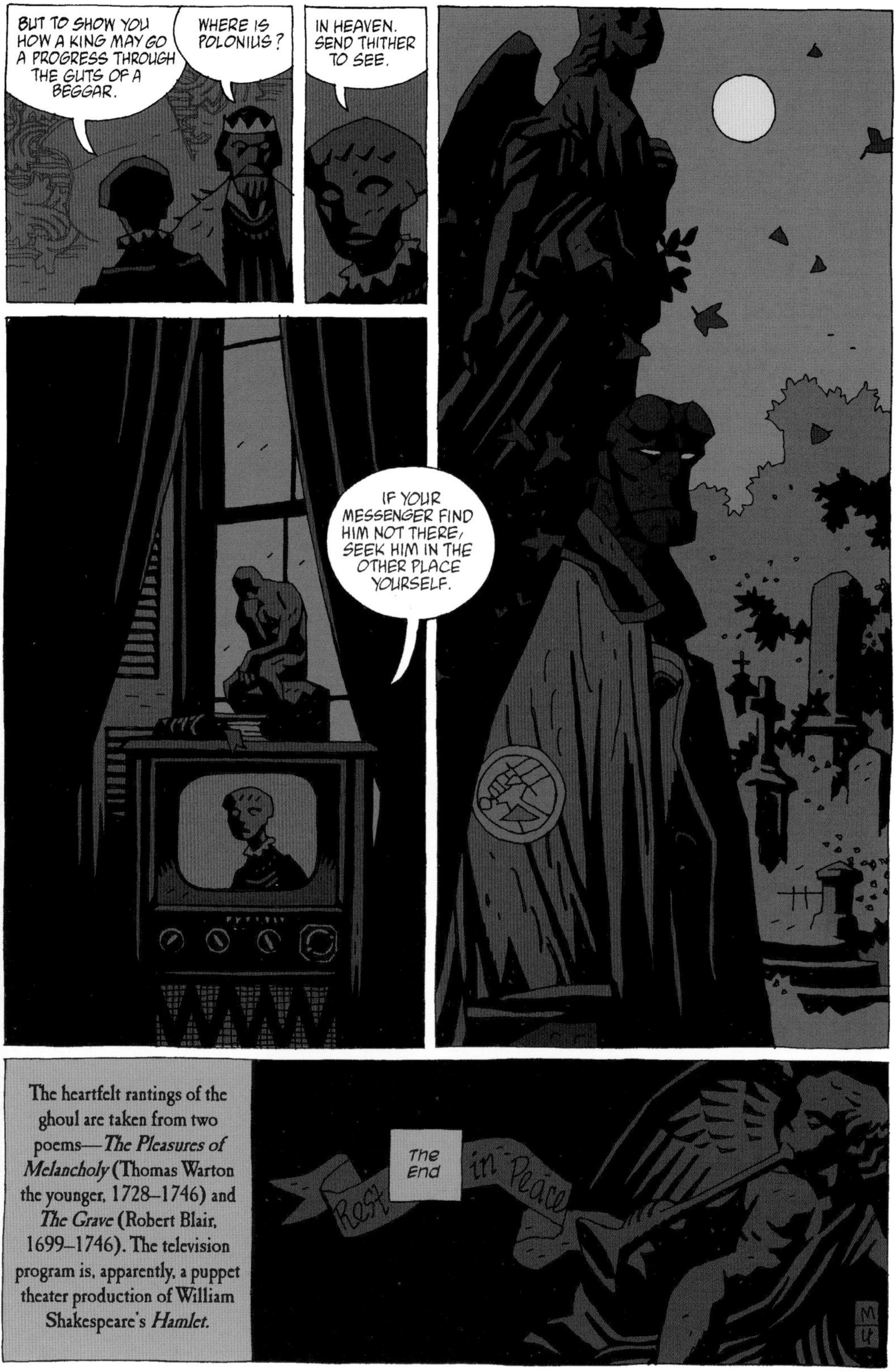
BUT TO SHOW YOU HOW A KING MAY GO A PROGRESS THROUGH THE GUTS OF A BEGGAR.
WHERE IS POLONIUS?
IN HEAVEN. SEND THITHER TO SEE.
IF YOUR MESSENGER FIND HIM NOT THERE, SEEK HIM IN THE OTHER PLACE YOURSELF.
The heartfelt rantings of the ghoul are taken from two poems—*The Pleasures of Melancholy* (Thomas Warton the younger, 1728–1746) and *The Grave* (Robert Blair, 1699–1746). The television program is, apparently, a puppet theater production of William Shakespeare's *Hamlet.*
Rest in Peace
The End

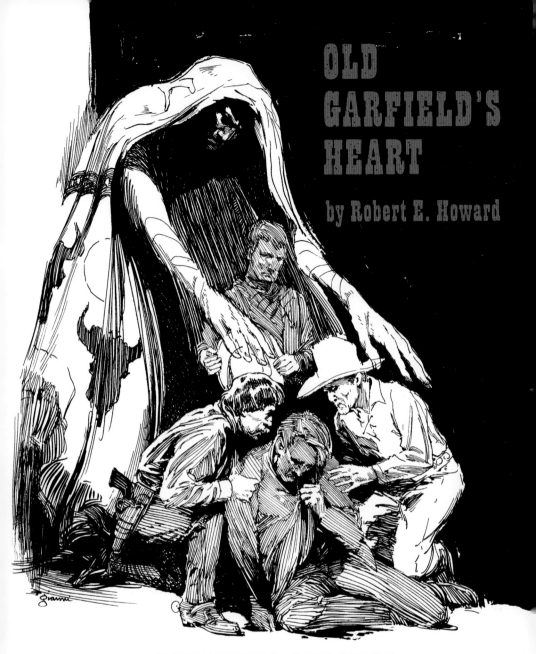

OLD GARFIELD'S HEART

by Robert E. Howard

ILLUSTRATIONS *by* GARY GIANNI

I was sitting on the porch when my grandfather hobbled out and sank down on his favorite chair with the cushioned seat, and began to stuff tobacco in his old corncob pipe.

"I thought you'd be goin' to the dance," he said.

"I'm waiting for Doc Blaine," I answered. "I'm going over to old man Garfield's with him."

My grandfather sucked at his pipe awhile before he spoke again.

"Old Jim purty bad off?"

"Doc says he hasn't a chance."

"Who's takin' care of him?"

"Joe Braxton—against Garfield's wishes. But somebody had to stay with him."

My grandfather sucked his pipe noisily, and watched the heat lightning playing away off up in the hills; then he said: "You think old Jim's the biggest liar in this county, don't you?"

"He tells some pretty tall tales," I admitted. "Some of the things he claimed he took part in, must have happened before he was born."

"I came from Tennessee to Texas in 1870," my grandfather said abruptly. "I saw this town of Lost Knob grow up from nothin'. There wasn't even a log-hut store here when I came. But old Jim Garfield was here, livin' in the same place he lives now, only then it was a log cabin. He didn't look a day older now than he did the first time I saw him."

"You never mentioned that before," I said in some surprise.

"I knew you'd put it down to an old man's maunderin's," he answered. "Old Jim was the first white man to settle in this country. He built his cabin a good fifty miles west of the frontier. God knows how he done it, for these hills swarmed with Comanches then.

"I remember the first time I ever saw him. Even then everybody called him 'old Jim.'

"I remember him tellin' me the same tales he's told you—how he was at the battle of San Jacinto when he was a youngster, and how he'd rode with Ewen Cameron and Jack Hayes. Only I believe him, and you don't."

"That was so long ago—" I protested.

"The last Indian raid through this country was in 1874," said my grandfather, engrossed in his own reminiscences. "I was in on that fight, and so was old Jim. I saw him knock old Yellow Tail off his mustang at seven hundred yards with a buffalo rifle.

"But before that I was with him in a fight up near the head of Locust Creek. A band of Comanches came down Mesquital, lootin' and burnin', rode through the hills and started back up Locust Creek, and a scout of us were hot on their heels. We ran on to them just at sundown in a mesquite flat. We killed seven of them, and the rest skinned out through the brush on foot. But three of our boys were killed, and Jim Garfield got a thrust in the breast with a lance.

"It was an awful wound. He lay like a dead man, and it seemed sure nobody could live after a wound like that. But an old Indian came out of the brush, and when we aimed our guns at him, he made the peace sign and spoke to us in Spanish. I don't know why the boys didn't shoot him in his tracks, because our blood was heated with the fightin' and killin', but

somethin' about him made us hold our fire. He said he wasn't a Comanche, but was an old friend of Garfield's, and wanted to help him. He asked us to carry Jim into a clump of mesquite, and leave him alone with him, and to this day I don't know why we did, but we did. It was an awful time—the wounded moanin' and callin' for water, the starin' corpses strewn about the camp, night comin' on, and no way of knowin' that the Indians wouldn't return when dark fell.

"We made camp right there, because the horses were fagged out, and we watched all night, but the Comanches didn't come back. I don't know what went on out in the mesquite where Jim Garfield's body lay, because I never saw that strange Indian again, but durin' the night I kept hearin' a weird moanin' that wasn't made by the dyin' men, and an owl hooted from midnight till dawn.

"And at sunrise Jim Garfield came walkin' out of the mesquite, pale and haggard, but alive, and already the wound in his breast had closed and begun to heal. And since then he's never mentioned that wound, nor that fight, nor the strange Indian who came and went so mysteriously. And he hasn't aged a bit; he looks now just like he did then—a man of about fifty."

In the silence that followed, a car began to purr down the road, and twin shafts of light cut through the dusk.

"That's Doc Blaine," I said. "When I come back I'll tell you how Garfield is."

Doc Blaine was prompt with his predictions as we drove the three miles of post oak-covered hills that lay between Lost Knob and the Garfield farm.

"I'll be surprised to find him alive," he said, "smashed up like he is. A man his age ought to have more sense than to try to break a young horse."

"He doesn't look so old," I remarked.

"I'll be fifty, my next birthday," answered Doc Blaine. "I've known him all my life, and he must have been at least fifty the first time I ever saw him. His looks are deceiving."

Old Garfield's dwelling place was reminiscent of the past. The boards of the low, squat house had never known paint. Orchard fence and corrals were built of rails.

Old Jim lay on his rude bed, tended crudely but efficiently by the man Doc Blaine had hired over the old man's protests. As I looked at him, I was impressed anew by his evident vitality. His frame was stooped but unwithered, his limbs rounded out with springy muscles. In his corded neck and in his face, drawn though it was with suffering, was apparent an innate virility. His eyes, though partly glazed with pain, burned with the same unquenchable element.

"He's been ravin'," said Joe Braxton stolidly.

"First white man in this country," muttered old Jim, becoming intelligible. "Hills no white man ever set foot in before. Gettin' too old. Have to settle down. Can't move on like I used to. Settle down here. Good country before it filled up with cow-men and squatters. Wish Ewen Cameron could see this country. The Mexicans shot him. Damn 'em!"

Doc Blaine shook his head. "He's all smashed up inside. He won't live till daylight."

Garfield unexpectedly lifted his head and looked at us with clear eyes.

"Wrong, Doc," he wheezed, his breath whistling with pain. "I'll live. What's broken bones and twisted guts? Nothin'! It's the heart that counts. Long as the heart keeps pumpin', a man can't die. My heart's sound. Listen to it! Feel of it!"

He groped painfully for Doc Blaine's wrist, dragged his hand to his bosom and held it there, staring up into the doctor's face with avid intensity.

"Regular dynamo, ain't it?" he gasped. "Stronger'n a gasoline engine!"

Blaine beckoned me. "Lay your hand here," he said, placing my hand on the old man's bare breast. "He does have a remarkable heart action."

I noted, in the light of the coal-oil lamp, a great livid scar as might be made by a flint-headed spear. I laid my hand directly on this scar, and an exclamation escaped my lips.

Under my hand old Jim Garfield's heart pulsed, but its throb was like no other heart action I have ever observed. Its power was astounding; his ribs vibrated to its steady throb. It felt more like the vibrating of a dynamo than the action of a human organ. I could feel its amazing vitality radiating from his breast, stealing up into my hand and up my arm, until my own heart seemed to speed up in response.

"I can't die," old Jim gasped. "Not so long as my heart's in my breast. Only a bullet through the brain can kill me. And even then I wouldn't be rightly dead, as long as my heart beats in my breast. Yet it ain't rightly mine, either. It belongs to Ghost Man, the Lipan chief. It was the heart of a god the Lipans worshipped before the Comanches drove 'em out of their native hills.

"I knew Ghost Man down on the Rio Grande, when I was with Ewen Cameron. I saved his life from the Mexicans once. He tied the string of ghost wampum between him and me—the wampum no man but me and him can see or feel. He came when he knowed I needed him, in that fight up on the headwaters of Locust Creek, when I got this scar.

"I was dead as a man can be. My heart was sliced in two, like the heart of a butchered beef steer.

"All night Ghost Man did magic, callin' my ghost back from spirit-land. I remember that flight, a little. It was dark, and gray-like, and I drifted through gray mists and heard the dead wailin' past me in the mist. But Ghost Man brought me back.

"He took out what was left of my mortal heart, and put the heart of the god in my bosom. But it's his, and when I'm through with it, he'll come for it. It's kept me alive and strong for the lifetime of a man. Age can't touch me. What do I care if these fools around here call me an old liar? What I know, I know. But hark'ee!"

His fingers became claws, clamping fiercely on Doc Blaine's wrist. His old eyes, old yet strangely young, burned fierce as those of an eagle under his bushy brows.

"If by some mischance I *should* die, now or later, promise me this! Cut into my bosom and take out the heart Ghost Man lent me so long ago! It's his. And as long as it beats in my body, my spirit'll be tied to that body, though my head be crushed like an egg underfoot! A livin' thing in a rottin' body! Promise!"

"All right, I promise," replied Doc Blaine, to humor him, and old Jim Garfield sank back with a whistling sigh of relief.

He did not die that night, nor the next, nor the next. I well remember the next day, because it was that day that I had the fight with Jack Kirby.

People will take a good deal from a bully, rather than to spill blood. Because nobody had gone to the trouble of killing him, Kirby thought the whole countryside was afraid of him.

He had bought a steer from my father, and when my father went to collect for it, Kirby told him that he had paid the money to me—which was a lie. I went looking for Kirby, and came upon him in a bootleg joint, boasting of his toughness, and telling the crowd that he was going to beat me up and

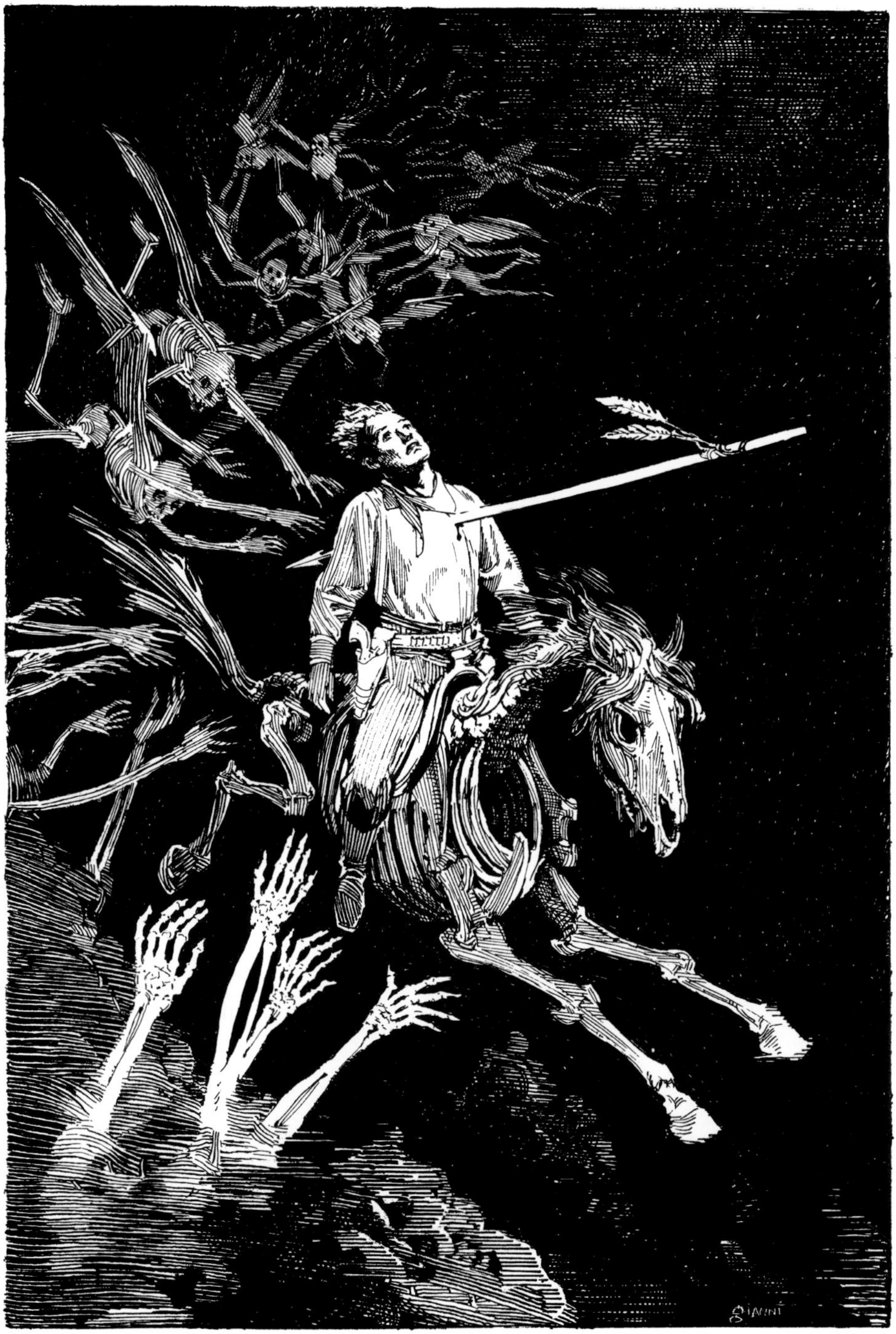

make me say that he had paid me the money, and that I had stuck it into my own pocket. When I heard him say that, I saw red, and ran in on him with a stockman's knife, and cut him across the face, and in the neck, side, breast and belly, and the only thing that saved his life was the fact that the crowd pulled me off.

There was a preliminary hearing, and I was indicted on a charge of assault, and my trial was set for the following term of court. Kirby was as tough-fibered as a post-oak, country bully ought to be, and he recovered, swearing vengeance, for he was vain of his looks, though God knows why, and I had permanently impaired them.

And while Jack Kirby was recovering, old man Garfield recovered, too, to the amazement of everybody, especially Doc Blaine.

I well remember the night Doc Blaine took me again out to old Jim Garfield's farm. I was in Shifty Corlan's joint, trying to drink enough of the slop he called beer to get a kick out of it, when Doc Blaine came in and persuaded me to go with him.

As we drove along the winding old road in Doc's car, I asked: "Why are you insistent that I go with you this particular night? This isn't a professional call, is it?"

"No," he said. "You couldn't kill old Jim with a post-oak maul. He's completely recovered from injuries that ought to have killed an ox. To tell you the truth, Jack Kirby is in Lost Knob, swearing he'll shoot you on sight."

"Well, for God's sake!" I exclaimed angrily. "Now everybody'll think I left town because I was afraid of him. Turn around and take me back, damn it!"

"Be reasonable," said Doc. "Everybody knows you're not afraid of Kirby. Nobody's afraid of him now. His bluff's broken, and that's why he's so wild against you. But you can't afford to have any more trouble with him now, and your trial only a short time off."

I laughed and said: "Well, if he's looking for me hard enough, he can find me as easily at old Garfield's as in town, because Shifty Corlan heard you say where we were going. And Shifty's hated me ever since I skinned him in that horse swap last fall. He'll tell Kirby where I went."

"I never thought of that," said Doc Blaine, worried.

"Hell, forget it," I advised. "Kirby hasn't got guts enough to do anything but blow."

But I was mistaken. Puncture a bully's vanity and you touch his one vital spot.

Old Jim had not gone to bed when we got there. He was sitting in the room opening on to his sagging porch, the room which was at once living room and bedroom, smoking his old cob pipe and trying to read a newspaper by the light of his coal-oil lamp. All the windows and doors were wide open for the coolness, and the insects which swarmed in and fluttered around the lamp didn't seem to bother him.

We sat down and discussed the weather—which isn't so inane as one might suppose, in a country where a man's livelihood depends on sun and rain, and is at the mercy of wind and drouth. The talk drifted into the other kindred channels, and after some time, Doc Blaine bluntly spoke of something that hung in his mind.

"Jim," he said, "that night I thought you were dying, you babbled a lot of stuff about your heart, and an Indian who lent you his. How much of that was delirium?"

"None, Doc," said Garfield, pulling at his pipe. "It was gospel truth. Ghost Man, the Lipan priest of the Gods of Night, replaced my dead, torn heart with one from somethin' he worshipped. I ain't sure myself just what that somethin' is—somethin' from a way back and a long way off, he said. But bein' a god, it can do without a heart for a while. But when I die—if I ever get my head smashed so my consciousness is destroyed—the heart must be given back to Ghost Man."

"You mean you were in earnest about the cutting out your heart?" demanded Doc Blaine.

"It has to be," answered old Garfield. "A livin' thing in a dead thing is opposed to nat'er. That's what Ghost Man said."

"Who the devil was Ghost Man?"

"I told you. A witch-doctor of the Lipans, who dwelt in this country before the Comanches came down from the Staked Plains and drove 'em south across the Rio Grande. I was a friend to 'em. I reckon Ghost Man is the only one left alive."

"Alive? Now?"

"I dunno," confessed old Jim. "I dunno whether he's alive or dead. I dunno whether he was alive when he came to me after the fight on Locust Creek, or even if he was alive when I knowed him in the southern country. Alive as we understand life, I mean."

"What balderdash is this?" demanded Doc Blaine uneasily, and I felt a slight stirring in my hair. Outside was stillness, and the stars, and the black shadows of the post-oak woods. The lamp cast old Garfield's shadow grotesquely on the wall, so that it did not at all resemble that of a human, and his words were strange as words heard in a nightmare.

"I knowed you wouldn't understand," said old Jim. "I don't understand myself, and I ain't got the words to explain them things I feel and know without understandin'. The Lipans were kin to the Apaches, and the Apaches learnt curious things from the Pueblos. Ghost Man *was*. That's all I can say—alive or dead, I don't know, but he *was*. What's more, he *is*."

"Is it you or me that's crazy?" asked Doc Blaine.

"Well," said old Jim, "I'll tell you this much—Ghost Man knew Coronado."

"Crazy as a loon!" murmured Doc Blaine. Then he lifted his head. "What's that?"

"Horse turning in from the road," I said. "Sounds like it stopped."

I stepped to the door, like a fool, and stood etched in the light behind me. I got a glimpse of a shadowy bulk I knew to be a man on a horse; then Doc Blaine yelled: "Look out!" and threw himself against me, knocking us both sprawling. At the same instant I heard the smashing report of a rifle, and old Garfield grunted and fell heavily.

"Jack Kirby!" screamed Doc Blaine. "He's killed Jim!"

I scrambled up, hearing the clatter of retreating hoofs, snatched old Jim's shotgun from the wall, rushed recklessly out on to the sagging porch and let go both barrels at the fleeing shape, dim in the starlight. The charge was too light to kill at that range, but the bird-shot stung the horse and maddened him. He swerved, crashed headlong through a rail fence and charged across the orchard, and a peach tree limb knocked his rider out of the saddle. He never moved after he hit the ground. I ran out there and looked down at him. It was Jack Kirby, right enough, and his neck was broken like a rotten branch.

I let him lie, and ran back to the house. Doc Blaine had stretched old Garfield out on a bench he'd dragged in from the porch, and Doc's face was whiter than I'd ever seen it. Old Jim was a ghastly sight; he had been shot with an old-fashioned .45-70, and at that range the heavy ball had literally torn off the top of his head. His features were masked with blood and brains. He had been directly behind me, poor old devil, and he had stopped the slug meant for me.

Doc Blaine was trembling, though he was anything but a stranger to such sights.

"Would you pronounce him dead?" he asked.

"That's for you to say," I answered. "But even a fool could tell that he's dead."

"He *is* dead," said Doc Blaine in a strained unnatural voice. "Rigor mortis is already setting in. But feel his heart!"

I did, and cried out. The flesh was already cold and clammy; but beneath it that mysterious heart still hammered steadily away, like a dynamo in a deserted house. No blood coursed through those veins; yet the heart pounded, pounded, pounded, like the pulse of Eternity.

"A living thing in a dead thing," whispered Doc Blaine, cold sweat on his face. "This is opposed to nature. I am going to keep the promise I made him. I'll assume full responsibility. This is too monstrous to ignore."

Our implements were a butcher-knife and a hack-saw. Outside only the still stars looked down on the black post-oak shadows and the dead man that lay in the orchard. Inside, the oil lamp flickered, making strange shadows move and shiver and cringe in the corners, and glistened on the blood on the floor, and the red-dabbled figure on the bench. The only sound inside was the crunch of the saw-edge in bone; outside an owl began to hoot weirdly.

Doc Blaine thrust a red-stained hand into the aperture he had made, and drew out a red, pulsing object that caught the lamplight. With a choked cry he recoiled, and the thing slipped from his fingers and fell on the table. And I, too, cried out involuntarily. For it did not fall with a soft meaty thud, as a piece of flesh should fall. It *thumped* hard on the table.

Impelled by an irresistible urge, I bent and gingerly picked up old Garfield's heart. The feel of it was brittle, unyielding, like steel or stone, but smoother than either. In size and shape it was the duplicate of a human heart, but it was slick and smooth, and its crimson surface reflected the lamplight like a jewel more lambent than any ruby; and in my hand it still throbbed mightily, sending vibratory radiations of energy up my arm until my own heart seemed swelling and bursting in response. It was cosmic *power*, beyond my comprehension, concentrated into the likeness of a human heart.

The thought came to me that here was a dynamo of life, the nearest approach to immortality that is possible for the destructible human body, the materialization of a cosmic secret more wonderful than the fabulous fountain sought for by Ponce de Leon. My soul was drawn into that unterrestrial gleam, and I suddenly wished passionately that it hammered and thundered in my own bosom in place of my paltry heart of tissue and muscle.

Doc Blaine ejaculated incoherently. I wheeled.

The noise of his coming had been no greater than the whispering of a night wind through the corn. There in the doorway he stood, tall, dark, inscrutable—an Indian warrior, in the paint, war bonnet, breech-clout and moccasins of an elder age. His dark eyes burned like fires gleaming deep under fathomless black lakes. Silently he extended his hand, and I dropped Jim Garfield's heart into it. Then without a word he turned and stalked into the night. But when Doc Blaine and I rushed out into the yard an instant later, there was no sign of any human being. He had vanished like a phantom of the night, and only something that looked like an owl was flying, dwindling from sight, into the rising moon.

The End

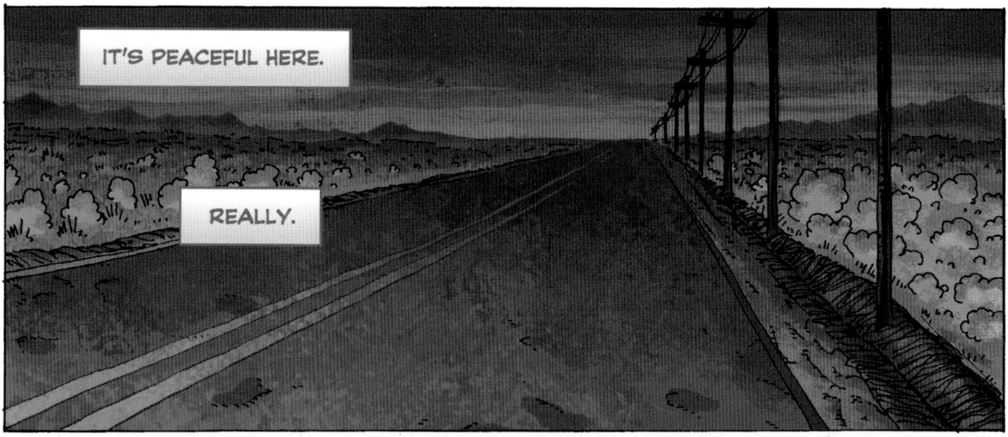
IT'S PEACEFUL HERE.
REALLY.

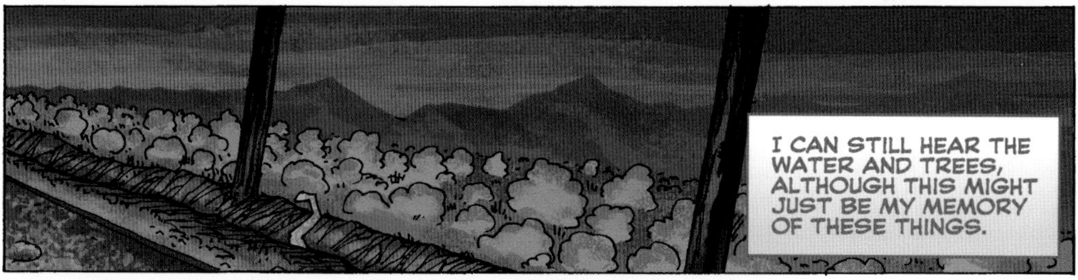
I CAN STILL HEAR THE WATER AND TREES, ALTHOUGH THIS MIGHT JUST BE MY MEMORY OF THESE THINGS.

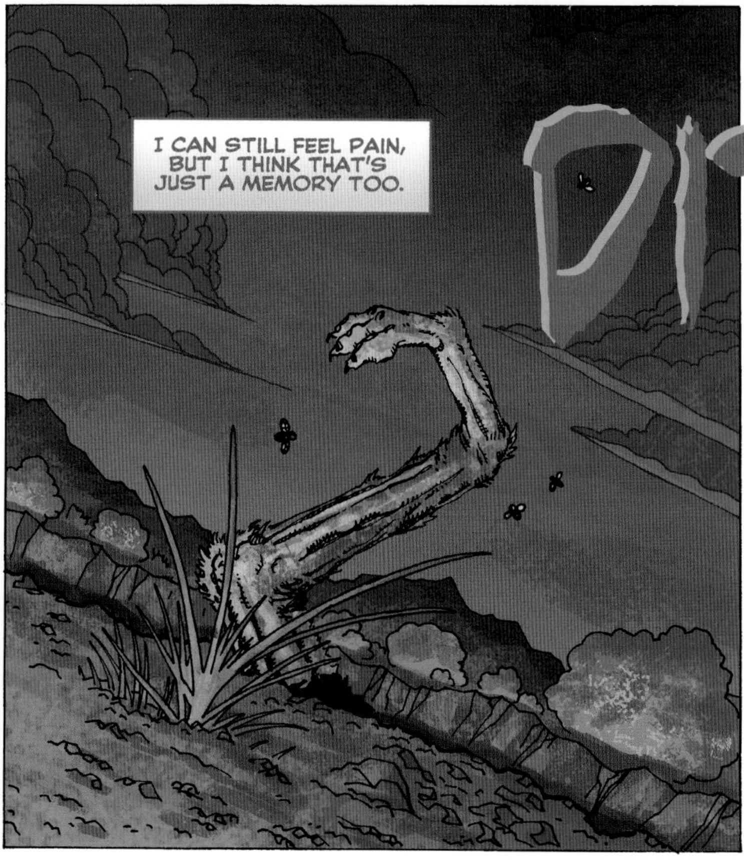
I CAN STILL FEEL PAIN, BUT I THINK THAT'S JUST A MEMORY TOO.

THE DITCH

STORY
DAVID CROUSE

ART
TODD HERMAN

COLOR
DAVE STEWART

LETTERS
RICHARD STARKINGS

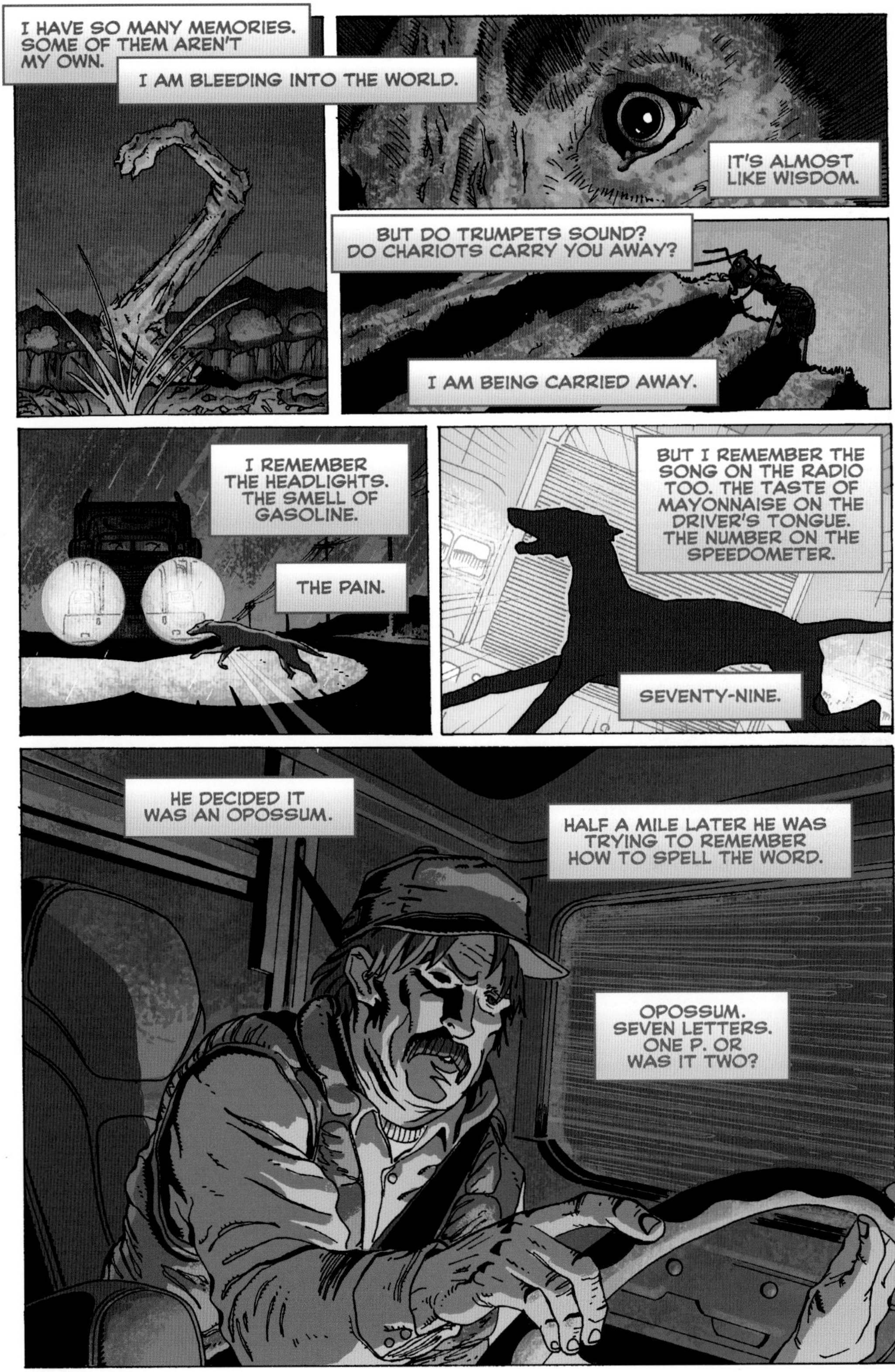
I HAVE SO MANY MEMORIES. SOME OF THEM AREN'T MY OWN.
I AM BLEEDING INTO THE WORLD.
IT'S ALMOST LIKE WISDOM.
BUT DO TRUMPETS SOUND? DO CHARIOTS CARRY YOU AWAY?
I AM BEING CARRIED AWAY.
I REMEMBER THE HEADLIGHTS. THE SMELL OF GASOLINE.
THE PAIN.
BUT I REMEMBER THE SONG ON THE RADIO TOO. THE TASTE OF MAYONNAISE ON THE DRIVER'S TONGUE. THE NUMBER ON THE SPEEDOMETER.
SEVENTY-NINE.
HE DECIDED IT WAS AN OPOSSUM.
HALF A MILE LATER HE WAS TRYING TO REMEMBER HOW TO SPELL THE WORD.
OPOSSUM. SEVEN LETTERS. ONE P. OR WAS IT TWO?

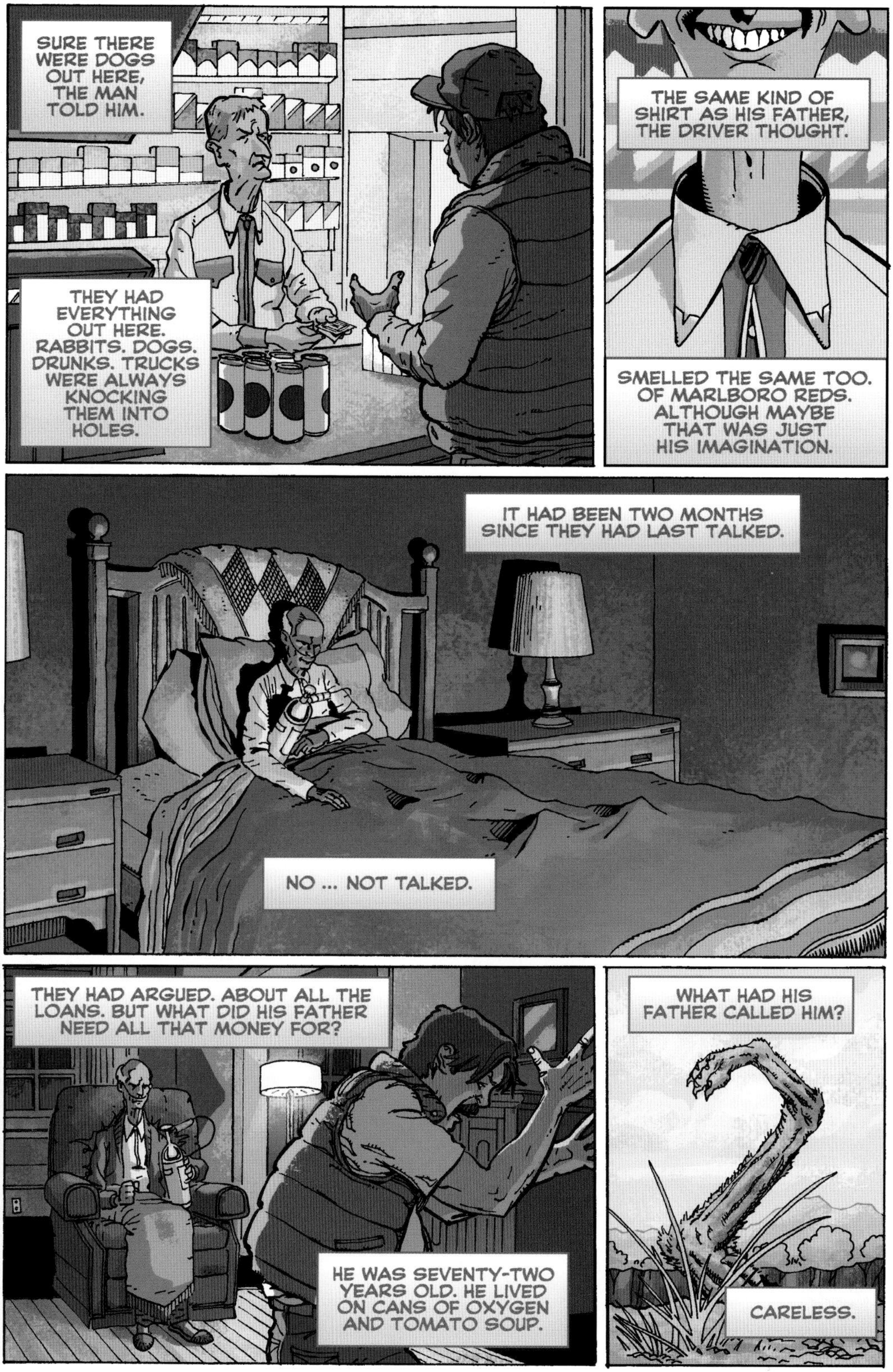
SURE THERE WERE DOGS OUT HERE, THE MAN TOLD HIM.
THEY HAD EVERYTHING OUT HERE. RABBITS. DOGS. DRUNKS. TRUCKS WERE ALWAYS KNOCKING THEM INTO HOLES.
THE SAME KIND OF SHIRT AS HIS FATHER, THE DRIVER THOUGHT.
SMELLED THE SAME TOO. OF MARLBORO REDS. ALTHOUGH MAYBE THAT WAS JUST HIS IMAGINATION.
IT HAD BEEN TWO MONTHS SINCE THEY HAD LAST TALKED.
NO ... NOT TALKED.
THEY HAD ARGUED. ABOUT ALL THE LOANS. BUT WHAT DID HIS FATHER NEED ALL THAT MONEY FOR?
HE WAS SEVENTY-TWO YEARS OLD. HE LIVED ON CANS OF OXYGEN AND TOMATO SOUP.
WHAT HAD HIS FATHER CALLED HIM?
CARELESS.

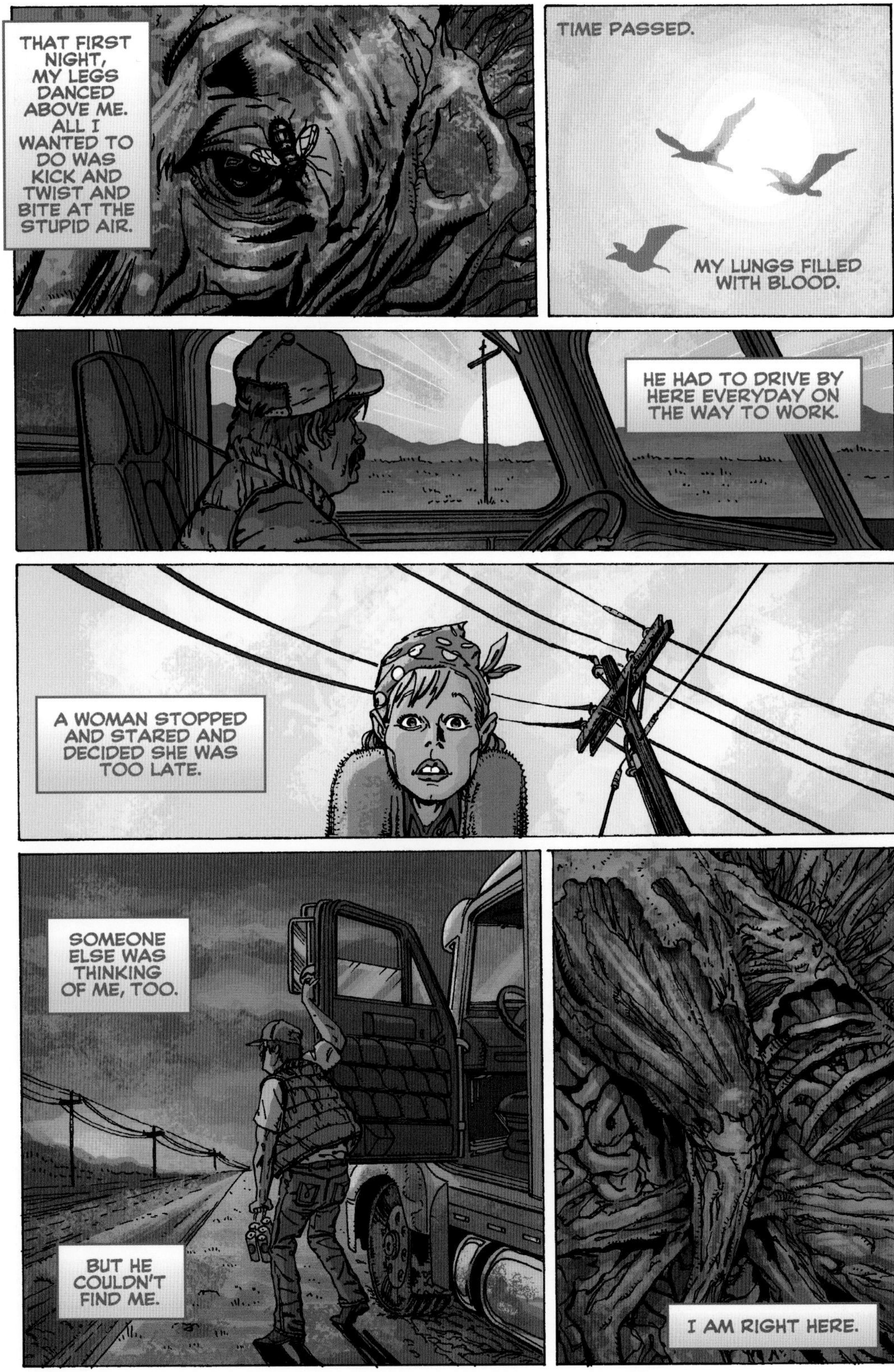
THAT FIRST NIGHT, MY LEGS DANCED ABOVE ME. ALL I WANTED TO DO WAS KICK AND TWIST AND BITE AT THE STUPID AIR.
TIME PASSED.
MY LUNGS FILLED WITH BLOOD.
HE HAD TO DRIVE BY HERE EVERYDAY ON THE WAY TO WORK.
A WOMAN STOPPED AND STARED AND DECIDED SHE WAS TOO LATE.
SOMEONE ELSE WAS THINKING OF ME, TOO.
BUT HE COULDN'T FIND ME.
I AM RIGHT HERE.

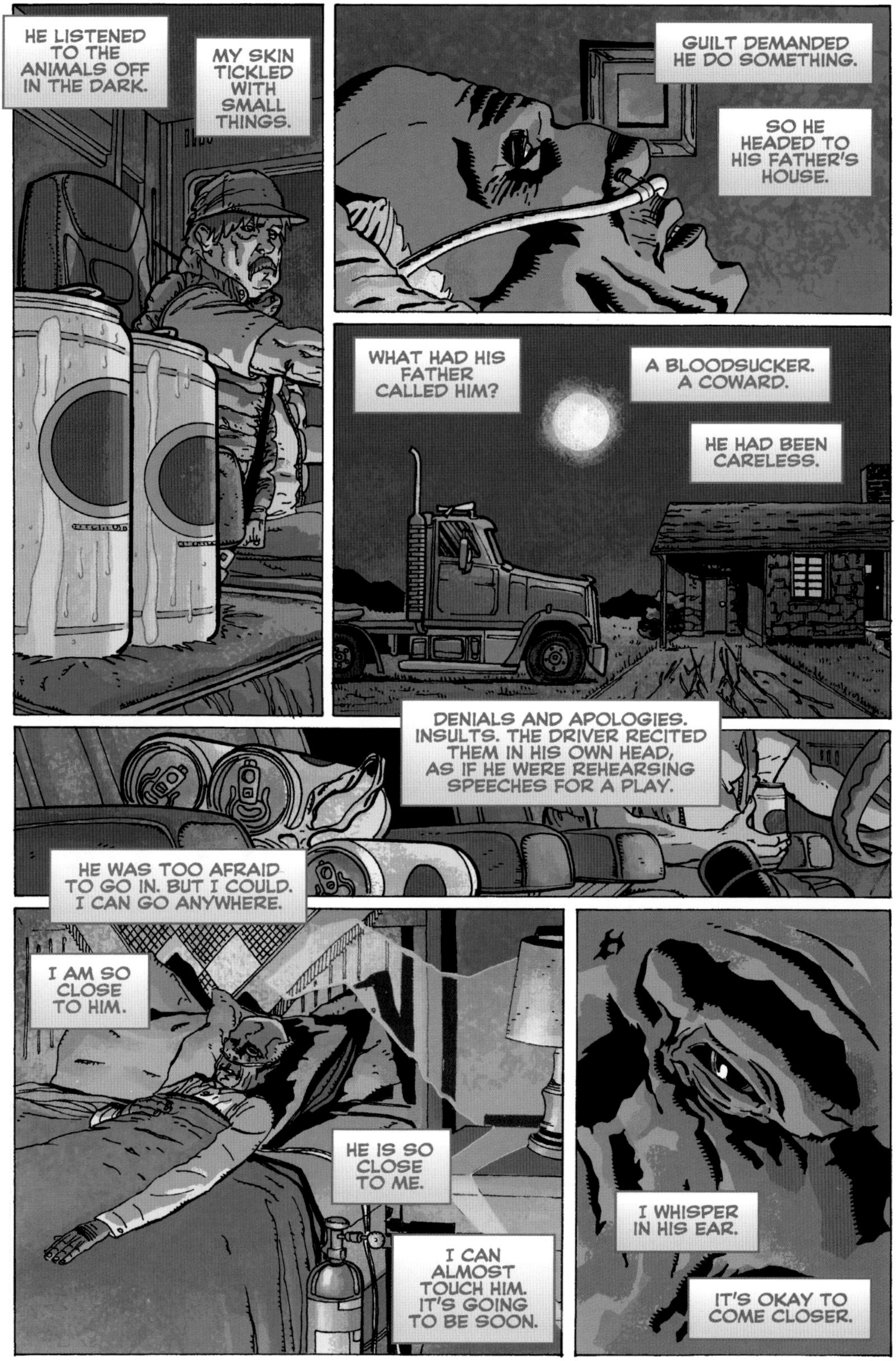
HE LISTENED TO THE ANIMALS OFF IN THE DARK.
MY SKIN TICKLED WITH SMALL THINGS.
GUILT DEMANDED HE DO SOMETHING.
SO HE HEADED TO HIS FATHER'S HOUSE.
WHAT HAD HIS FATHER CALLED HIM?
A BLOODSUCKER. A COWARD.
HE HAD BEEN CARELESS.
DENIALS AND APOLOGIES. INSULTS. THE DRIVER RECITED THEM IN HIS OWN HEAD, AS IF HE WERE REHEARSING SPEECHES FOR A PLAY.
HE WAS TOO AFRAID TO GO IN. BUT I COULD. I CAN GO ANYWHERE.
I AM SO CLOSE TO HIM.
HE IS SO CLOSE TO ME.
I CAN ALMOST TOUCH HIM. IT'S GOING TO BE SOON.
I WHISPER IN HIS EAR.
IT'S OKAY TO COME CLOSER.

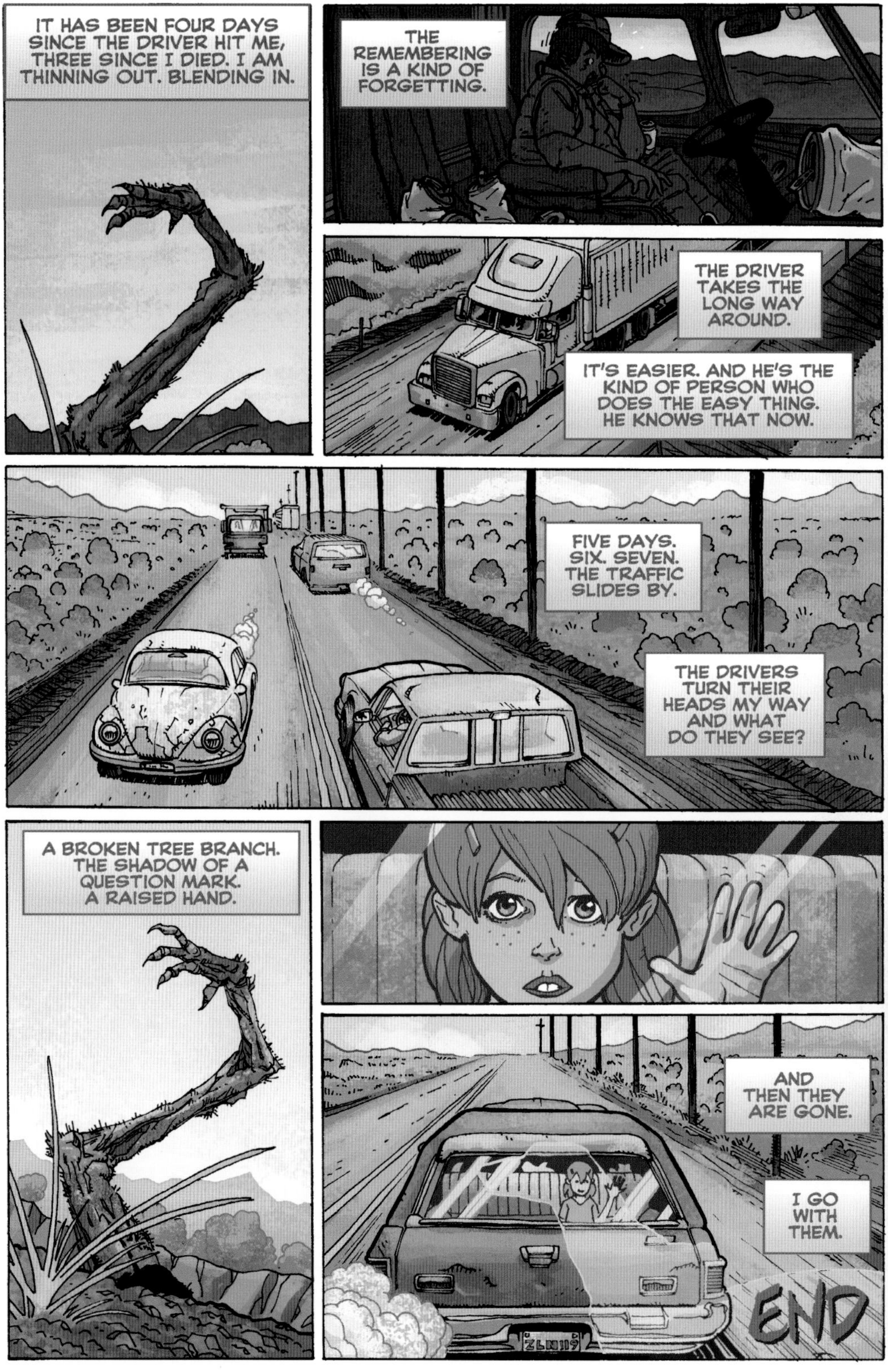
IT HAS BEEN FOUR DAYS SINCE THE DRIVER HIT ME, THREE SINCE I DIED. I AM THINNING OUT. BLENDING IN.
THE REMEMBERING IS A KIND OF FORGETTING.
THE DRIVER TAKES THE LONG WAY AROUND.
IT'S EASIER. AND HE'S THE KIND OF PERSON WHO DOES THE EASY THING. HE KNOWS THAT NOW.
FIVE DAYS. SIX. SEVEN. THE TRAFFIC SLIDES BY.
THE DRIVERS TURN THEIR HEADS MY WAY AND WHAT DO THEY SEE?
A BROKEN TREE BRANCH. THE SHADOW OF A QUESTION MARK. A RAISED HAND.
AND THEN THEY ARE GONE.
I GO WITH THEM.
ZLN119
END

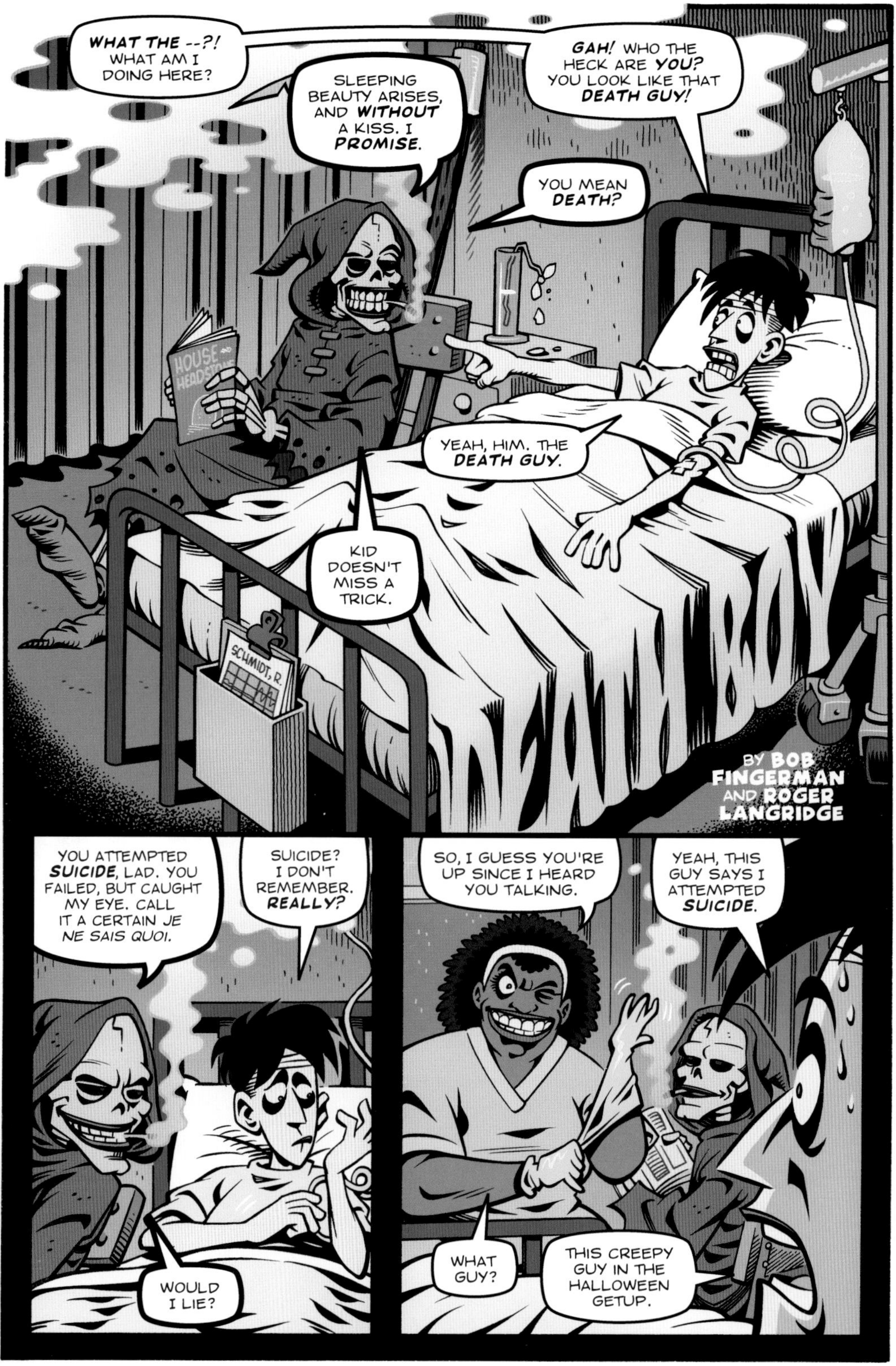
WHAT THE --?! WHAT AM I DOING HERE?
SLEEPING BEAUTY ARISES, AND WITHOUT A KISS. I PROMISE.
GAH! WHO THE HECK ARE YOU? YOU LOOK LIKE THAT DEATH GUY!
YOU MEAN DEATH?
YEAH, HIM. THE DEATH GUY.
KID DOESN'T MISS A TRICK.
HOUSE AND HEADSTONE
SCHMIDT, R.
DEATH BOY
BY BOB FINGERMAN AND ROGER LANGRIDGE
YOU ATTEMPTED SUICIDE, LAD. YOU FAILED, BUT CAUGHT MY EYE. CALL IT A CERTAIN JE NE SAIS QUOI.
SUICIDE? I DON'T REMEMBER. REALLY?
WOULD I LIE?
SO, I GUESS YOU'RE UP SINCE I HEARD YOU TALKING.
YEAH, THIS GUY SAYS I ATTEMPTED SUICIDE.
WHAT GUY?
THIS CREEPY GUY IN THE HALLOWEEN GETUP.

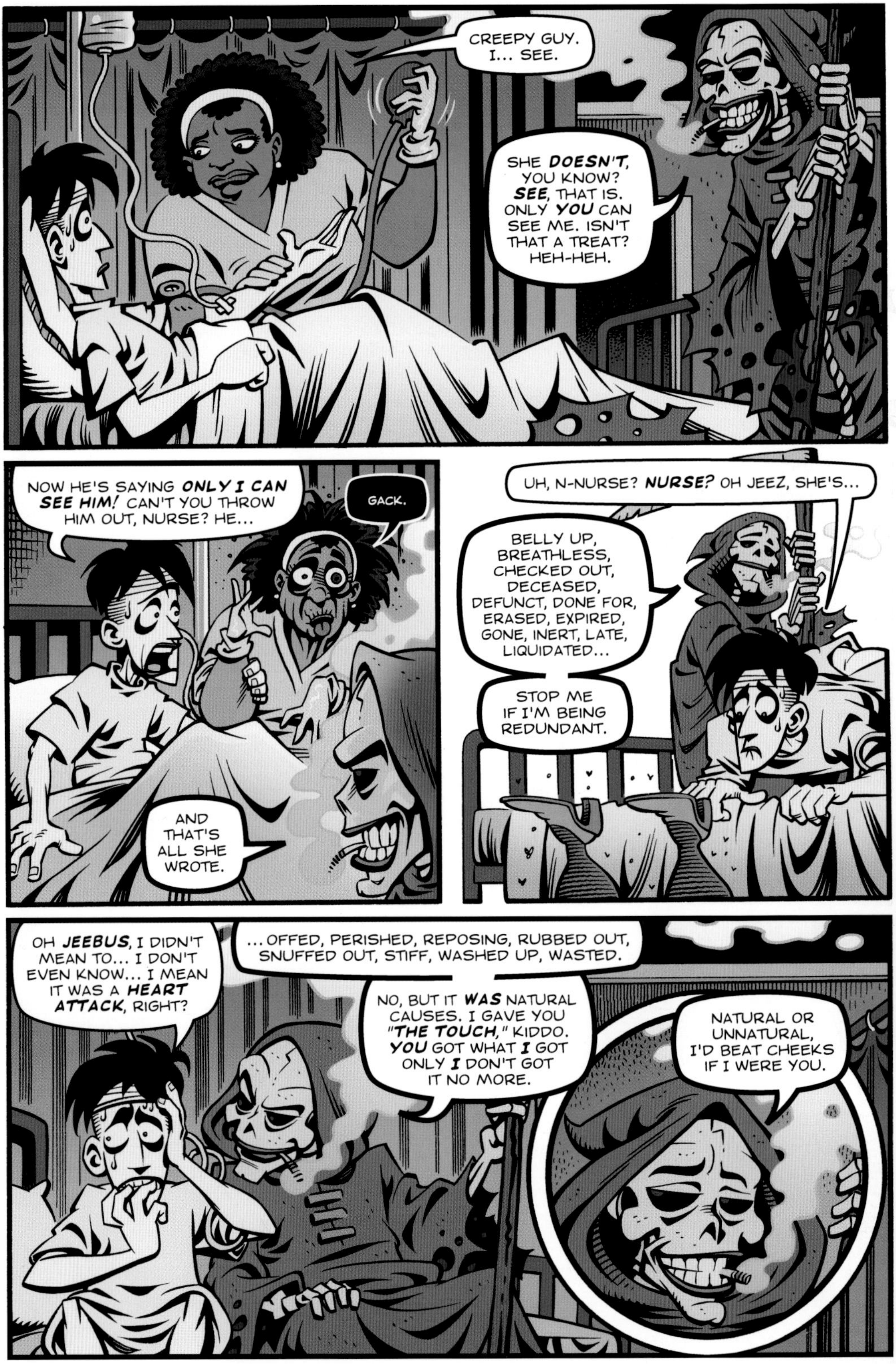
CREEPY GUY. I... SEE.
SHE DOESN'T, YOU KNOW? SEE, THAT IS. ONLY YOU CAN SEE ME. ISN'T THAT A TREAT? HEH-HEH.
NOW HE'S SAYING ONLY I CAN SEE HIM! CAN'T YOU THROW HIM OUT, NURSE? HE...
GACK.
AND THAT'S ALL SHE WROTE.
UH, N-NURSE? NURSE? OH JEEZ, SHE'S...
BELLY UP, BREATHLESS, CHECKED OUT, DECEASED, DEFUNCT, DONE FOR, ERASED, EXPIRED, GONE, INERT, LATE, LIQUIDATED...
STOP ME IF I'M BEING REDUNDANT.
OH JEEBUS, I DIDN'T MEAN TO... I DON'T EVEN KNOW... I MEAN IT WAS A HEART ATTACK, RIGHT?
...OFFED, PERISHED, REPOSING, RUBBED OUT, SNUFFED OUT, STIFF, WASHED UP, WASTED.
NO, BUT IT WAS NATURAL CAUSES. I GAVE YOU "THE TOUCH," KIDDO. YOU GOT WHAT I GOT ONLY I DON'T GOT IT NO MORE.
NATURAL OR UNNATURAL, I'D BEAT CHEEKS IF I WERE YOU.

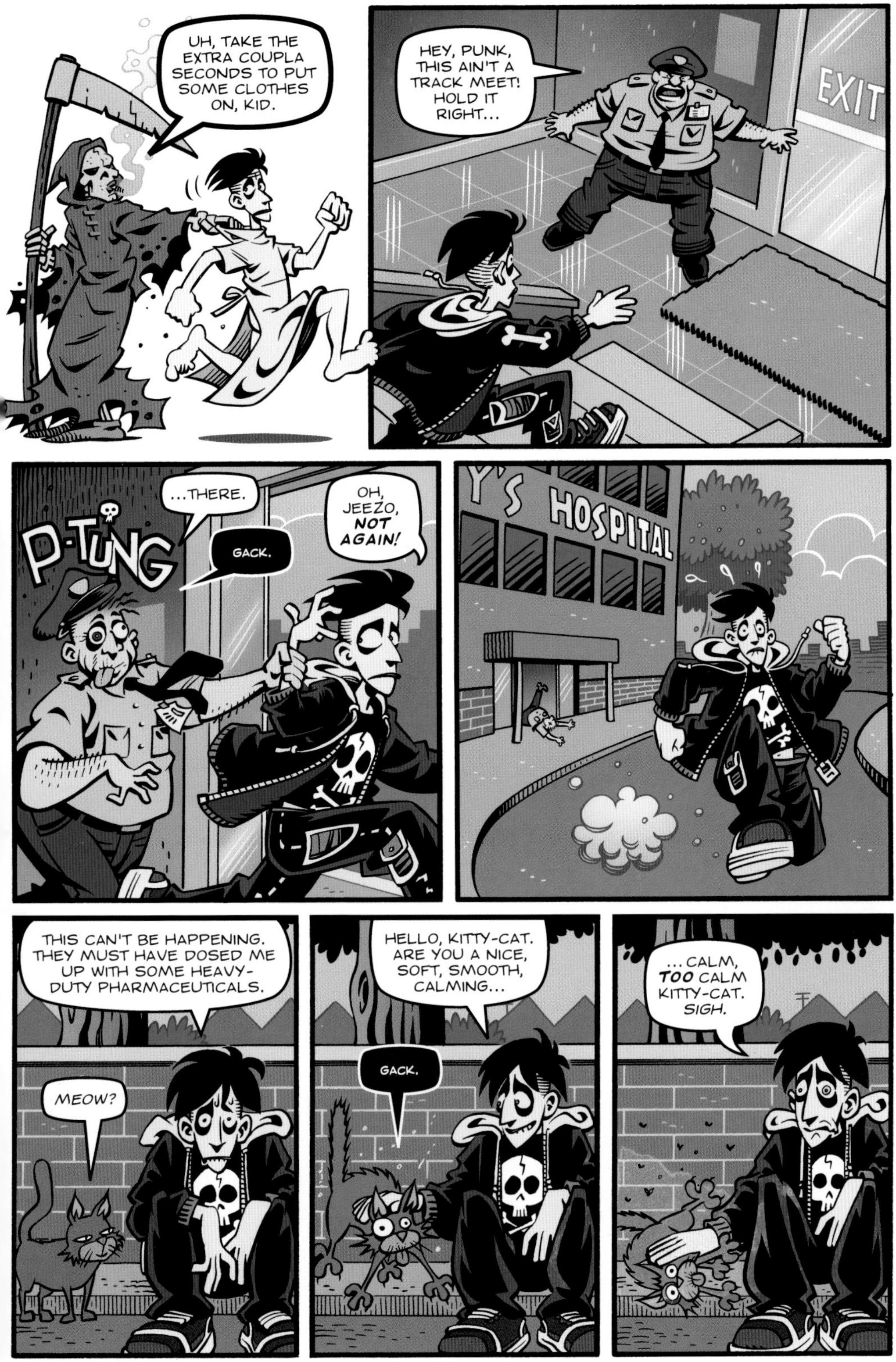
UH, TAKE THE EXTRA COUPLA SECONDS TO PUT SOME CLOTHES ON, KID.
HEY, PUNK, THIS AIN'T A TRACK MEET! HOLD IT RIGHT...
EXIT
...THERE.
P-TUNG
GACK.
OH, JEEZO, NOT AGAIN!
HOSPITAL
THIS CAN'T BE HAPPENING. THEY MUST HAVE DOSED ME UP WITH SOME HEAVY-DUTY PHARMACEUTICALS.
MEOW?
HELLO, KITTY-CAT. ARE YOU A NICE, SOFT, SMOOTH, CALMING...
GACK.
...CALM, TOO CALM KITTY-CAT. SIGH.

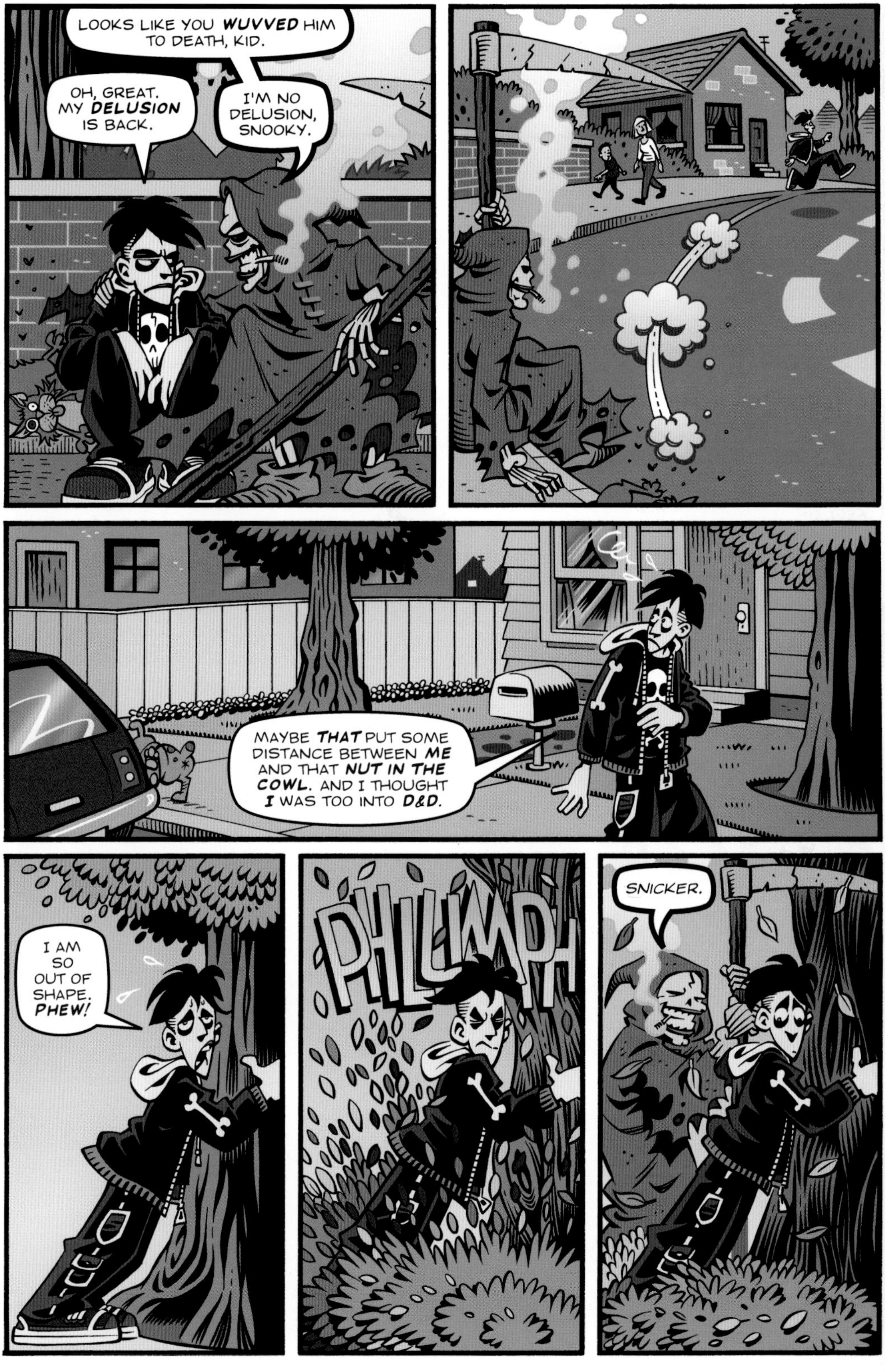
LOOKS LIKE YOU WUVVED HIM TO DEATH, KID.
OH, GREAT. MY DELUSION IS BACK.
I'M NO DELUSION, SNOOKY.
MAYBE THAT PUT SOME DISTANCE BETWEEN ME AND THAT NUT IN THE COWL. AND I THOUGHT I WAS TOO INTO D&D.
I AM SO OUT OF SHAPE. PHEW!
PHLUMPH
SNICKER.

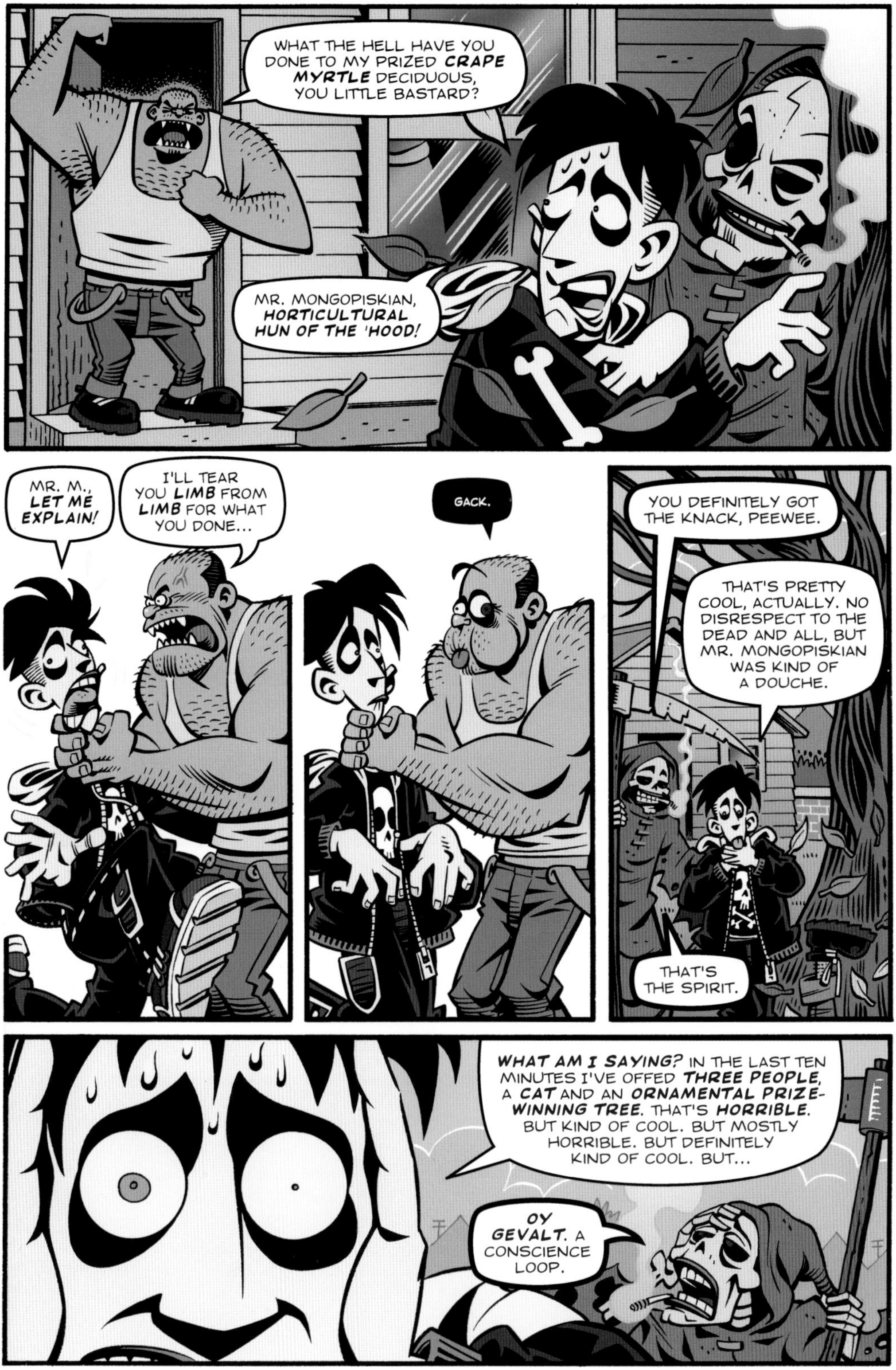
WHAT THE HELL HAVE YOU DONE TO MY PRIZED **CRAPE MYRTLE** DECIDUOUS, YOU LITTLE BASTARD?
MR. MONGOPISKIAN, **HORTICULTURAL HUN OF THE 'HOOD!**
MR. M., **LET ME EXPLAIN!**
I'LL TEAR YOU **LIMB** FROM **LIMB** FOR WHAT YOU DONE...
GACK.
YOU DEFINITELY GOT THE KNACK, PEEWEE.
THAT'S PRETTY COOL, ACTUALLY. NO DISRESPECT TO THE DEAD AND ALL, BUT MR. MONGOPISKIAN WAS KIND OF A DOUCHE.
THAT'S THE SPIRIT.
WHAT AM I SAYING? IN THE LAST TEN MINUTES I'VE OFFED **THREE PEOPLE**, A **CAT** AND AN **ORNAMENTAL PRIZE-WINNING TREE**. THAT'S **HORRIBLE**. BUT KIND OF COOL. BUT MOSTLY HORRIBLE. BUT DEFINITELY KIND OF COOL. BUT...
OY GEVALT. A CONSCIENCE LOOP.

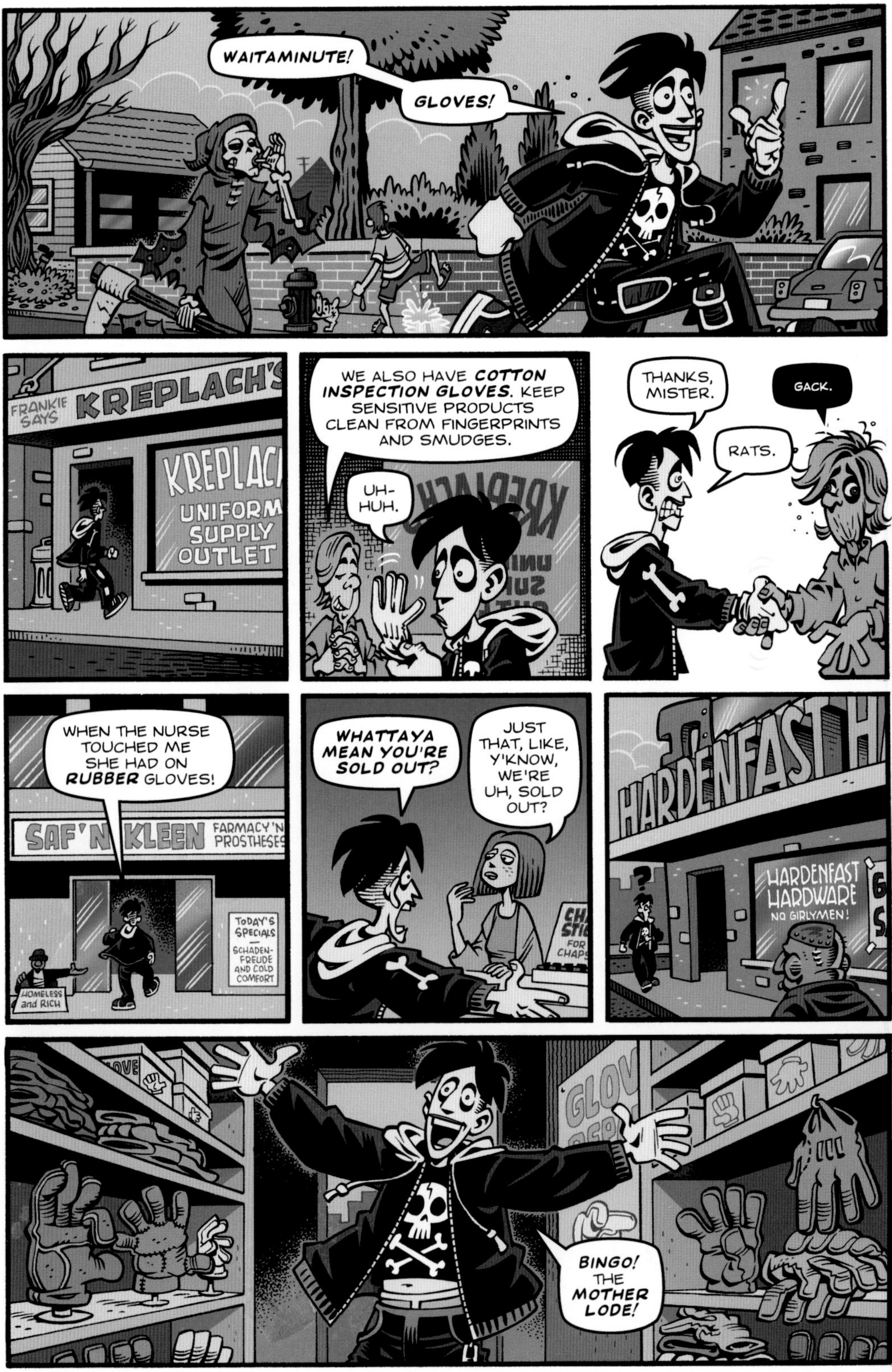
WAITAMINUTE!
GLOVES!
FRANKIE SAYS
KREPLACH'S
KREPLACH UNIFORM SUPPLY OUTLET
WE ALSO HAVE COTTON INSPECTION GLOVES. KEEP SENSITIVE PRODUCTS CLEAN FROM FINGERPRINTS AND SMUDGES.
UH-HUH.
THANKS, MISTER.
GACK.
RATS.
WHEN THE NURSE TOUCHED ME SHE HAD ON RUBBER GLOVES!
SAF'N KLEEN
FARMACY'N PROSTHESES
TODAY'S SPECIALS
SCHADEN-FREUDE AND COLD COMFORT
HOMELESS and RICH
WHATTAYA MEAN YOU'RE SOLD OUT?
JUST THAT, LIKE, Y'KNOW, WE'RE UH, SOLD OUT?
HARDENFAST
HARDENFAST HARDWARE
NO GIRLYMEN!
BINGO! THE MOTHER LODE!

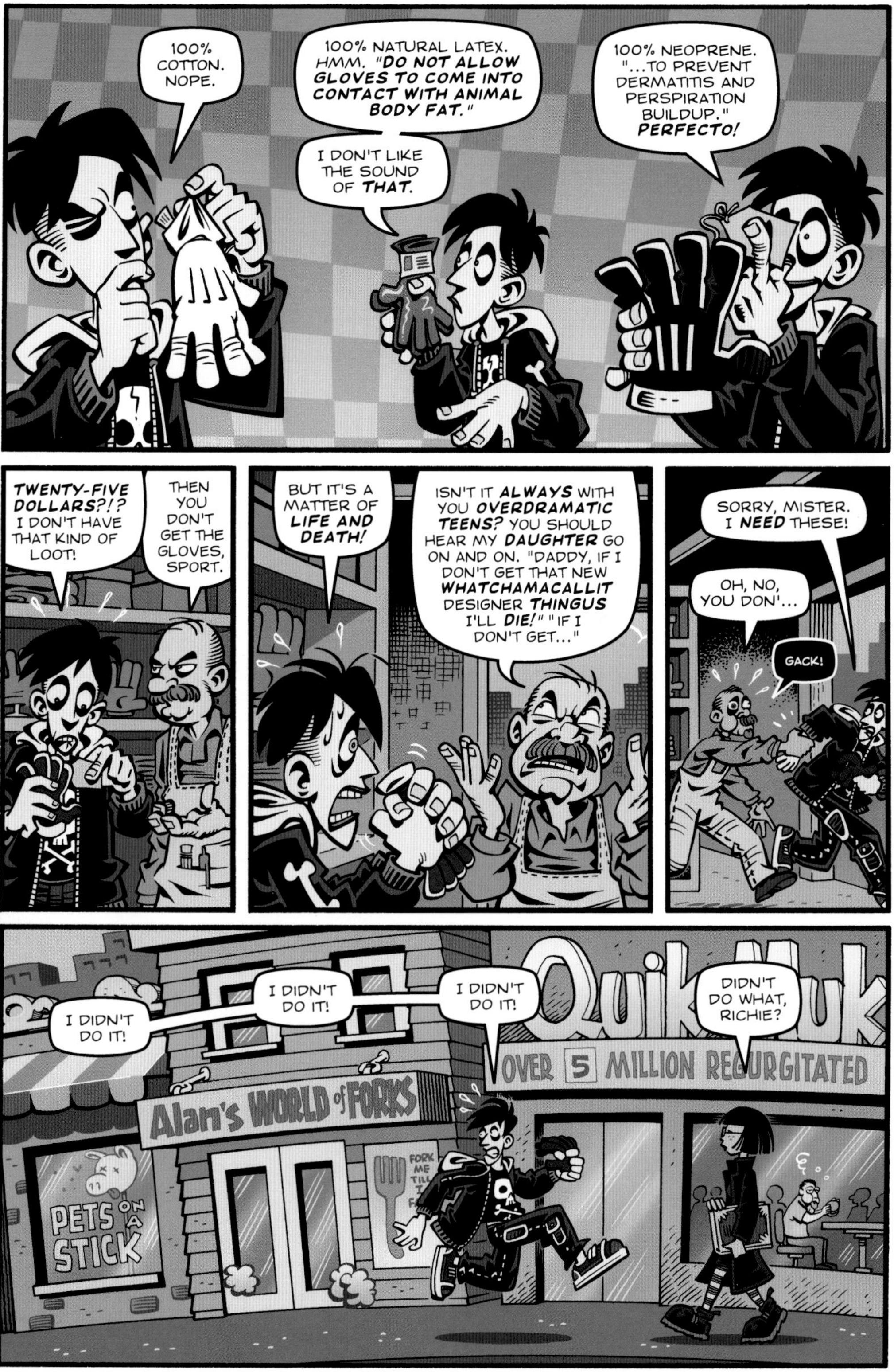
100% COTTON. NOPE.
100% NATURAL LATEX. HMM. "DO NOT ALLOW GLOVES TO COME INTO CONTACT WITH ANIMAL BODY FAT."
I DON'T LIKE THE SOUND OF THAT.
100% NEOPRENE. "...TO PREVENT DERMATITIS AND PERSPIRATION BUILDUP." PERFECTO!
TWENTY-FIVE DOLLARS?!? I DON'T HAVE THAT KIND OF LOOT!
THEN YOU DON'T GET THE GLOVES, SPORT.
BUT IT'S A MATTER OF LIFE AND DEATH!
ISN'T IT ALWAYS WITH YOU OVERDRAMATIC TEENS? YOU SHOULD HEAR MY DAUGHTER GO ON AND ON. "DADDY, IF I DON'T GET THAT NEW WHATCHAMACALLIT DESIGNER THINGUS I'LL DIE!" "IF I DON'T GET..."
SORRY, MISTER. I NEED THESE!
OH, NO, YOU DON'...
GACK!
I DIDN'T DO IT!
I DIDN'T DO IT!
I DIDN'T DO IT!
DIDN'T DO WHAT, RICHIE?
OVER 5 MILLION REGURGITATED
Alan's WORLD of FORKS
PETS ON A STICK

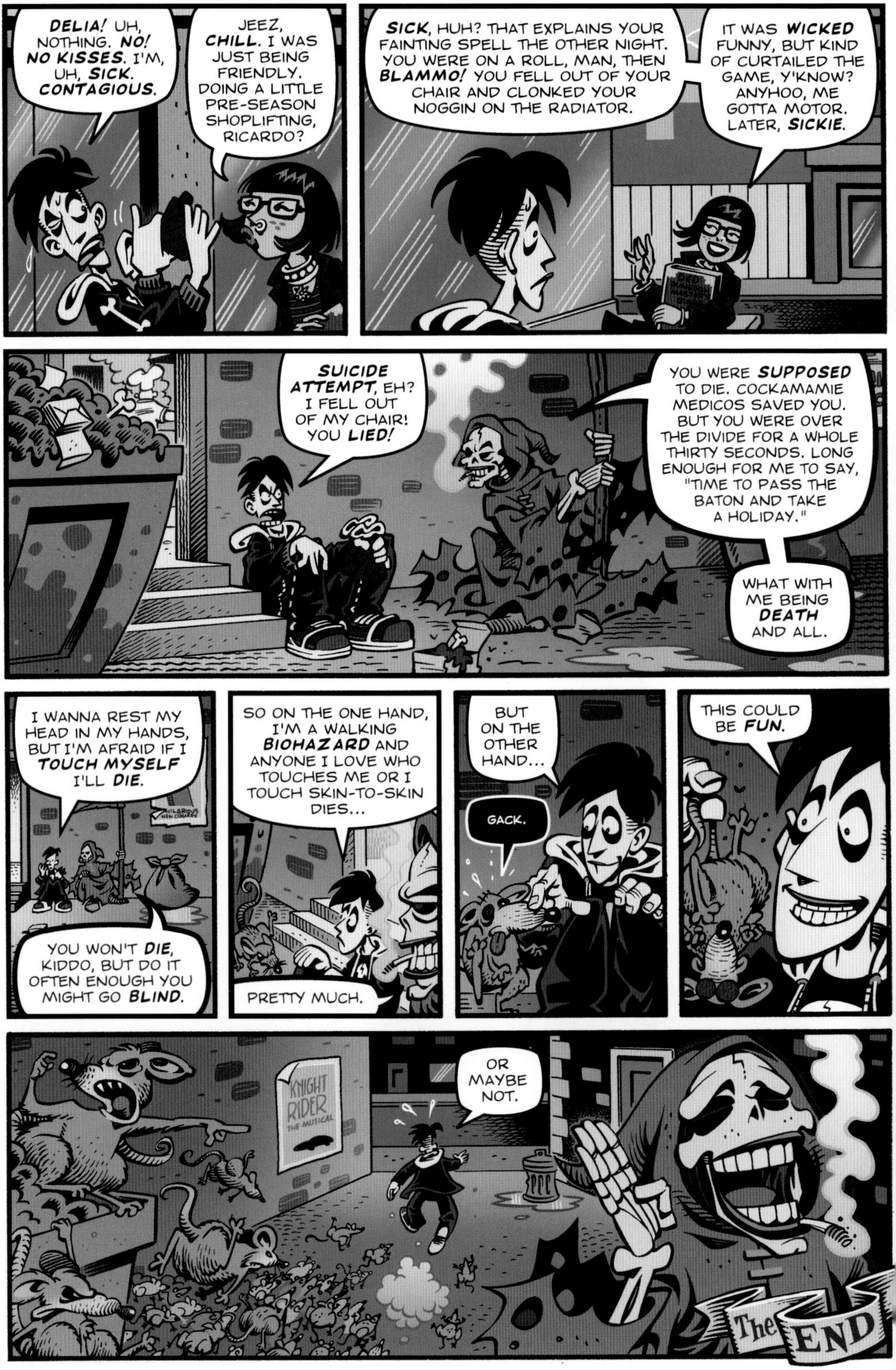
DELIA! UH, NOTHING. NO! NO KISSES. I'M, UH, SICK. CONTAGIOUS.
JEEZ, CHILL. I WAS JUST BEING FRIENDLY. DOING A LITTLE PRE-SEASON SHOPLIFTING, RICARDO?
SICK, HUH? THAT EXPLAINS YOUR FAINTING SPELL THE OTHER NIGHT. YOU WERE ON A ROLL, MAN, THEN BLAMMO! YOU FELL OUT OF YOUR CHAIR AND CLONKED YOUR NOGGIN ON THE RADIATOR.
IT WAS WICKED FUNNY, BUT KIND OF CURTAILED THE GAME, Y'KNOW? ANYHOO, ME GOTTA MOTOR. LATER, SICKIE.
SUICIDE ATTEMPT, EH? I FELL OUT OF MY CHAIR! YOU LIED!
YOU WERE SUPPOSED TO DIE. COCKAMAMIE MEDICOS SAVED YOU. BUT YOU WERE OVER THE DIVIDE FOR A WHOLE THIRTY SECONDS. LONG ENOUGH FOR ME TO SAY, "TIME TO PASS THE BATON AND TAKE A HOLIDAY."
WHAT WITH ME BEING DEATH AND ALL.
I WANNA REST MY HEAD IN MY HANDS, BUT I'M AFRAID IF I TOUCH MYSELF I'LL DIE.
HILARIOUS NEW COMEDY
YOU WON'T DIE, KIDDO, BUT DO IT OFTEN ENOUGH YOU MIGHT GO BLIND.
SO ON THE ONE HAND, I'M A WALKING BIOHAZARD AND ANYONE I LOVE WHO TOUCHES ME OR I TOUCH SKIN-TO-SKIN DIES...
PRETTY MUCH.
BUT ON THE OTHER HAND...
GACK.
THIS COULD BE FUN.
KNIGHT RIDER THE MUSICAL
OR MAYBE NOT.
The END

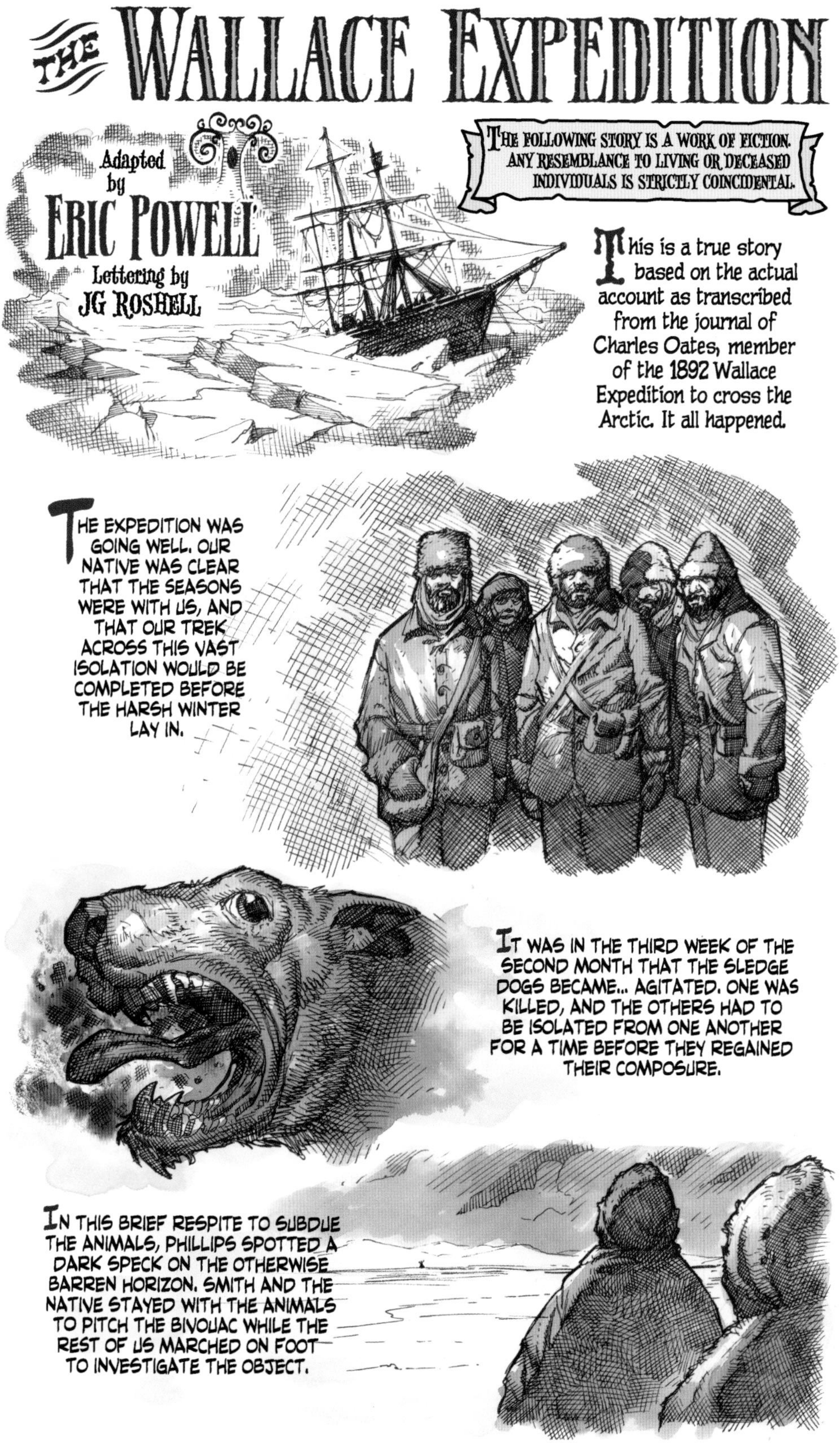
THE WALLACE EXPEDITION
Adapted by
ERIC POWELL
Lettering by
JG ROSHELL
THE FOLLOWING STORY IS A WORK OF FICTION. ANY RESEMBLANCE TO LIVING OR DECEASED INDIVIDUALS IS STRICTLY COINCIDENTAL.
This is a true story based on the actual account as transcribed from the journal of Charles Oates, member of the 1892 Wallace Expedition to cross the Arctic. It all happened.
THE EXPEDITION WAS GOING WELL. OUR NATIVE WAS CLEAR THAT THE SEASONS WERE WITH US, AND THAT OUR TREK ACROSS THIS VAST ISOLATION WOULD BE COMPLETED BEFORE THE HARSH WINTER LAY IN.
IT WAS IN THE THIRD WEEK OF THE SECOND MONTH THAT THE SLEDGE DOGS BECAME... AGITATED. ONE WAS KILLED, AND THE OTHERS HAD TO BE ISOLATED FROM ONE ANOTHER FOR A TIME BEFORE THEY REGAINED THEIR COMPOSURE.
IN THIS BRIEF RESPITE TO SUBDUE THE ANIMALS, PHILLIPS SPOTTED A DARK SPECK ON THE OTHERWISE BARREN HORIZON. SMITH AND THE NATIVE STAYED WITH THE ANIMALS TO PITCH THE BIVOUAC WHILE THE REST OF US MARCHED ON FOOT TO INVESTIGATE THE OBJECT.

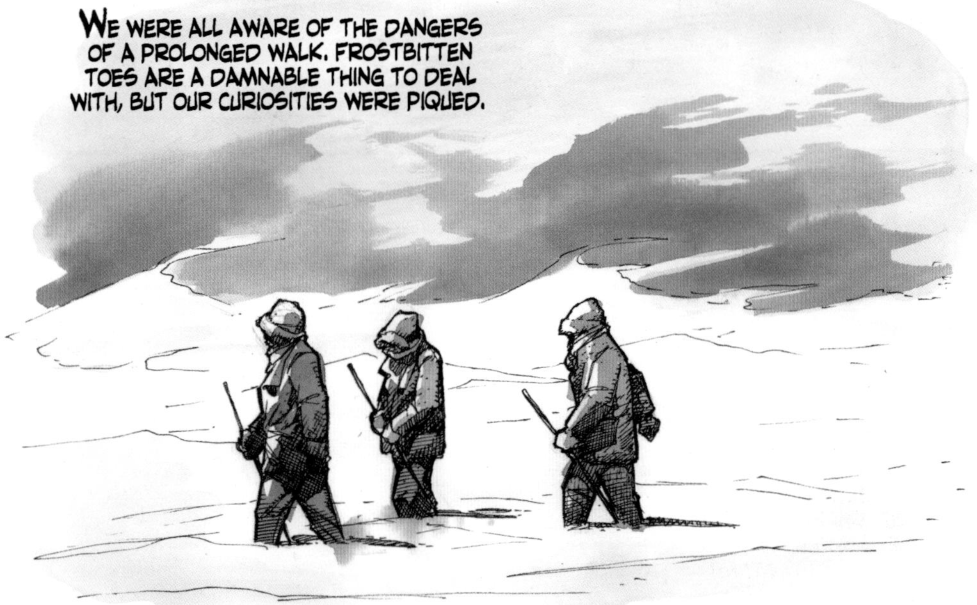
WE WERE ALL AWARE OF THE DANGERS OF A PROLONGED WALK. FROSTBITTEN TOES ARE A DAMNABLE THING TO DEAL WITH, BUT OUR CURIOSITIES WERE PIQUED.

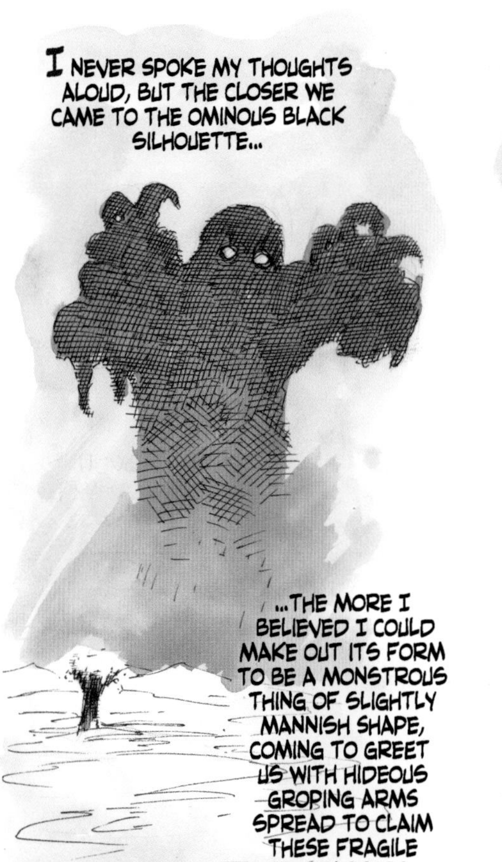
I NEVER SPOKE MY THOUGHTS ALOUD, BUT THE CLOSER WE CAME TO THE OMINOUS BLACK SILHOUETTE...
...THE MORE I BELIEVED I COULD MAKE OUT ITS FORM TO BE A MONSTROUS THING OF SLIGHTLY MANNISH SHAPE, COMING TO GREET US WITH HIDEOUS GROPING ARMS SPREAD TO CLAIM THESE FRAGILE TRESPASSERS.

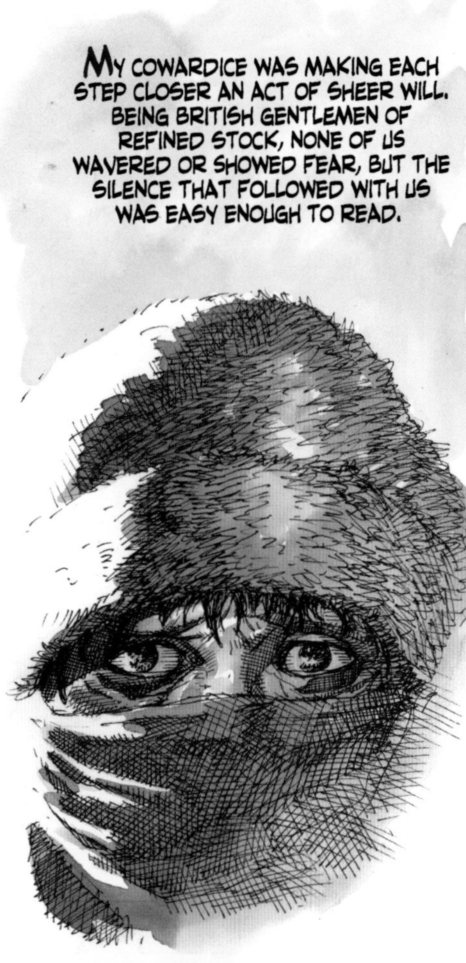
MY COWARDICE WAS MAKING EACH STEP CLOSER AN ACT OF SHEER WILL. BEING BRITISH GENTLEMEN OF REFINED STOCK, NONE OF US WAVERED OR SHOWED FEAR, BUT THE SILENCE THAT FOLLOWED WITH US WAS EASY ENOUGH TO READ.

WHEN WE FINALLY CAME CLOSE ENOUGH TO CONFIRM THE OBJECT'S TRUE SHAPE, IT WAS NO LESS SHOCKING THAN THE HORRORS MY MIND HAD ENVISIONED.

STANDING LIKE THE MONUMENT OF SOME DEAD PAGAN KING WAS A TREMENDOUS BLACK TREE, ITS APPEARANCE DEAD... OMINOUS... AND ALL THE MORE UNEARTHLY BECAUSE OF ITS LONELINESS IN THE WHITE LANDSCAPE.

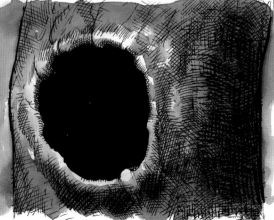

THE FEATURE THAT BROUGHT ME THE MOST UNEASE WAS THE KNOTHOLE IN THE CENTER OF THE TRUNK. THE OPAQUE BLACKNESS OF THIS CHASM SEEMED TOO DEEP... TOO REMOTE TO BE THE HOLLOW OF THIS DECREPIT, MISPLACED THING.

I DON'T KNOW HOW LONG WE STOOD GAZING UP AT IT, BUT NOT A WORD WAS SPOKEN BEFORE WE SLOWLY BACKED AWAY IN UNISON. WE WERE A GOOD DISTANCE AWAY BEFORE THE SILENCE WAS BROKEN. IT WAS ALMOST AS IF WE WERE AFRAID IT WOULD HEAR US.

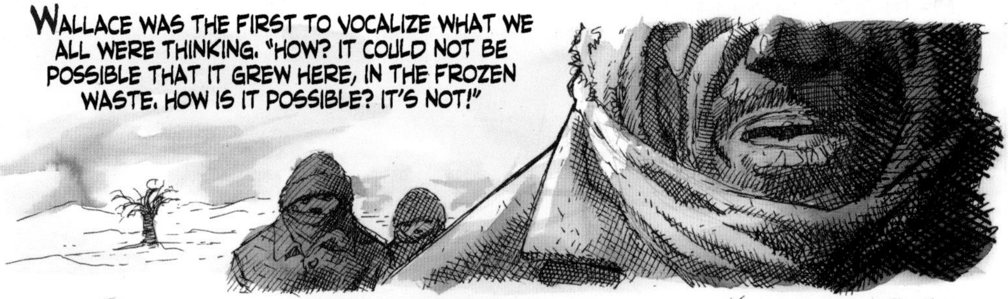
WALLACE WAS THE FIRST TO VOCALIZE WHAT WE ALL WERE THINKING. "HOW? IT COULD NOT BE POSSIBLE THAT IT GREW HERE, IN THE FROZEN WASTE. HOW IS IT POSSIBLE? IT'S NOT!"

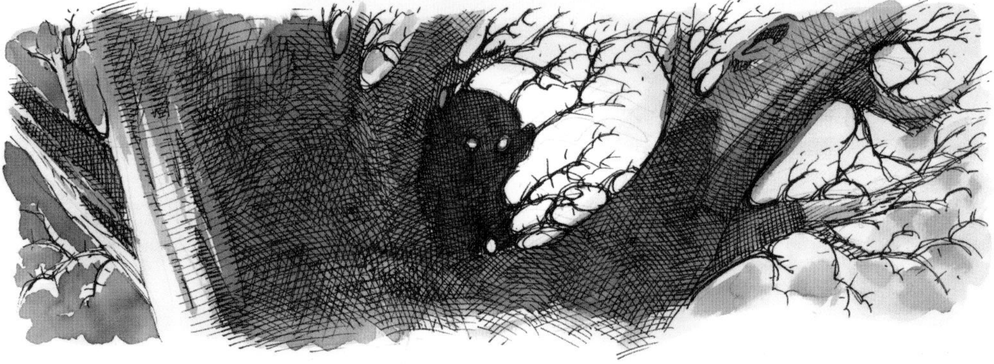

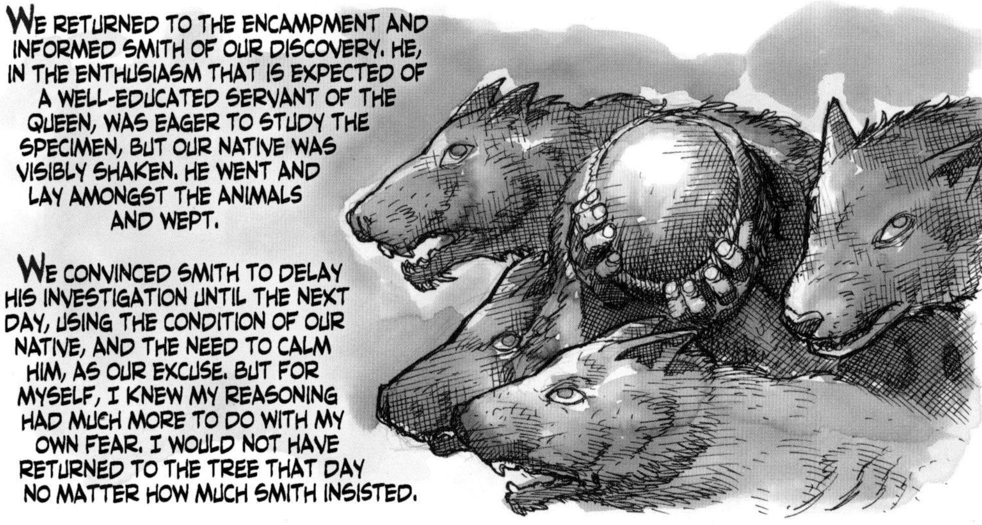
WE RETURNED TO THE ENCAMPMENT AND INFORMED SMITH OF OUR DISCOVERY. HE, IN THE ENTHUSIASM THAT IS EXPECTED OF A WELL-EDUCATED SERVANT OF THE QUEEN, WAS EAGER TO STUDY THE SPECIMEN, BUT OUR NATIVE WAS VISIBLY SHAKEN. HE WENT AND LAY AMONGST THE ANIMALS AND WEPT.
WE CONVINCED SMITH TO DELAY HIS INVESTIGATION UNTIL THE NEXT DAY, USING THE CONDITION OF OUR NATIVE, AND THE NEED TO CALM HIM, AS OUR EXCUSE. BUT FOR MYSELF, I KNEW MY REASONING HAD MUCH MORE TO DO WITH MY OWN FEAR. I WOULD NOT HAVE RETURNED TO THE TREE THAT DAY NO MATTER HOW MUCH SMITH INSISTED.

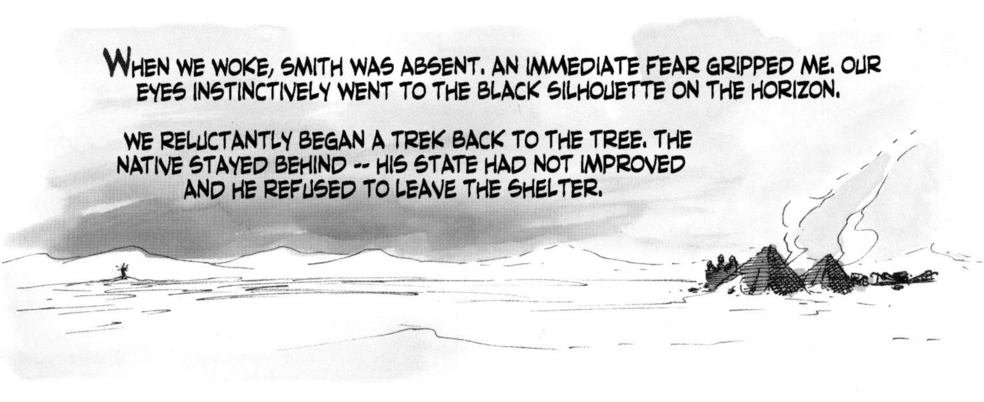
WHEN WE WOKE, SMITH WAS ABSENT. AN IMMEDIATE FEAR GRIPPED ME. OUR EYES INSTINCTIVELY WENT TO THE BLACK SILHOUETTE ON THE HORIZON.
WE RELUCTANTLY BEGAN A TREK BACK TO THE TREE. THE NATIVE STAYED BEHIND -- HIS STATE HAD NOT IMPROVED AND HE REFUSED TO LEAVE THE SHELTER.

AS WE APPROACHED, I BELIEVED MY MIND TO BE DECEIVING ME AS IT HAD THE DAY BEFORE WHEN I SAW THE THING AS A GIANT. IT SEEMED AS IF THE THING WAS NOW NESTLED IN A RING OF CRIMSON TURF. TO MY HORROR I REALIZED ONLY AS THE CRUMPLED FIGURE OF SMITH CAME INTO VIEW THAT IT WAS NOT TURF, BUT THE BLOOD-DRENCHED ICE.

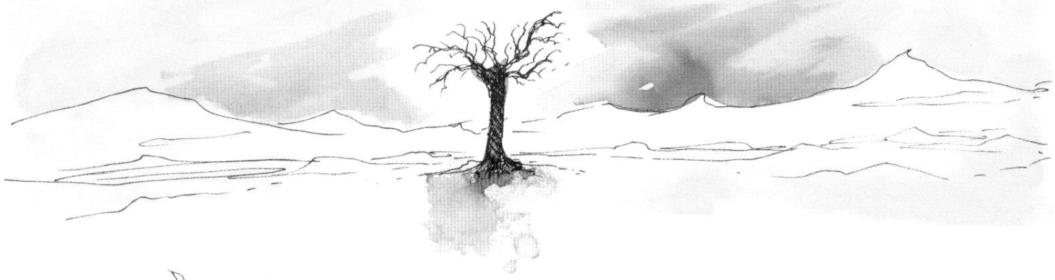

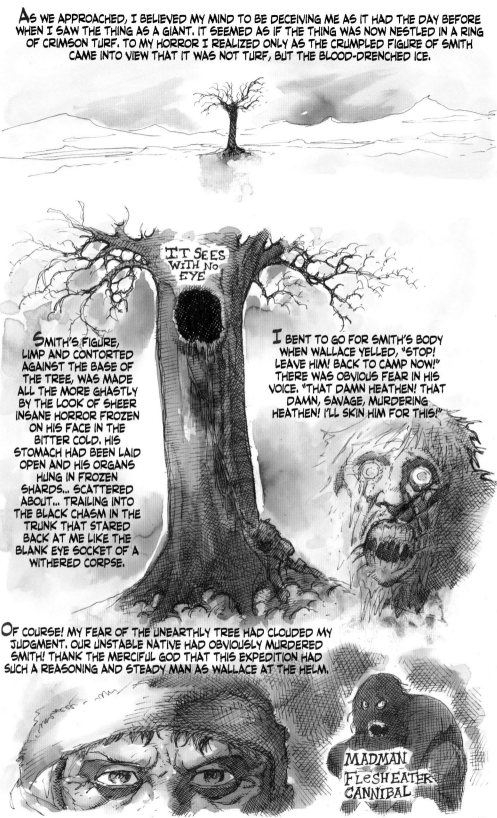

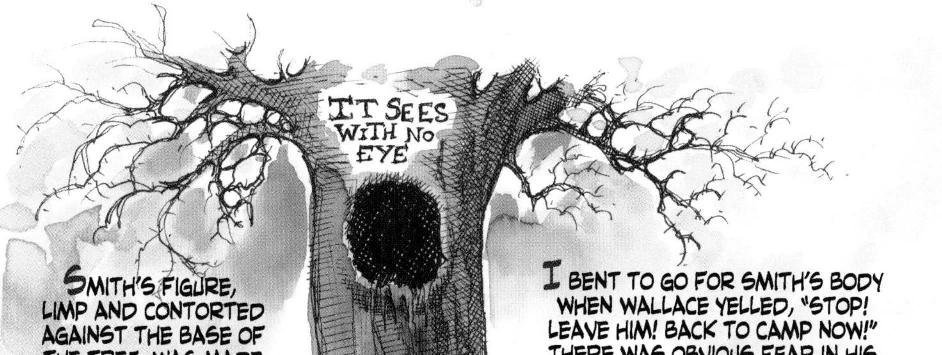
IT SEES WITH NO EYE

SMITH'S FIGURE, LIMP AND CONTORTED AGAINST THE BASE OF THE TREE, WAS MADE ALL THE MORE GHASTLY BY THE LOOK OF SHEER INSANE HORROR FROZEN ON HIS FACE IN THE BITTER COLD. HIS STOMACH HAD BEEN LAID OPEN AND HIS ORGANS HUNG IN FROZEN SHARDS... SCATTERED ABOUT... TRAILING INTO THE BLACK CHASM IN THE TRUNK THAT STARED BACK AT ME LIKE THE BLANK EYE SOCKET OF A WITHERED CORPSE.

I BENT TO GO FOR SMITH'S BODY WHEN WALLACE YELLED, "STOP! LEAVE HIM! BACK TO CAMP NOW!" THERE WAS OBVIOUS FEAR IN HIS VOICE. "THAT DAMN HEATHEN! THAT DAMN, SAVAGE, MURDERING HEATHEN! I'LL SKIN HIM FOR THIS!"

OF COURSE! MY FEAR OF THE UNEARTHLY TREE HAD CLOUDED MY JUDGMENT. OUR UNSTABLE NATIVE HAD OBVIOUSLY MURDERED SMITH! THANK THE MERCIFUL GOD THAT THIS EXPEDITION HAD SUCH A REASONING AND STEADY MAN AS WALLACE AT THE HELM.

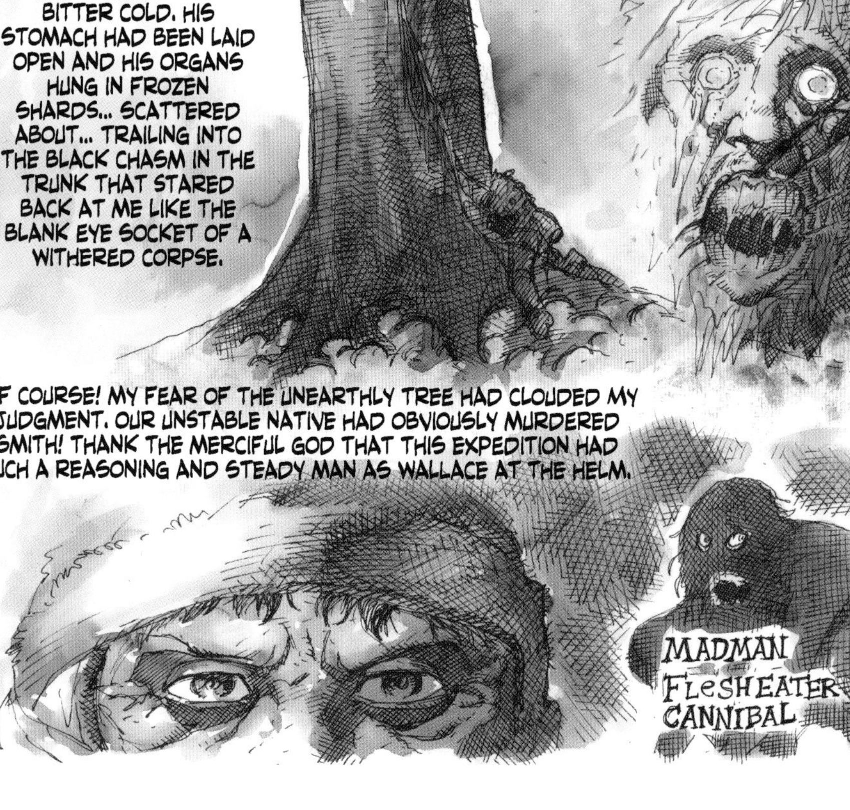
MADMAN
FLESHEATER
CANNIBAL

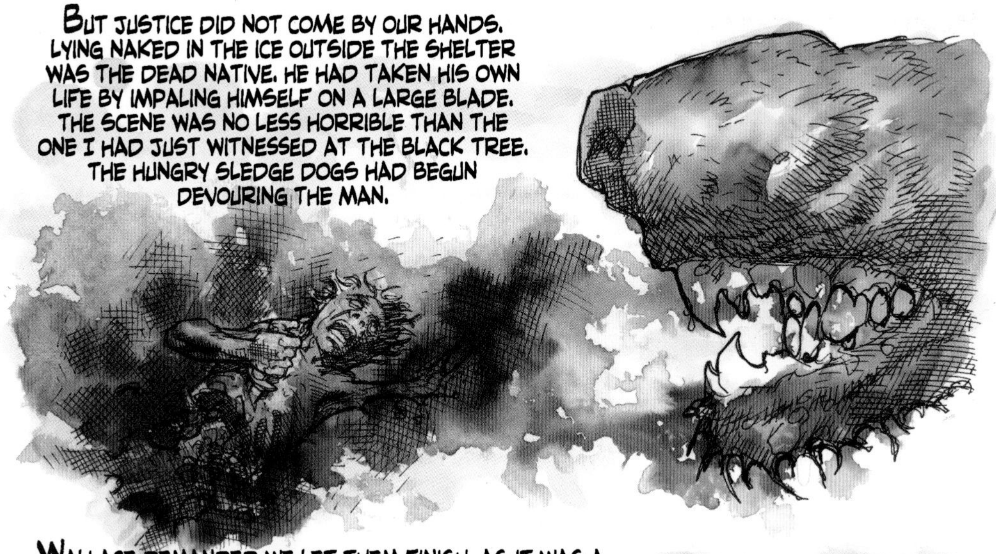
But justice did not come by our hands. Lying naked in the ice outside the shelter was the dead native. He had taken his own life by impaling himself on a large blade. The scene was no less horrible than the one I had just witnessed at the black tree. The hungry sledge dogs had begun devouring the man.

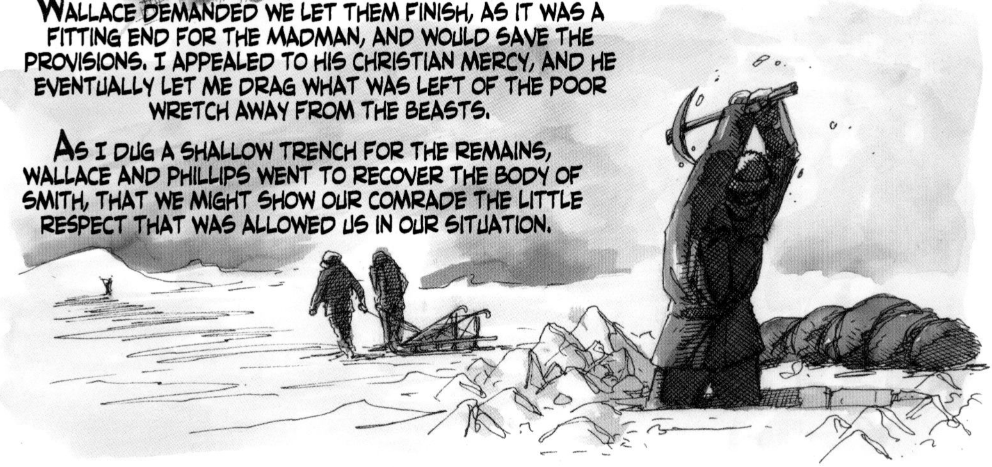
Wallace demanded we let them finish, as it was a fitting end for the madman, and would save the provisions. I appealed to his Christian mercy, and he eventually let me drag what was left of the poor wretch away from the beasts.
As I dug a shallow trench for the remains, Wallace and Phillips went to recover the body of Smith, that we might show our comrade the little respect that was allowed us in our situation.

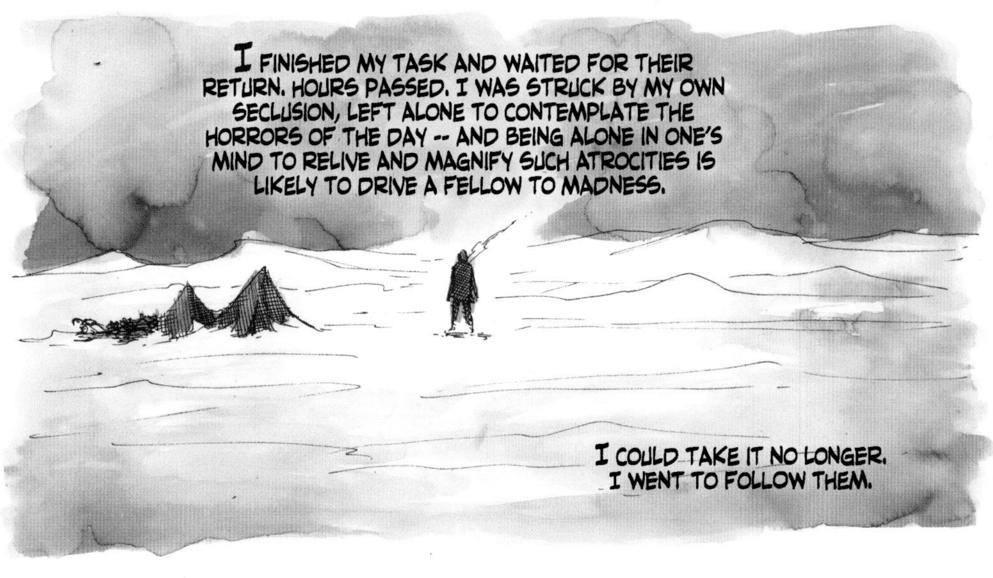
I finished my task and waited for their return. Hours passed. I was struck by my own seclusion, left alone to contemplate the horrors of the day -- and being alone in one's mind to relive and magnify such atrocities is likely to drive a fellow to madness.
I could take it no longer. I went to follow them.

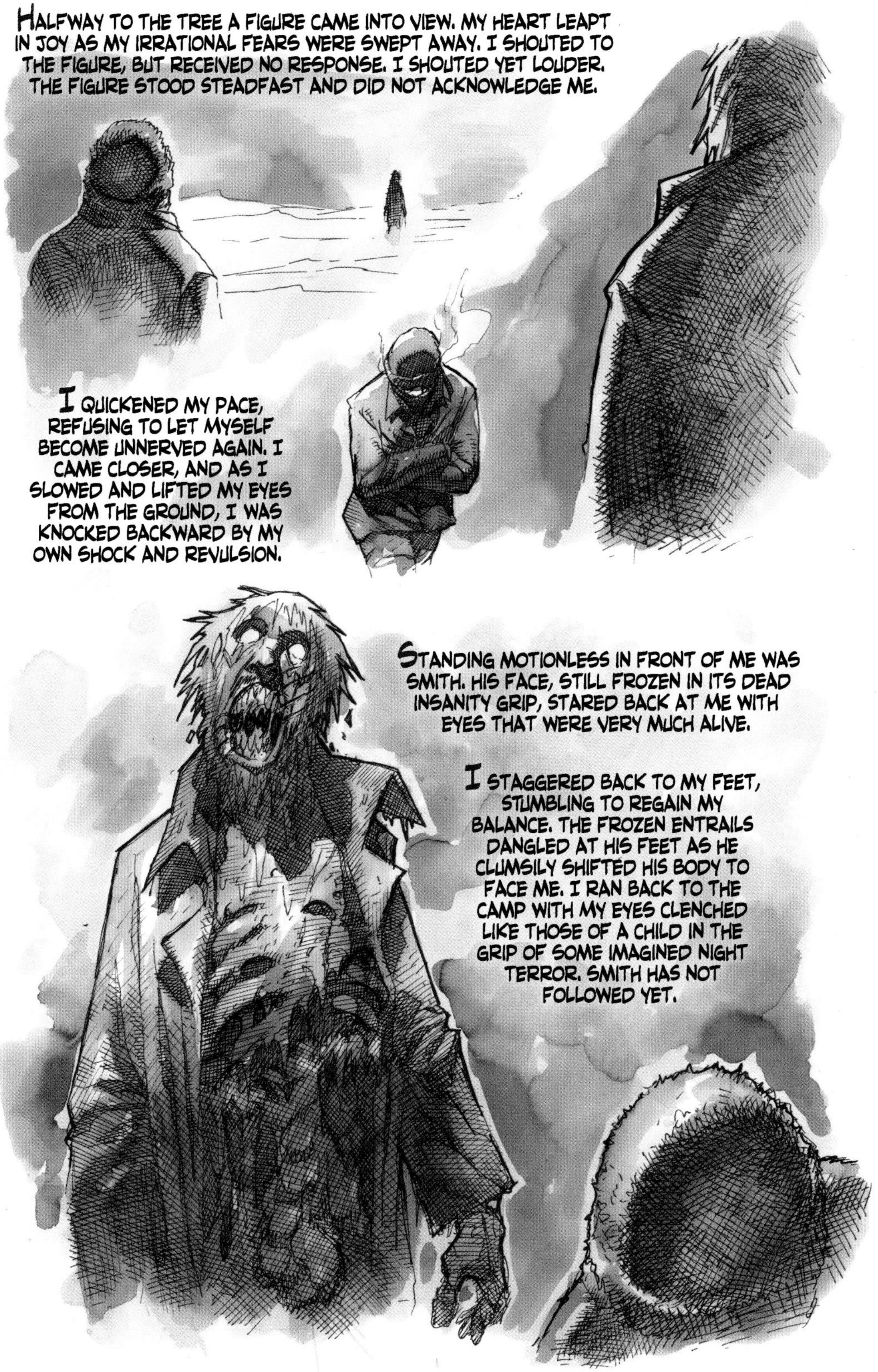
HALFWAY TO THE TREE A FIGURE CAME INTO VIEW. MY HEART LEAPT IN JOY AS MY IRRATIONAL FEARS WERE SWEPT AWAY. I SHOUTED TO THE FIGURE, BUT RECEIVED NO RESPONSE. I SHOUTED YET LOUDER. THE FIGURE STOOD STEADFAST AND DID NOT ACKNOWLEDGE ME.
I QUICKENED MY PACE, REFUSING TO LET MYSELF BECOME UNNERVED AGAIN. I CAME CLOSER, AND AS I SLOWED AND LIFTED MY EYES FROM THE GROUND, I WAS KNOCKED BACKWARD BY MY OWN SHOCK AND REVULSION.
STANDING MOTIONLESS IN FRONT OF ME WAS SMITH. HIS FACE, STILL FROZEN IN ITS DEAD INSANITY GRIP, STARED BACK AT ME WITH EYES THAT WERE VERY MUCH ALIVE.
I STAGGERED BACK TO MY FEET, STUMBLING TO REGAIN MY BALANCE. THE FROZEN ENTRAILS DANGLED AT HIS FEET AS HE CLUMSILY SHIFTED HIS BODY TO FACE ME. I RAN BACK TO THE CAMP WITH MY EYES CLENCHED LIKE THOSE OF A CHILD IN THE GRIP OF SOME IMAGINED NIGHT TERROR. SMITH HAS NOT FOLLOWED YET.

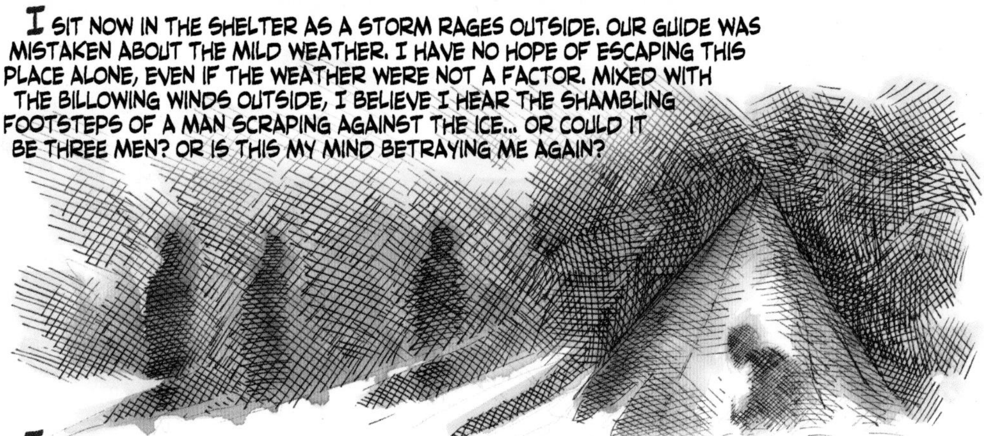
I SIT NOW IN THE SHELTER AS A STORM RAGES OUTSIDE. OUR GUIDE WAS MISTAKEN ABOUT THE MILD WEATHER. I HAVE NO HOPE OF ESCAPING THIS PLACE ALONE, EVEN IF THE WEATHER WERE NOT A FACTOR. MIXED WITH THE BILLOWING WINDS OUTSIDE, I BELIEVE I HEAR THE SHAMBLING FOOTSTEPS OF A MAN SCRAPING AGAINST THE ICE... OR COULD IT BE THREE MEN? OR IS THIS MY MIND BETRAYING ME AGAIN?

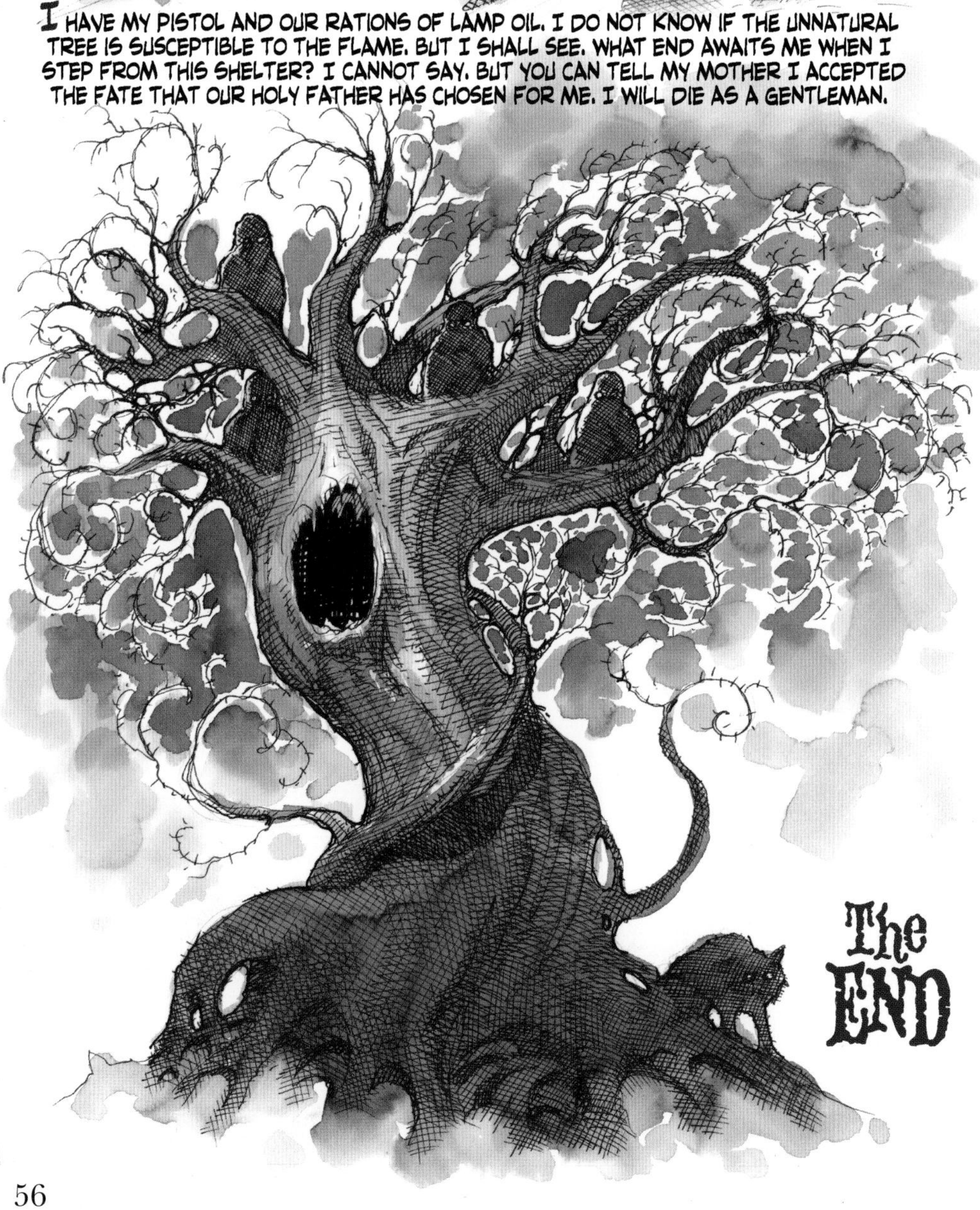
I HAVE MY PISTOL AND OUR RATIONS OF LAMP OIL. I DO NOT KNOW IF THE UNNATURAL TREE IS SUSCEPTIBLE TO THE FLAME. BUT I SHALL SEE. WHAT END AWAITS ME WHEN I STEP FROM THIS SHELTER? I CANNOT SAY. BUT YOU CAN TELL MY MOTHER I ACCEPTED THE FATE THAT OUR HOLY FATHER HAS CHOSEN FOR ME. I WILL DIE AS A GENTLEMAN.
The END

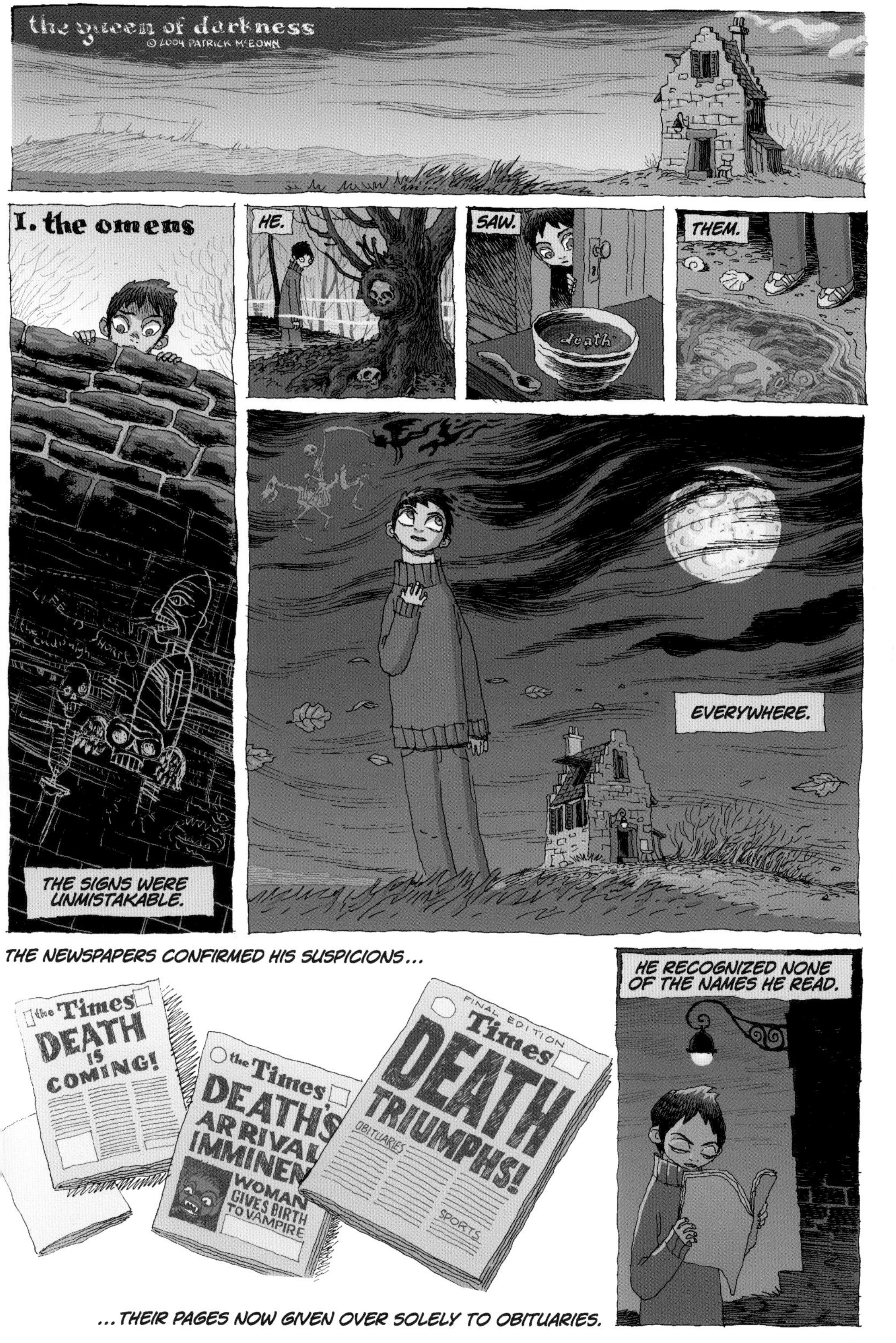

the queen of darkness
© 2004 PATRICK McEOWN
I. the omens
HE.
SAW.
death
THEM.
THE SIGNS WERE UNMISTAKABLE.
EVERYWHERE.
THE NEWSPAPERS CONFIRMED HIS SUSPICIONS...
the Times
DEATH IS COMING!
the Times
DEATH'S ARRIVAL IMMINEN
WOMAN GIVES BIRTH TO VAMPIRE
FINAL EDITION
Times
DEATH TRIUMPHS!
OBITUARIES
SPORTS
HE RECOGNIZED NONE OF THE NAMES HE READ.
...THEIR PAGES NOW GIVEN OVER SOLELY TO OBITUARIES.

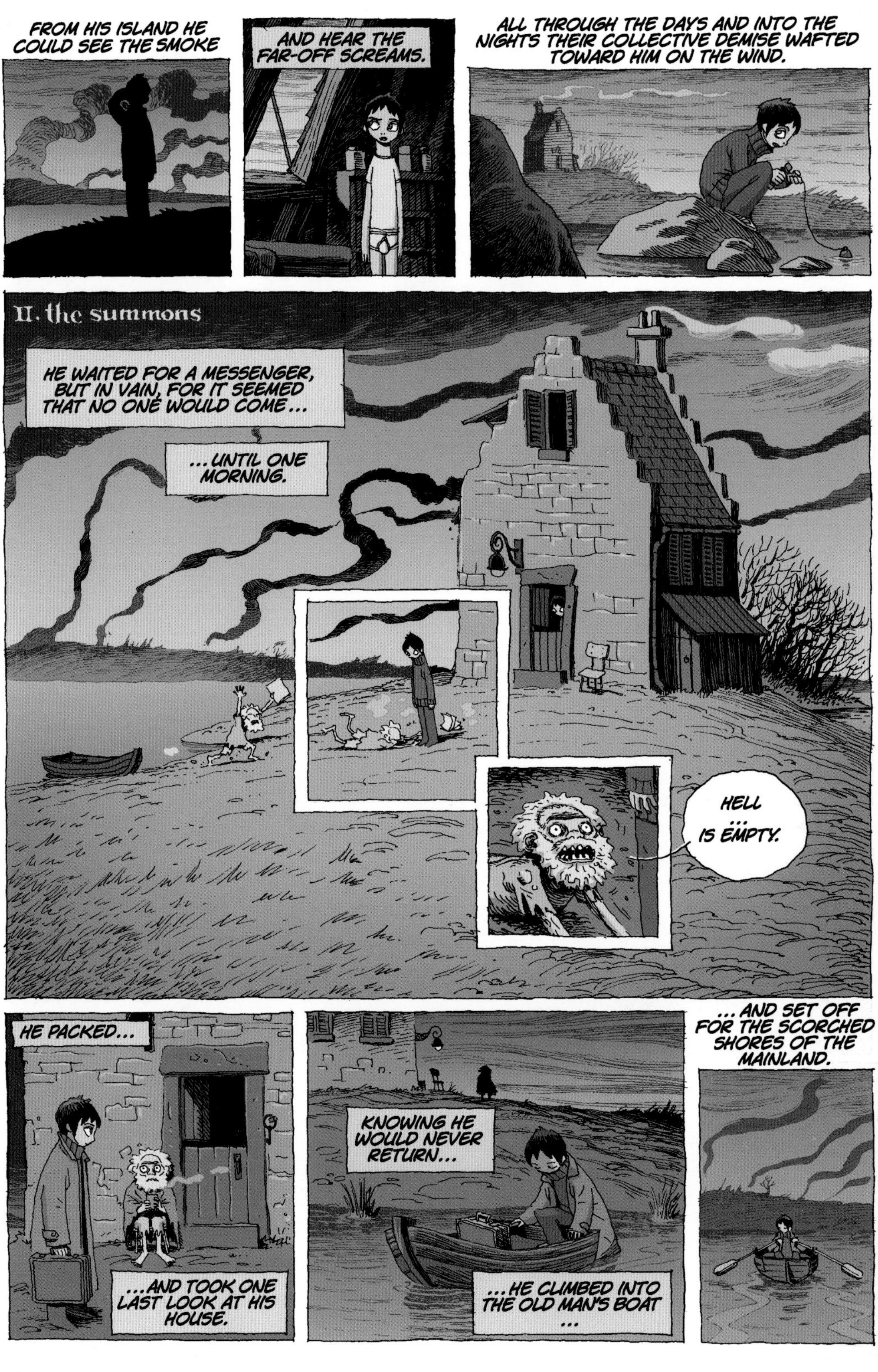
FROM HIS ISLAND HE COULD SEE THE SMOKE
AND HEAR THE FAR-OFF SCREAMS.
ALL THROUGH THE DAYS AND INTO THE NIGHTS THEIR COLLECTIVE DEMISE WAFTED TOWARD HIM ON THE WIND.
II. the summons
HE WAITED FOR A MESSENGER, BUT IN VAIN, FOR IT SEEMED THAT NO ONE WOULD COME...
...UNTIL ONE MORNING.
HELL ... IS EMPTY.
HE PACKED...
...AND TOOK ONE LAST LOOK AT HIS HOUSE.
KNOWING HE WOULD NEVER RETURN...
...HE CLIMBED INTO THE OLD MAN'S BOAT ...
... AND SET OFF FOR THE SCORCHED SHORES OF THE MAINLAND.

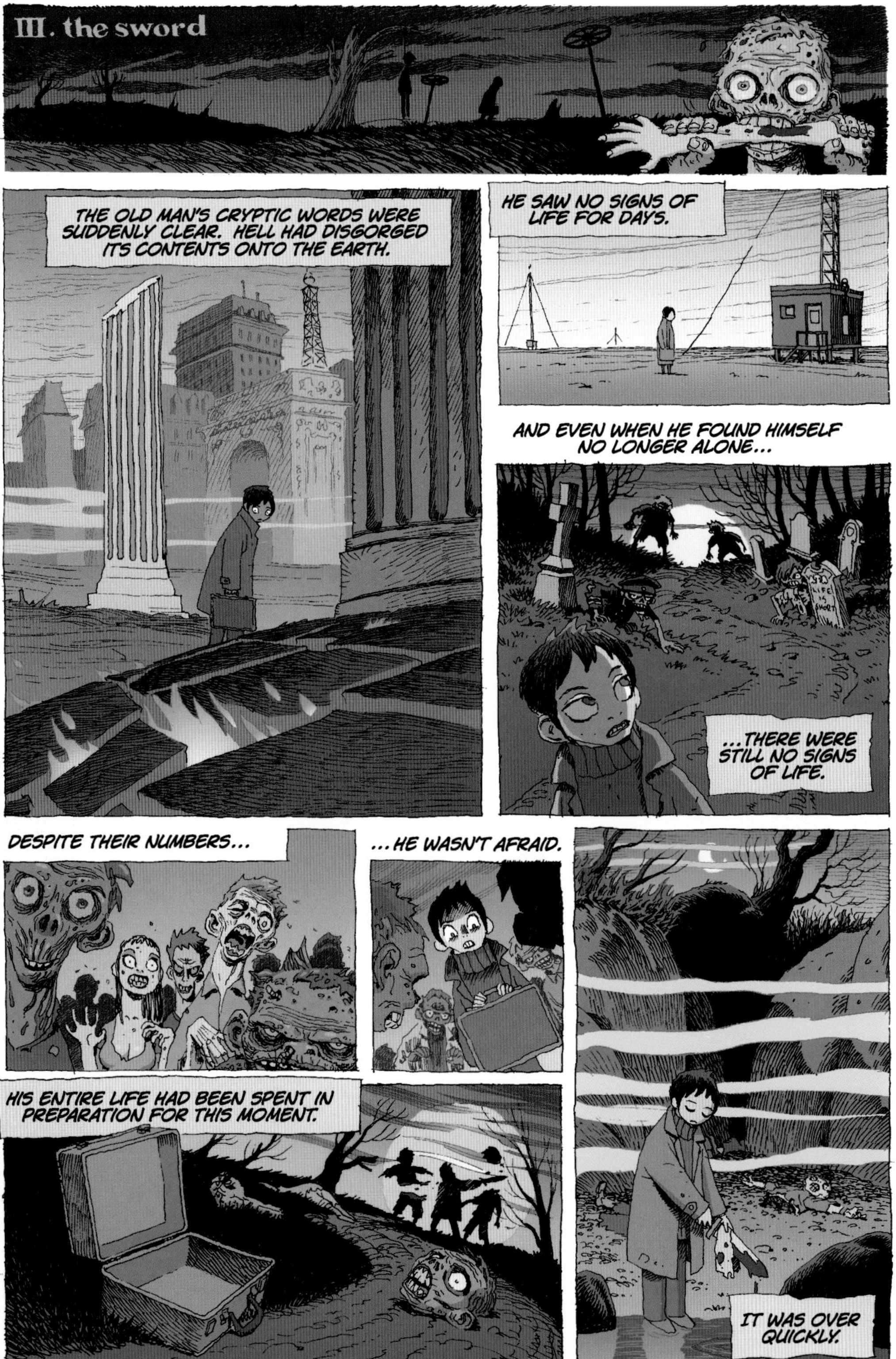
III. the sword
THE OLD MAN'S CRYPTIC WORDS WERE SUDDENLY CLEAR. HELL HAD DISGORGED ITS CONTENTS ONTO THE EARTH.
HE SAW NO SIGNS OF LIFE FOR DAYS.
AND EVEN WHEN HE FOUND HIMSELF NO LONGER ALONE...
LIFE IS SHORT
...THERE WERE STILL NO SIGNS OF LIFE.
DESPITE THEIR NUMBERS...
...HE WASN'T AFRAID.
HIS ENTIRE LIFE HAD BEEN SPENT IN PREPARATION FOR THIS MOMENT.
IT WAS OVER QUICKLY.

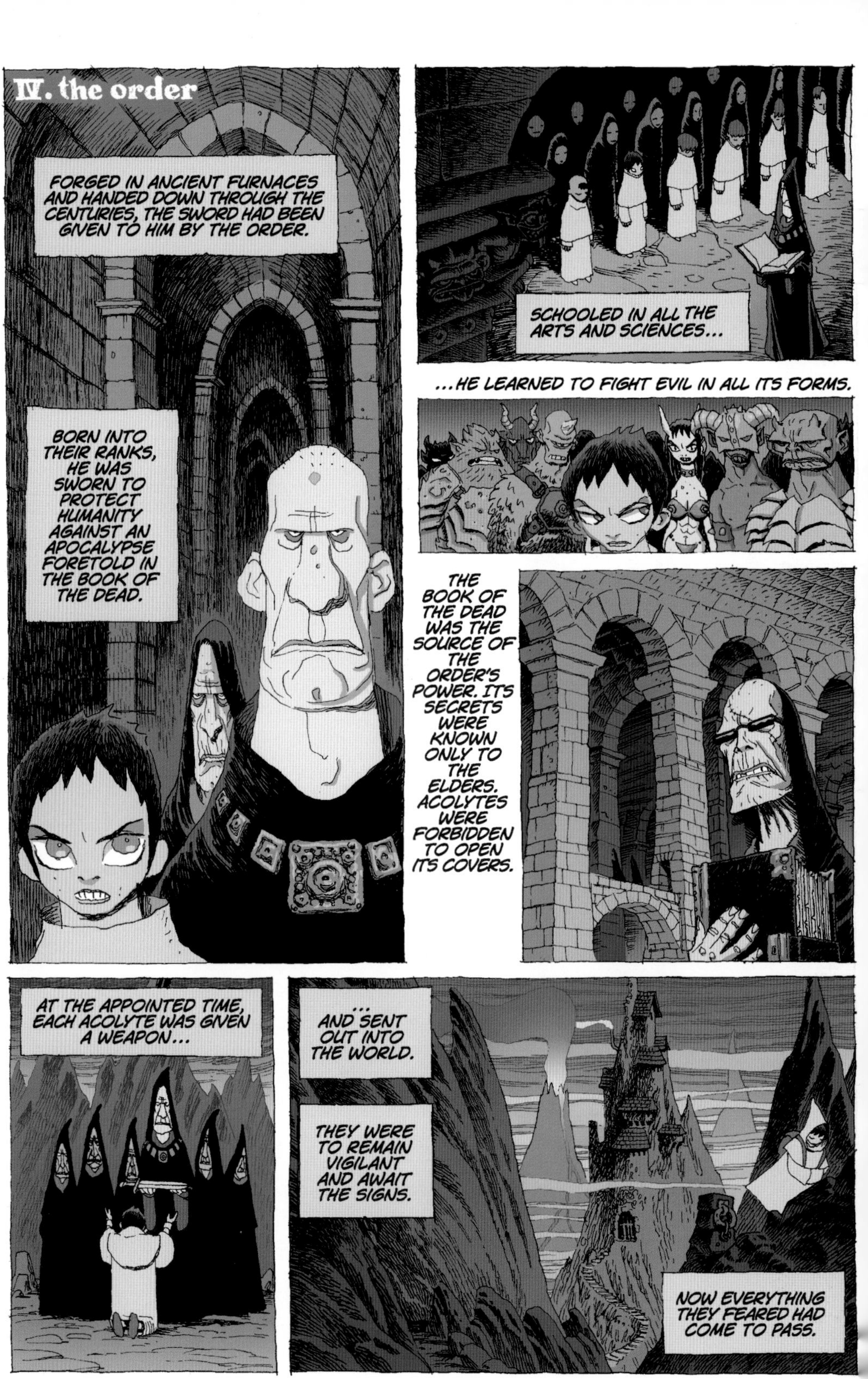
IV. the order
FORGED IN ANCIENT FURNACES AND HANDED DOWN THROUGH THE CENTURIES, THE SWORD HAD BEEN GIVEN TO HIM BY THE ORDER.
BORN INTO THEIR RANKS, HE WAS SWORN TO PROTECT HUMANITY AGAINST AN APOCALYPSE FORETOLD IN THE BOOK OF THE DEAD.
SCHOOLED IN ALL THE ARTS AND SCIENCES...
...HE LEARNED TO FIGHT EVIL IN ALL ITS FORMS.
THE BOOK OF THE DEAD WAS THE SOURCE OF THE ORDER'S POWER. ITS SECRETS WERE KNOWN ONLY TO THE ELDERS. ACOLYTES WERE FORBIDDEN TO OPEN ITS COVERS.
AT THE APPOINTED TIME, EACH ACOLYTE WAS GIVEN A WEAPON...
...AND SENT OUT INTO THE WORLD.
THEY WERE TO REMAIN VIGILANT AND AWAIT THE SIGNS.
NOW EVERYTHING THEY FEARED HAD COME TO PASS.

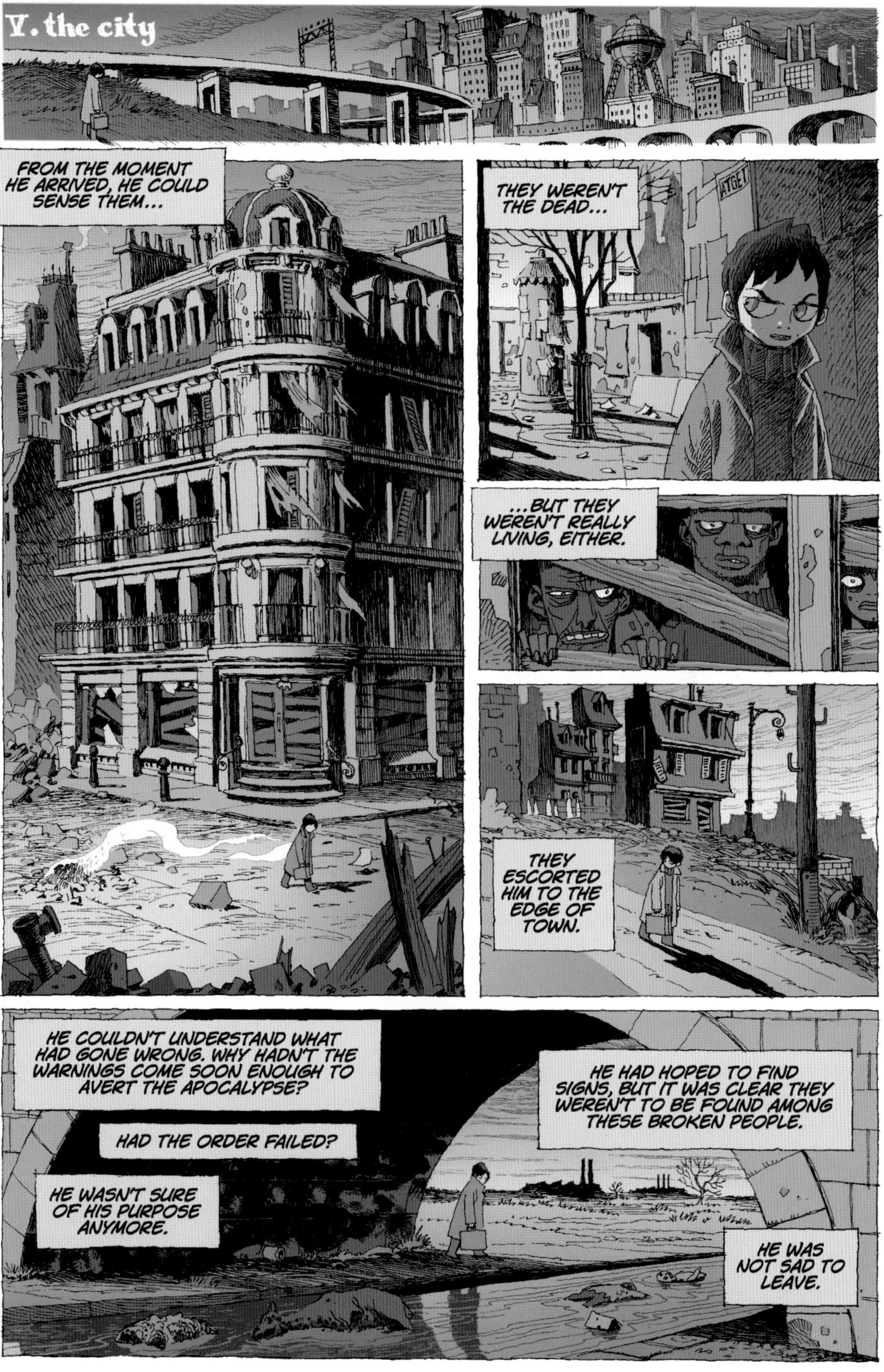
V. the city
FROM THE MOMENT HE ARRIVED, HE COULD SENSE THEM...
THEY WEREN'T THE DEAD...
ATGET
...BUT THEY WEREN'T REALLY LIVING, EITHER.
THEY ESCORTED HIM TO THE EDGE OF TOWN.
HE COULDN'T UNDERSTAND WHAT HAD GONE WRONG. WHY HADN'T THE WARNINGS COME SOON ENOUGH TO AVERT THE APOCALYPSE?
HAD THE ORDER FAILED?
HE WASN'T SURE OF HIS PURPOSE ANYMORE.
HE HAD HOPED TO FIND SIGNS, BUT IT WAS CLEAR THEY WEREN'T TO BE FOUND AMONG THESE BROKEN PEOPLE.
HE WAS NOT SAD TO LEAVE.

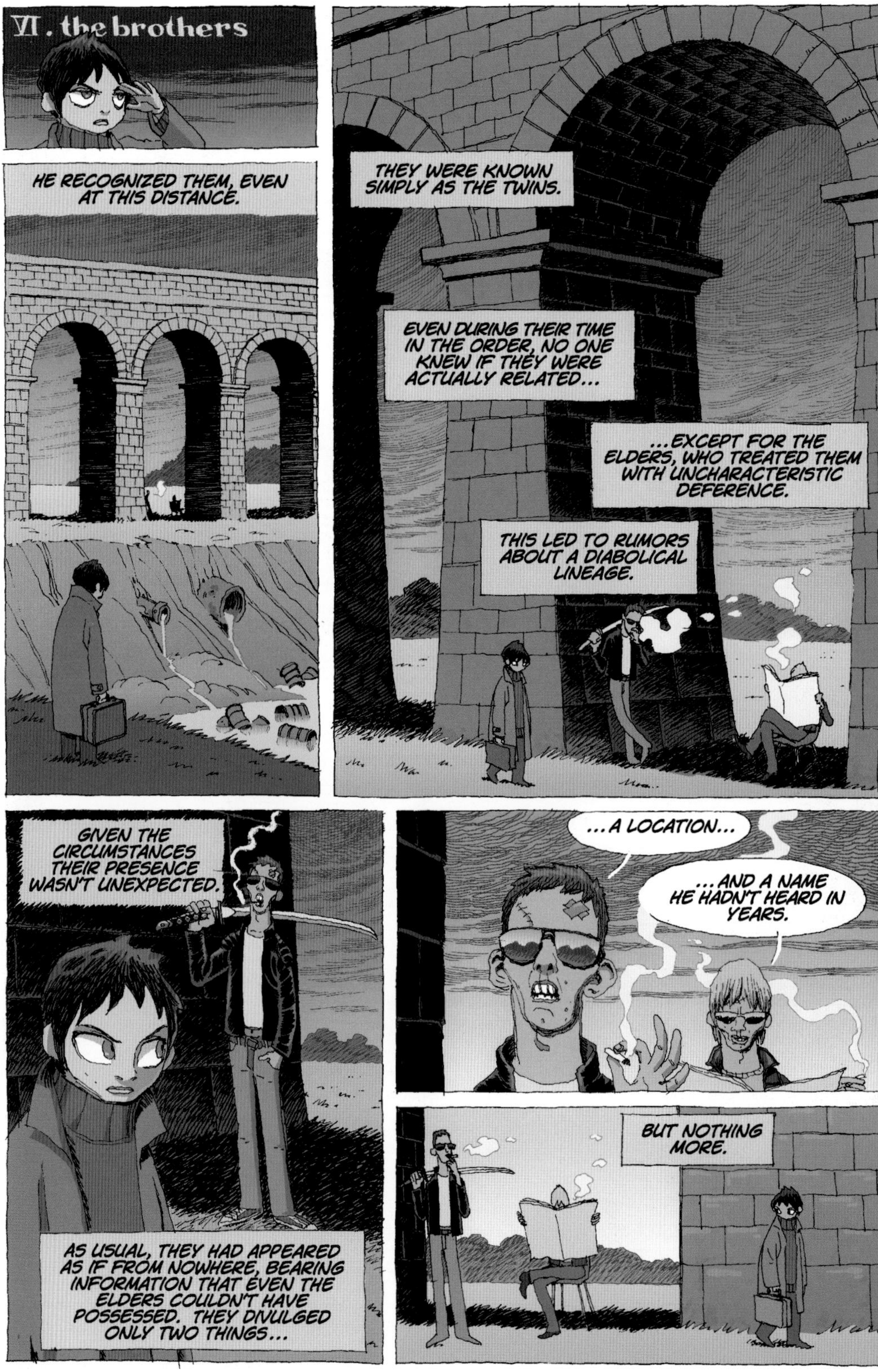
VI . the brothers
HE RECOGNIZED THEM, EVEN AT THIS DISTANCE.
THEY WERE KNOWN SIMPLY AS THE TWINS.
EVEN DURING THEIR TIME IN THE ORDER, NO ONE KNEW IF THEY WERE ACTUALLY RELATED...
...EXCEPT FOR THE ELDERS, WHO TREATED THEM WITH UNCHARACTERISTIC DEFERENCE.
THIS LED TO RUMORS ABOUT A DIABOLICAL LINEAGE.
GIVEN THE CIRCUMSTANCES THEIR PRESENCE WASN'T UNEXPECTED.
AS USUAL, THEY HAD APPEARED AS IF FROM NOWHERE, BEARING INFORMATION THAT EVEN THE ELDERS COULDN'T HAVE POSSESSED. THEY DIVULGED ONLY TWO THINGS...
...A LOCATION...
...AND A NAME HE HADN'T HEARD IN YEARS.
BUT NOTHING MORE.

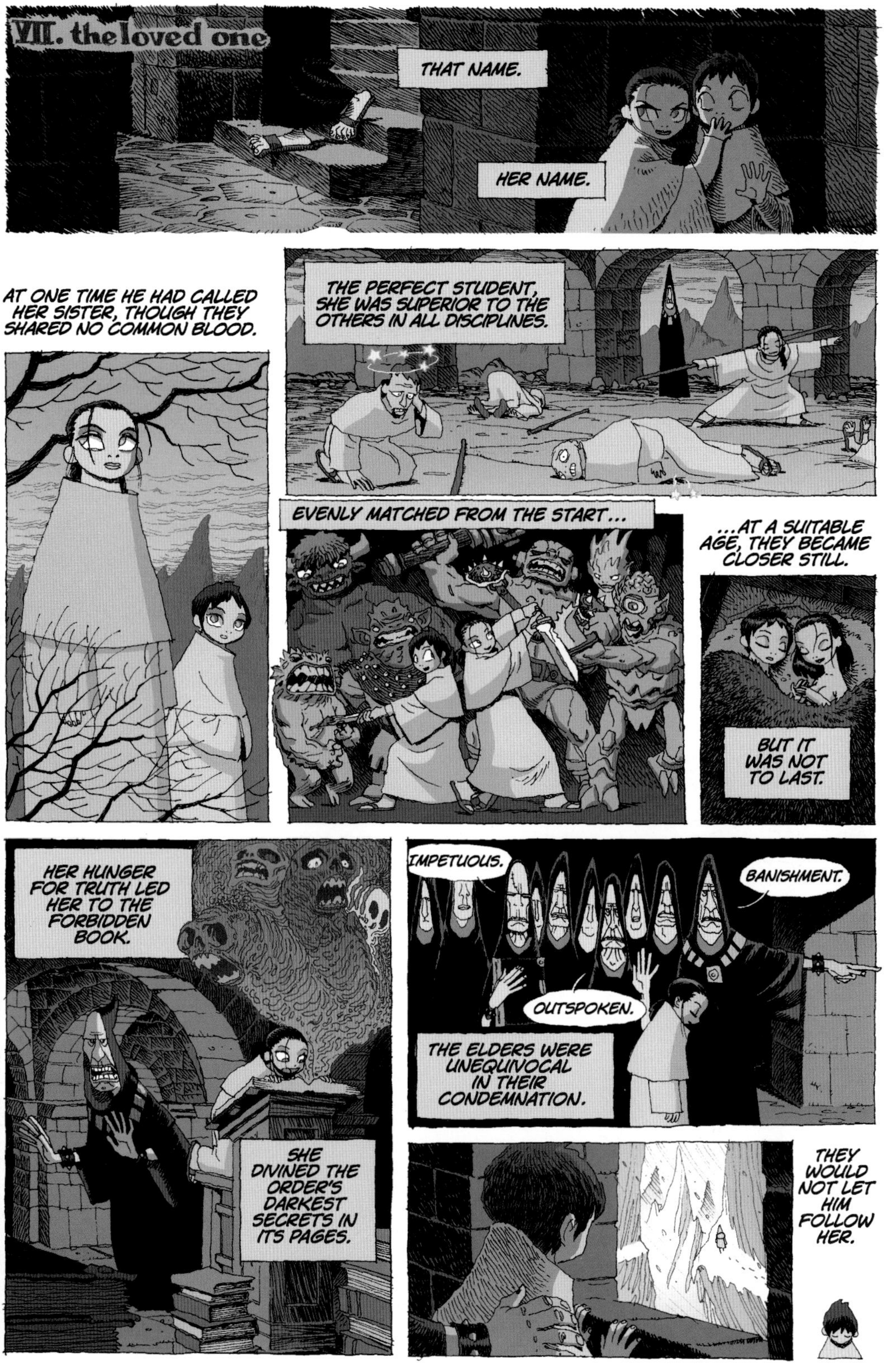
VII. the loved one
THAT NAME.
HER NAME.
AT ONE TIME HE HAD CALLED HER SISTER, THOUGH THEY SHARED NO COMMON BLOOD.
THE PERFECT STUDENT, SHE WAS SUPERIOR TO THE OTHERS IN ALL DISCIPLINES.
EVENLY MATCHED FROM THE START...
...AT A SUITABLE AGE, THEY BECAME CLOSER STILL.
BUT IT WAS NOT TO LAST.
HER HUNGER FOR TRUTH LED HER TO THE FORBIDDEN BOOK.
SHE DIVINED THE ORDER'S DARKEST SECRETS IN ITS PAGES.
IMPETUOUS.
BANISHMENT.
OUTSPOKEN.
THE ELDERS WERE UNEQUIVOCAL IN THEIR CONDEMNATION.
THEY WOULD NOT LET HIM FOLLOW HER.

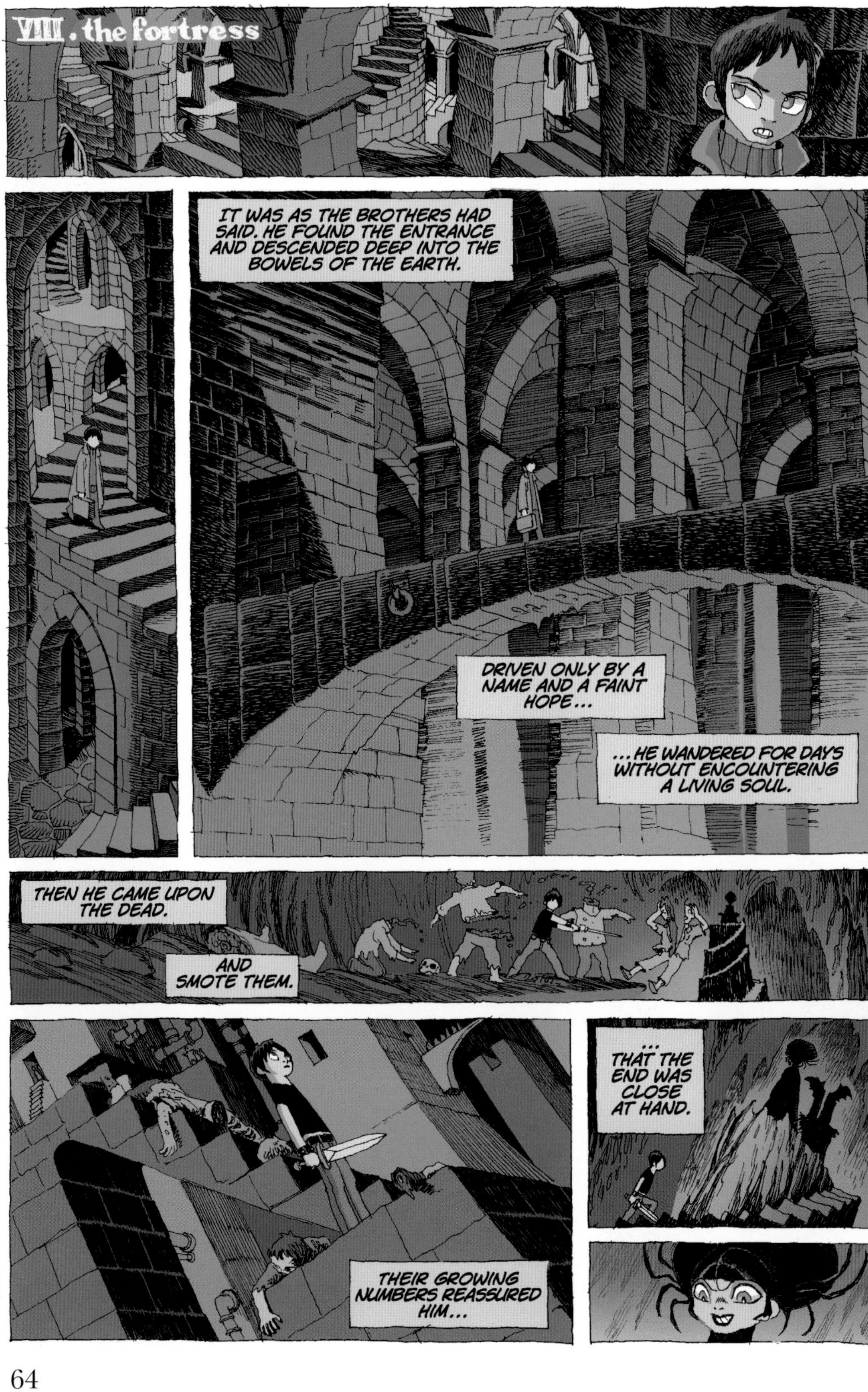
VIII . the fortress
IT WAS AS THE BROTHERS HAD SAID. HE FOUND THE ENTRANCE AND DESCENDED DEEP INTO THE BOWELS OF THE EARTH.
DRIVEN ONLY BY A NAME AND A FAINT HOPE...
...HE WANDERED FOR DAYS WITHOUT ENCOUNTERING A LIVING SOUL.
THEN HE CAME UPON THE DEAD.
AND SMOTE THEM.
THEIR GROWING NUMBERS REASSURED HIM...
...THAT THE END WAS CLOSE AT HAND.

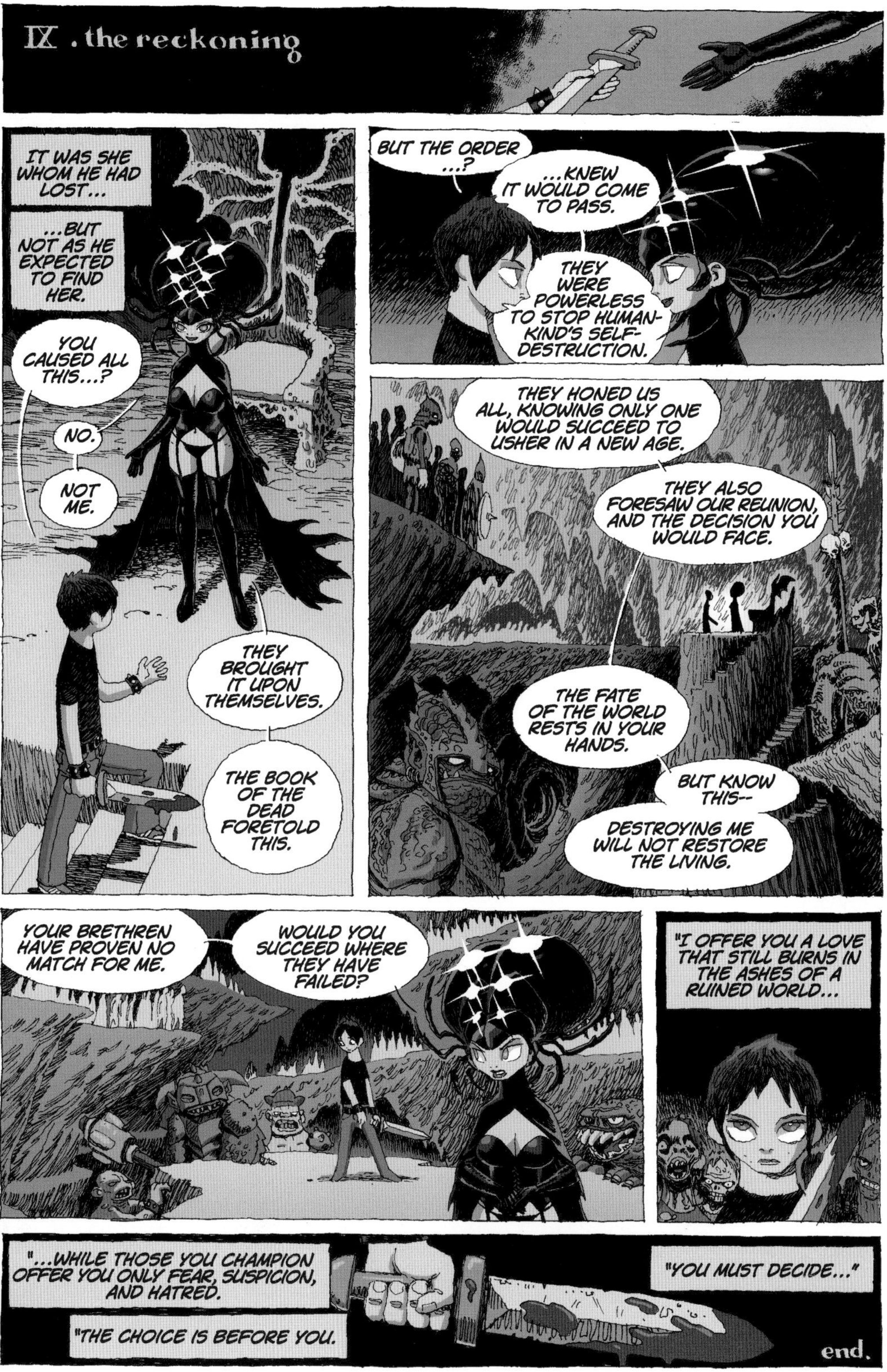
IX . the reckoning
IT WAS SHE WHOM HE HAD LOST...
...BUT NOT AS HE EXPECTED TO FIND HER.
YOU CAUSED ALL THIS...?
NO.
NOT ME.
THEY BROUGHT IT UPON THEMSELVES.
THE BOOK OF THE DEAD FORETOLD THIS.
BUT THE ORDER ...?
...KNEW IT WOULD COME TO PASS.
THEY WERE POWERLESS TO STOP HUMAN-KIND'S SELF-DESTRUCTION.
THEY HONED US ALL, KNOWING ONLY ONE WOULD SUCCEED TO USHER IN A NEW AGE.
THEY ALSO FORESAW OUR REUNION, AND THE DECISION YOU WOULD FACE.
THE FATE OF THE WORLD RESTS IN YOUR HANDS.
BUT KNOW THIS--
DESTROYING ME WILL NOT RESTORE THE LIVING.
YOUR BRETHREN HAVE PROVEN NO MATCH FOR ME.
WOULD YOU SUCCEED WHERE THEY HAVE FAILED?
"I OFFER YOU A LOVE THAT STILL BURNS IN THE ASHES OF A RUINED WORLD...
"...WHILE THOSE YOU CHAMPION OFFER YOU ONLY FEAR, SUSPICION, AND HATRED.
"THE CHOICE IS BEFORE YOU.
"YOU MUST DECIDE..."
end.

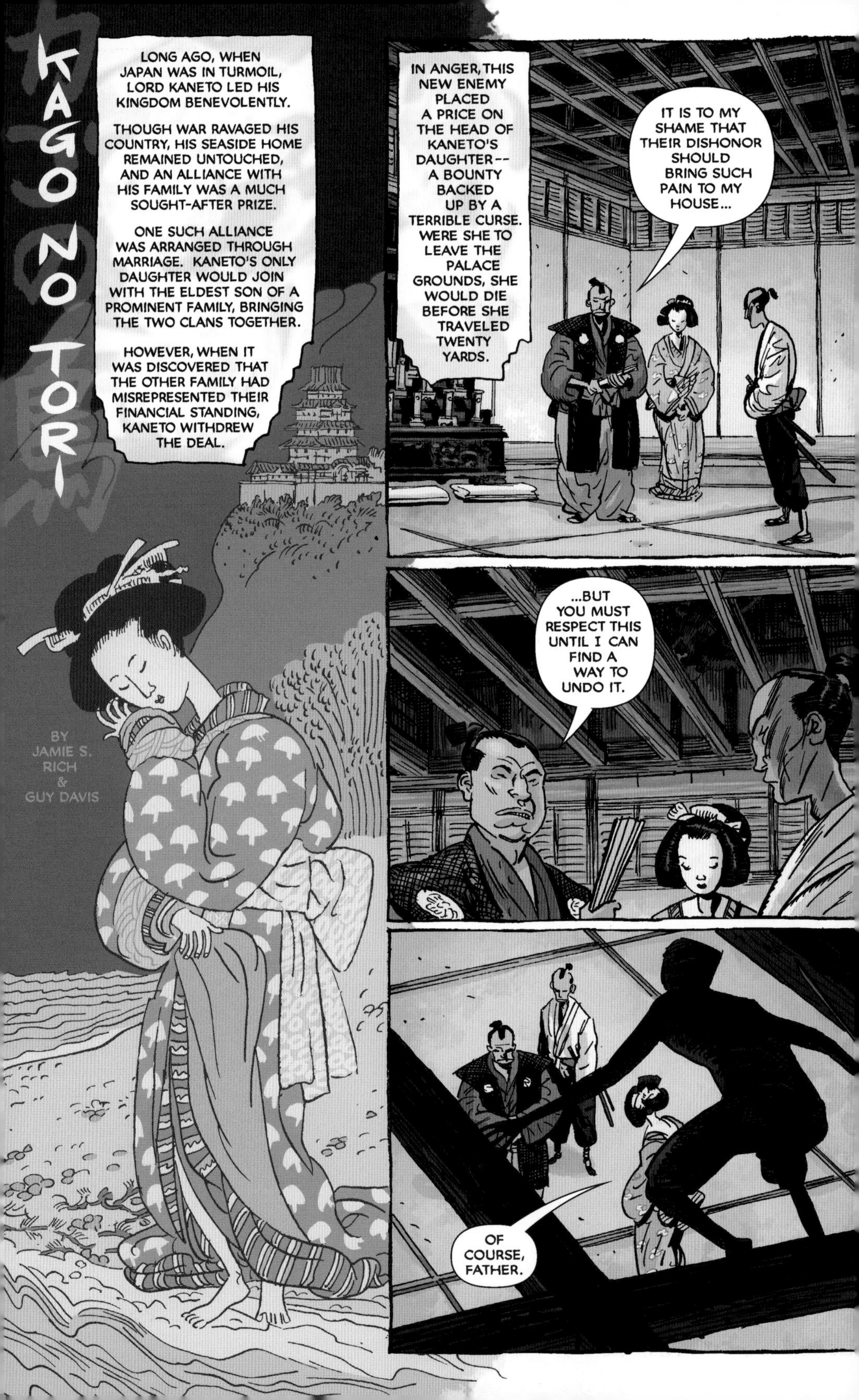
KAGO NO TORI
LONG AGO, WHEN JAPAN WAS IN TURMOIL, LORD KANETO LED HIS KINGDOM BENEVOLENTLY.
THOUGH WAR RAVAGED HIS COUNTRY, HIS SEASIDE HOME REMAINED UNTOUCHED, AND AN ALLIANCE WITH HIS FAMILY WAS A MUCH SOUGHT-AFTER PRIZE.
ONE SUCH ALLIANCE WAS ARRANGED THROUGH MARRIAGE. KANETO'S ONLY DAUGHTER WOULD JOIN WITH THE ELDEST SON OF A PROMINENT FAMILY, BRINGING THE TWO CLANS TOGETHER.
HOWEVER, WHEN IT WAS DISCOVERED THAT THE OTHER FAMILY HAD MISREPRESENTED THEIR FINANCIAL STANDING, KANETO WITHDREW THE DEAL.
BY JAMIE S. RICH & GUY DAVIS
IN ANGER, THIS NEW ENEMY PLACED A PRICE ON THE HEAD OF KANETO'S DAUGHTER-- A BOUNTY BACKED UP BY A TERRIBLE CURSE. WERE SHE TO LEAVE THE PALACE GROUNDS, SHE WOULD DIE BEFORE SHE TRAVELED TWENTY YARDS.
IT IS TO MY SHAME THAT THEIR DISHONOR SHOULD BRING SUCH PAIN TO MY HOUSE...
...BUT YOU MUST RESPECT THIS UNTIL I CAN FIND A WAY TO UNDO IT.
OF COURSE, FATHER.

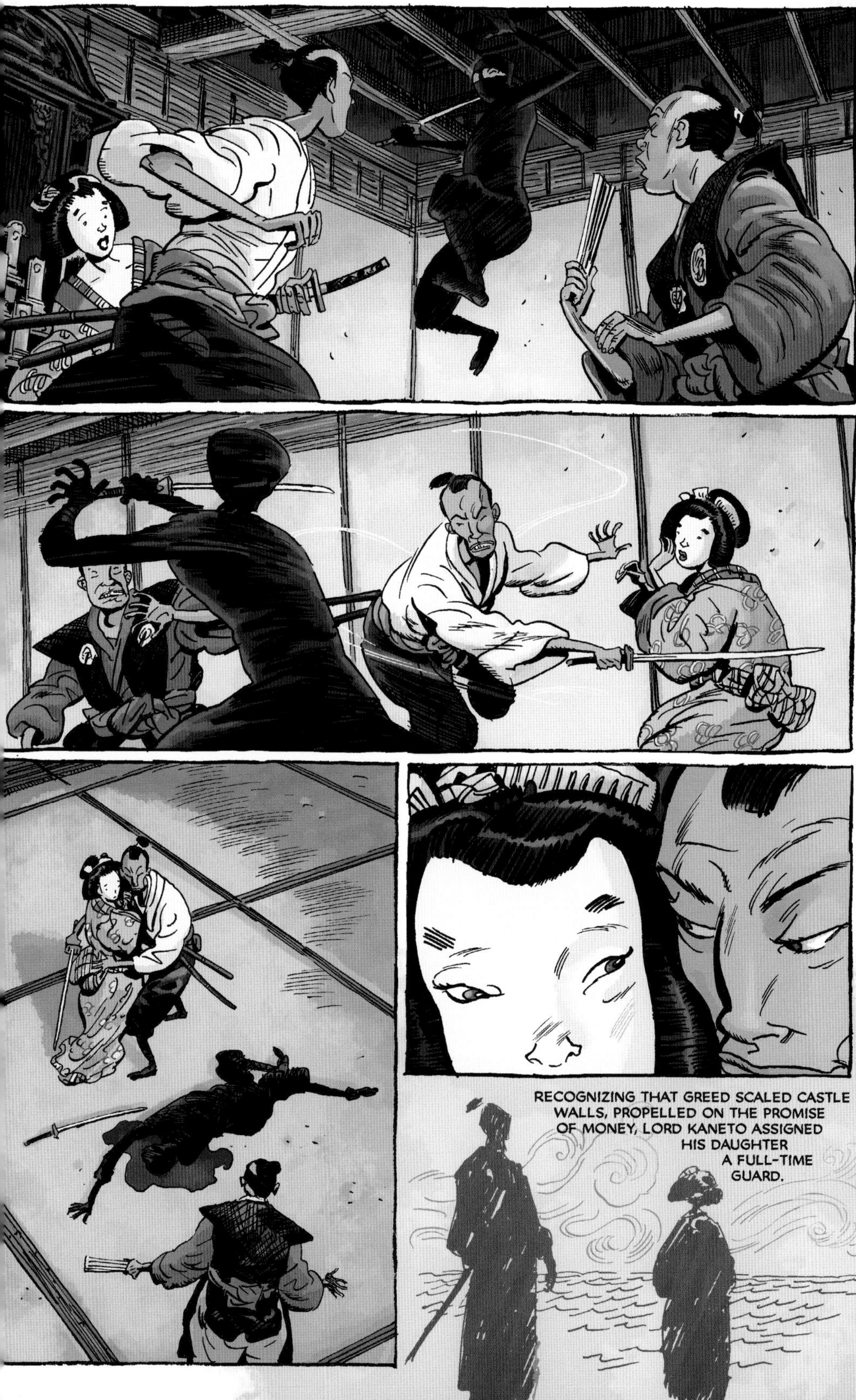
RECOGNIZING THAT GREED SCALED CASTLE WALLS, PROPELLED ON THE PROMISE OF MONEY, LORD KANETO ASSIGNED HIS DAUGHTER A FULL-TIME GUARD.

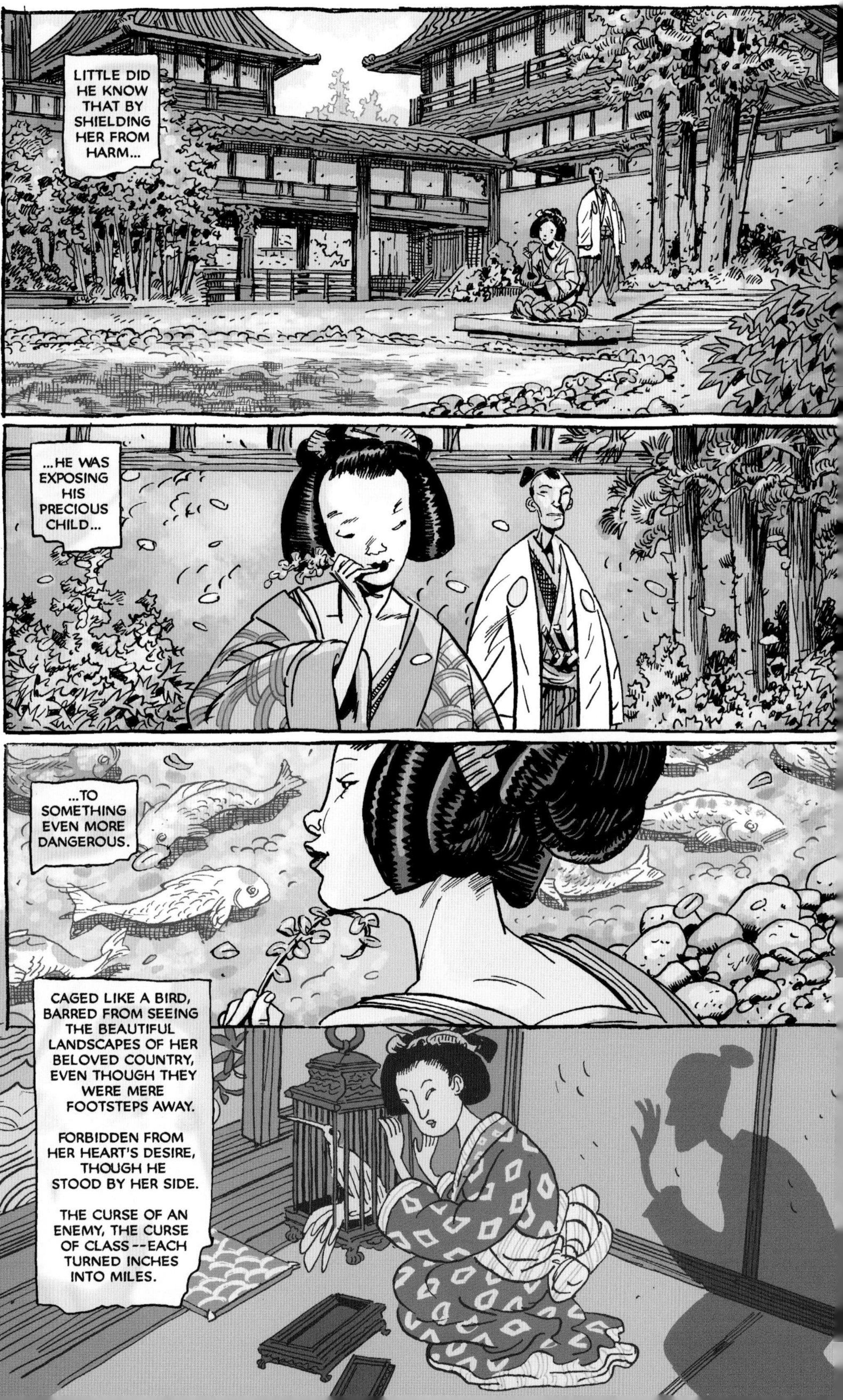
LITTLE DID HE KNOW THAT BY SHIELDING HER FROM HARM...
...HE WAS EXPOSING HIS PRECIOUS CHILD...
...TO SOMETHING EVEN MORE DANGEROUS.
CAGED LIKE A BIRD, BARRED FROM SEEING THE BEAUTIFUL LANDSCAPES OF HER BELOVED COUNTRY, EVEN THOUGH THEY WERE MERE FOOTSTEPS AWAY.
FORBIDDEN FROM HER HEART'S DESIRE, THOUGH HE STOOD BY HER SIDE.
THE CURSE OF AN ENEMY, THE CURSE OF CLASS--EACH TURNED INCHES INTO MILES.

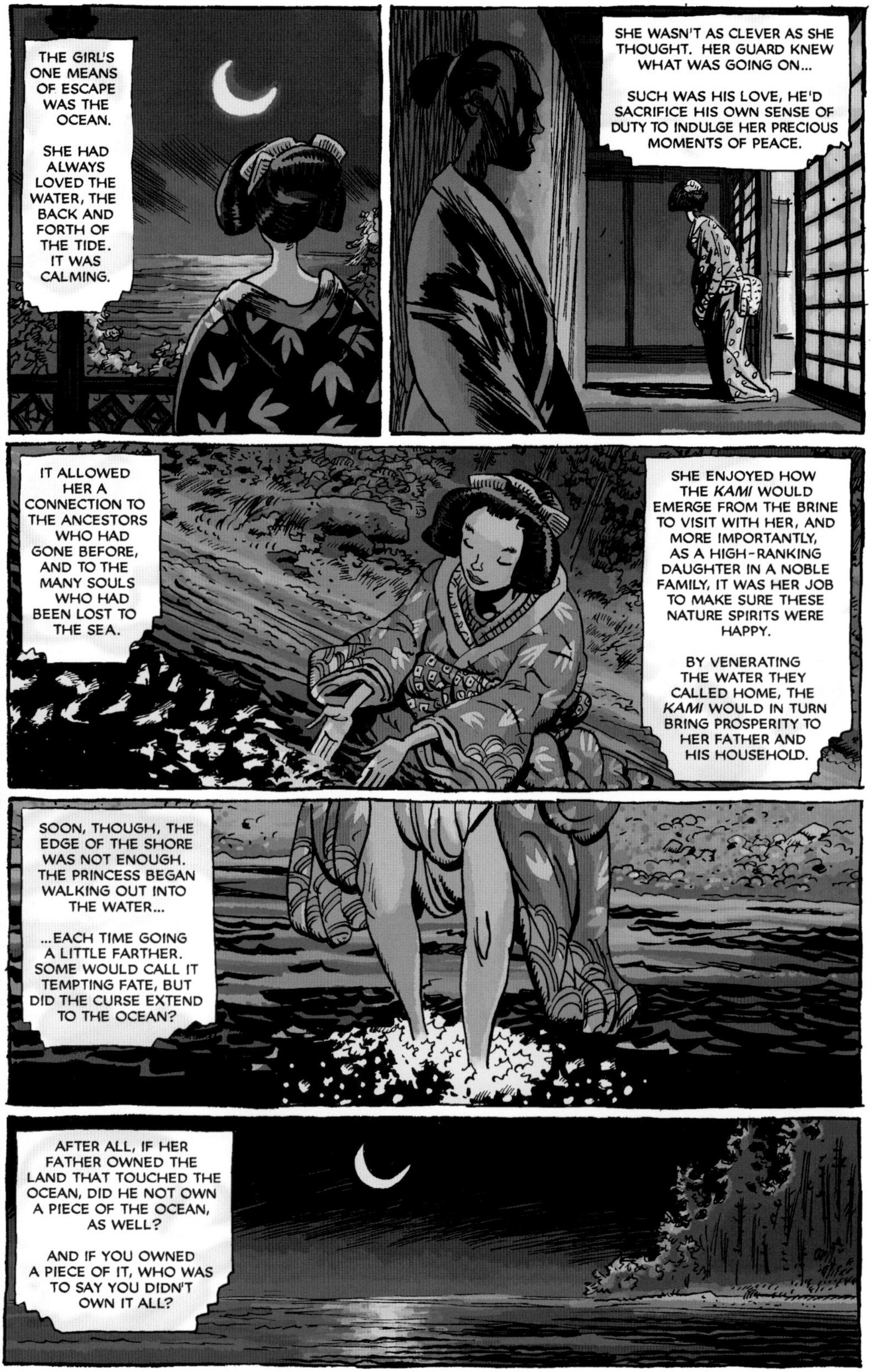

THE GIRL'S ONE MEANS OF ESCAPE WAS THE OCEAN.
SHE HAD ALWAYS LOVED THE WATER, THE BACK AND FORTH OF THE TIDE. IT WAS CALMING.
SHE WASN'T AS CLEVER AS SHE THOUGHT. HER GUARD KNEW WHAT WAS GOING ON...
SUCH WAS HIS LOVE, HE'D SACRIFICE HIS OWN SENSE OF DUTY TO INDULGE HER PRECIOUS MOMENTS OF PEACE.
IT ALLOWED HER A CONNECTION TO THE ANCESTORS WHO HAD GONE BEFORE, AND TO THE MANY SOULS WHO HAD BEEN LOST TO THE SEA.
SHE ENJOYED HOW THE *KAMI* WOULD EMERGE FROM THE BRINE TO VISIT WITH HER, AND MORE IMPORTANTLY, AS A HIGH-RANKING DAUGHTER IN A NOBLE FAMILY, IT WAS HER JOB TO MAKE SURE THESE NATURE SPIRITS WERE HAPPY.
BY VENERATING THE WATER THEY CALLED HOME, THE *KAMI* WOULD IN TURN BRING PROSPERITY TO HER FATHER AND HIS HOUSEHOLD.
SOON, THOUGH, THE EDGE OF THE SHORE WAS NOT ENOUGH. THE PRINCESS BEGAN WALKING OUT INTO THE WATER...
...EACH TIME GOING A LITTLE FARTHER. SOME WOULD CALL IT TEMPTING FATE, BUT DID THE CURSE EXTEND TO THE OCEAN?
AFTER ALL, IF HER FATHER OWNED THE LAND THAT TOUCHED THE OCEAN, DID HE NOT OWN A PIECE OF THE OCEAN, AS WELL?
AND IF YOU OWNED A PIECE OF IT, WHO WAS TO SAY YOU DIDN'T OWN IT ALL?

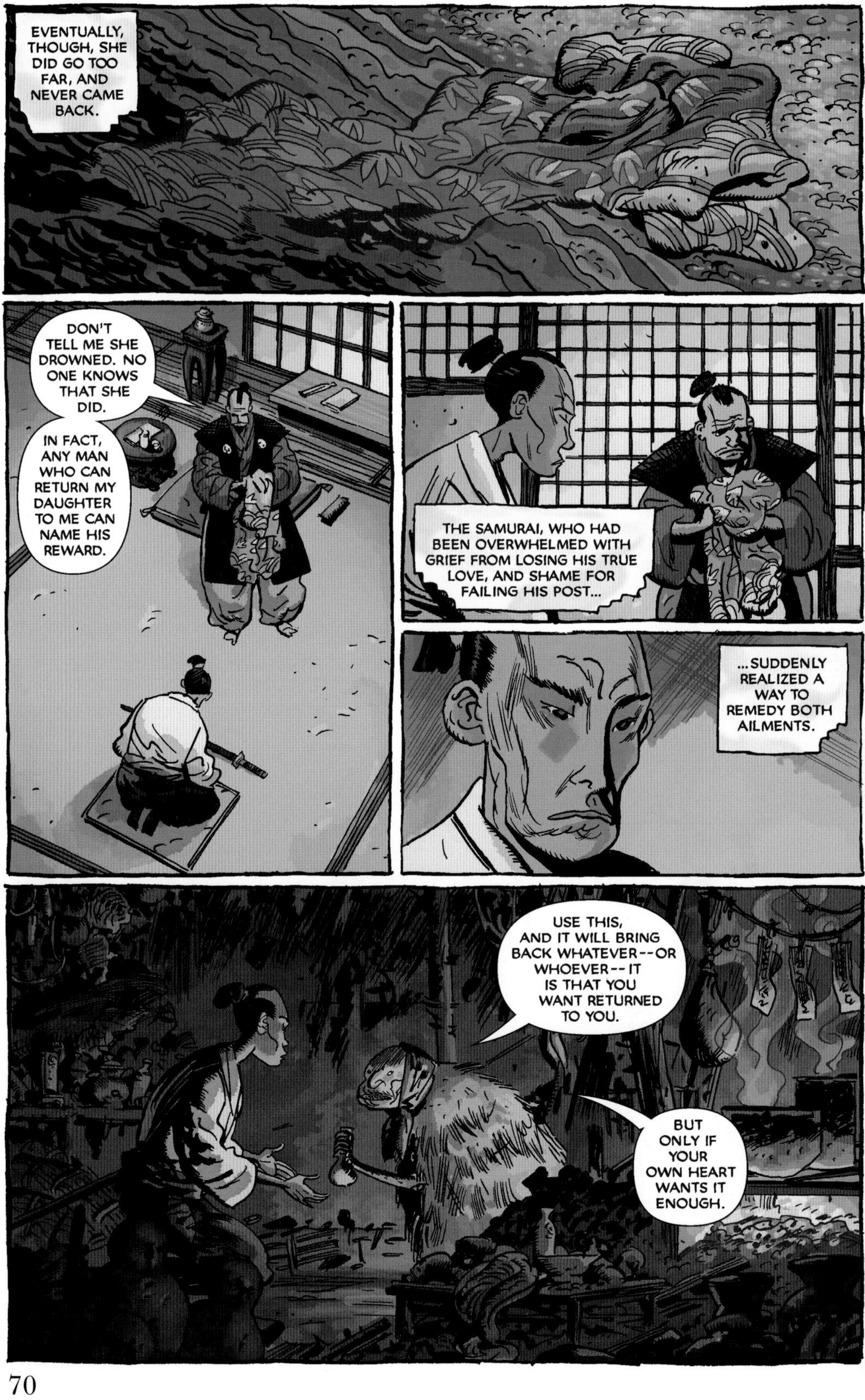
EVENTUALLY, THOUGH, SHE DID GO TOO FAR, AND NEVER CAME BACK.
DON'T TELL ME SHE DROWNED. NO ONE KNOWS THAT SHE DID.
IN FACT, ANY MAN WHO CAN RETURN MY DAUGHTER TO ME CAN NAME HIS REWARD.
THE SAMURAI, WHO HAD BEEN OVERWHELMED WITH GRIEF FROM LOSING HIS TRUE LOVE, AND SHAME FOR FAILING HIS POST...
...SUDDENLY REALIZED A WAY TO REMEDY BOTH AILMENTS.
USE THIS, AND IT WILL BRING BACK WHATEVER--OR WHOEVER--IT IS THAT YOU WANT RETURNED TO YOU.
BUT ONLY IF YOUR OWN HEART WANTS IT ENOUGH.

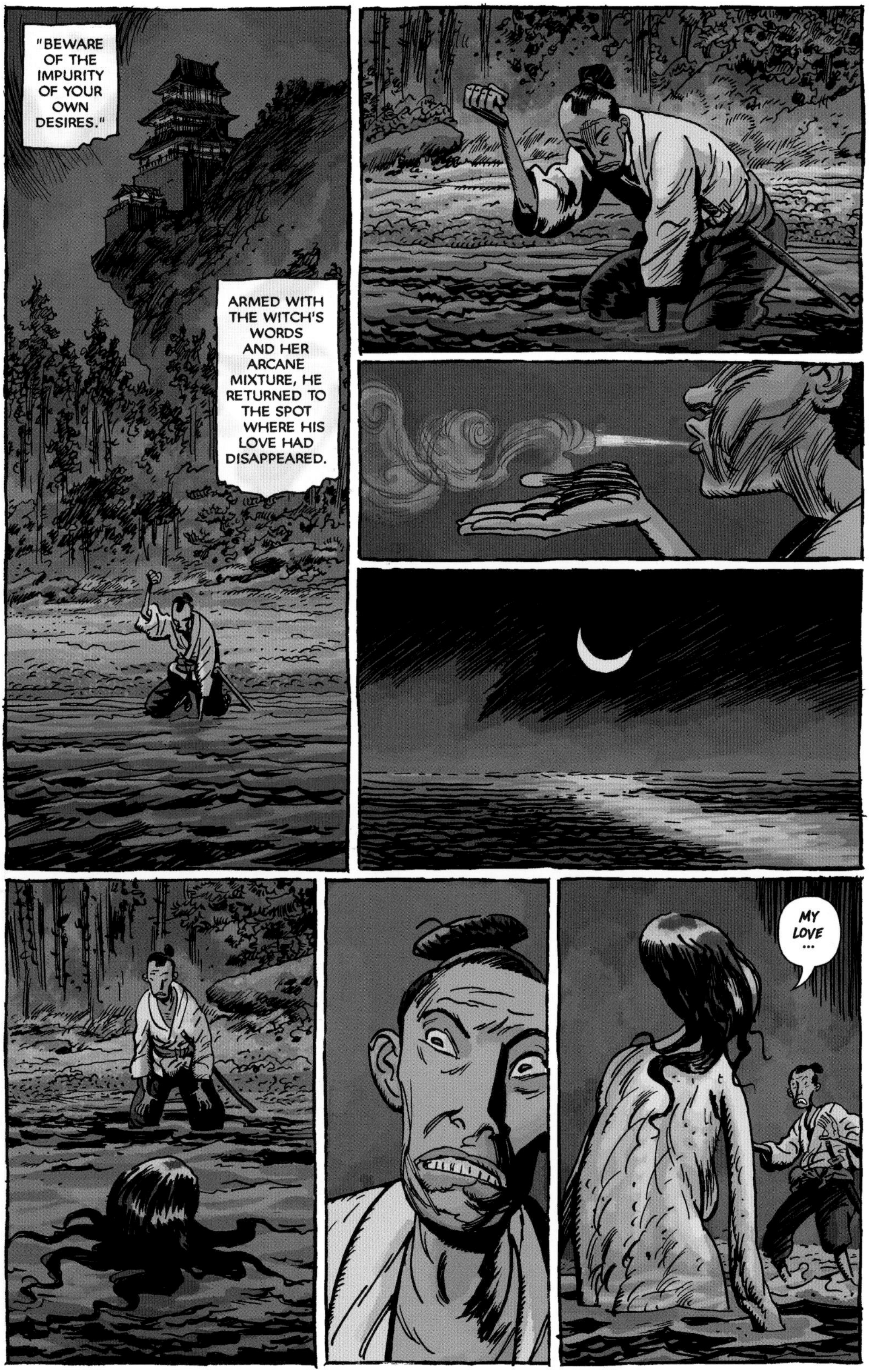
"BEWARE OF THE IMPURITY OF YOUR OWN DESIRES."
ARMED WITH THE WITCH'S WORDS AND HER ARCANE MIXTURE, HE RETURNED TO THE SPOT WHERE HIS LOVE HAD DISAPPEARED.
MY LOVE ...

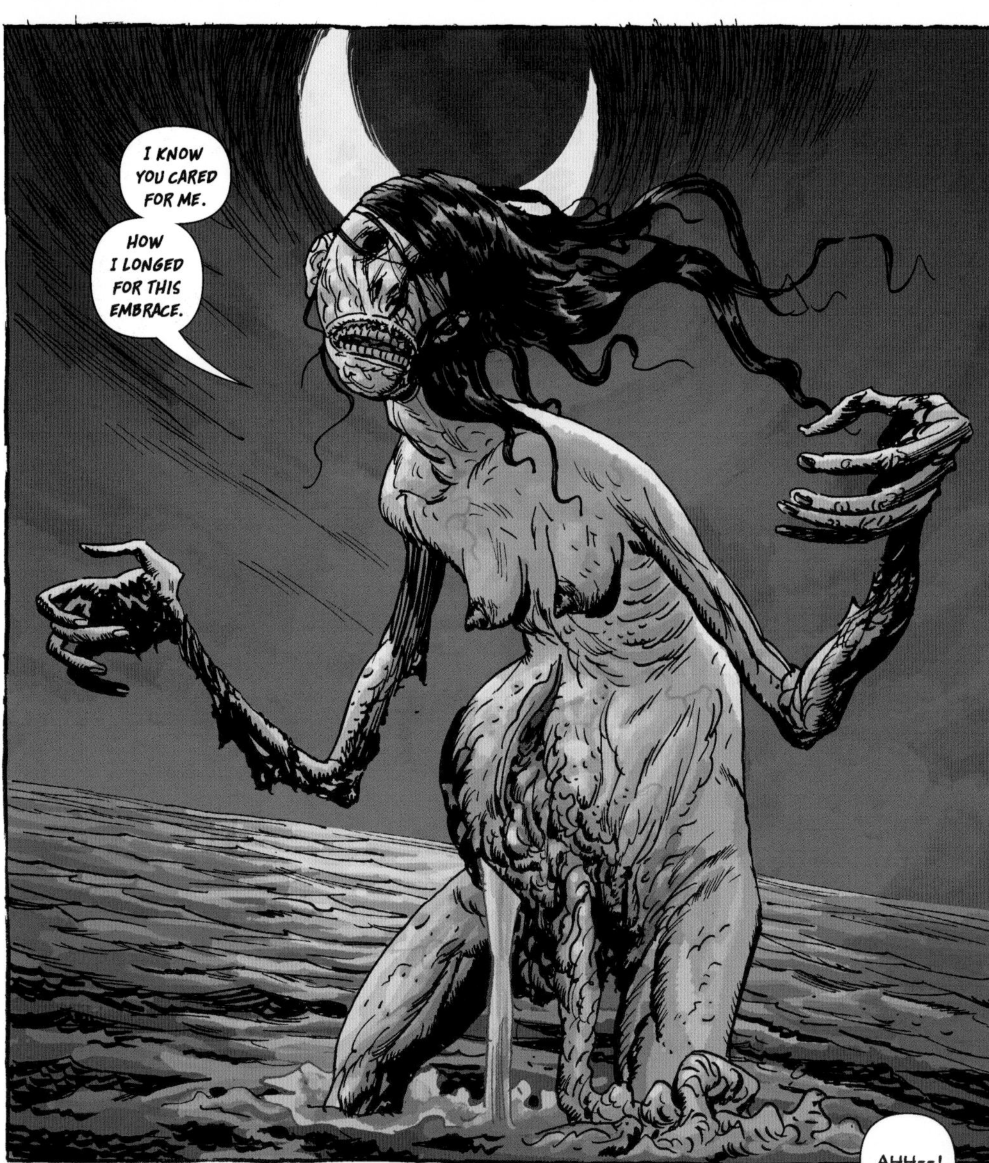
I KNOW YOU CARED FOR ME.
HOW I LONGED FOR THIS EMBRACE.

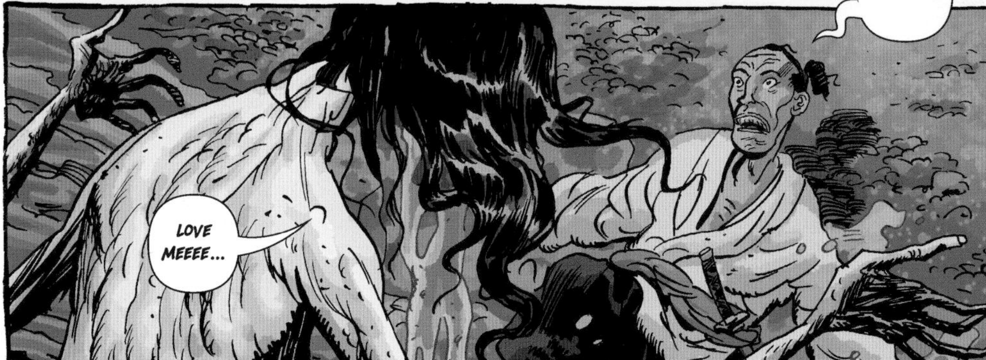
AHH--!
LOVE MEEEE...

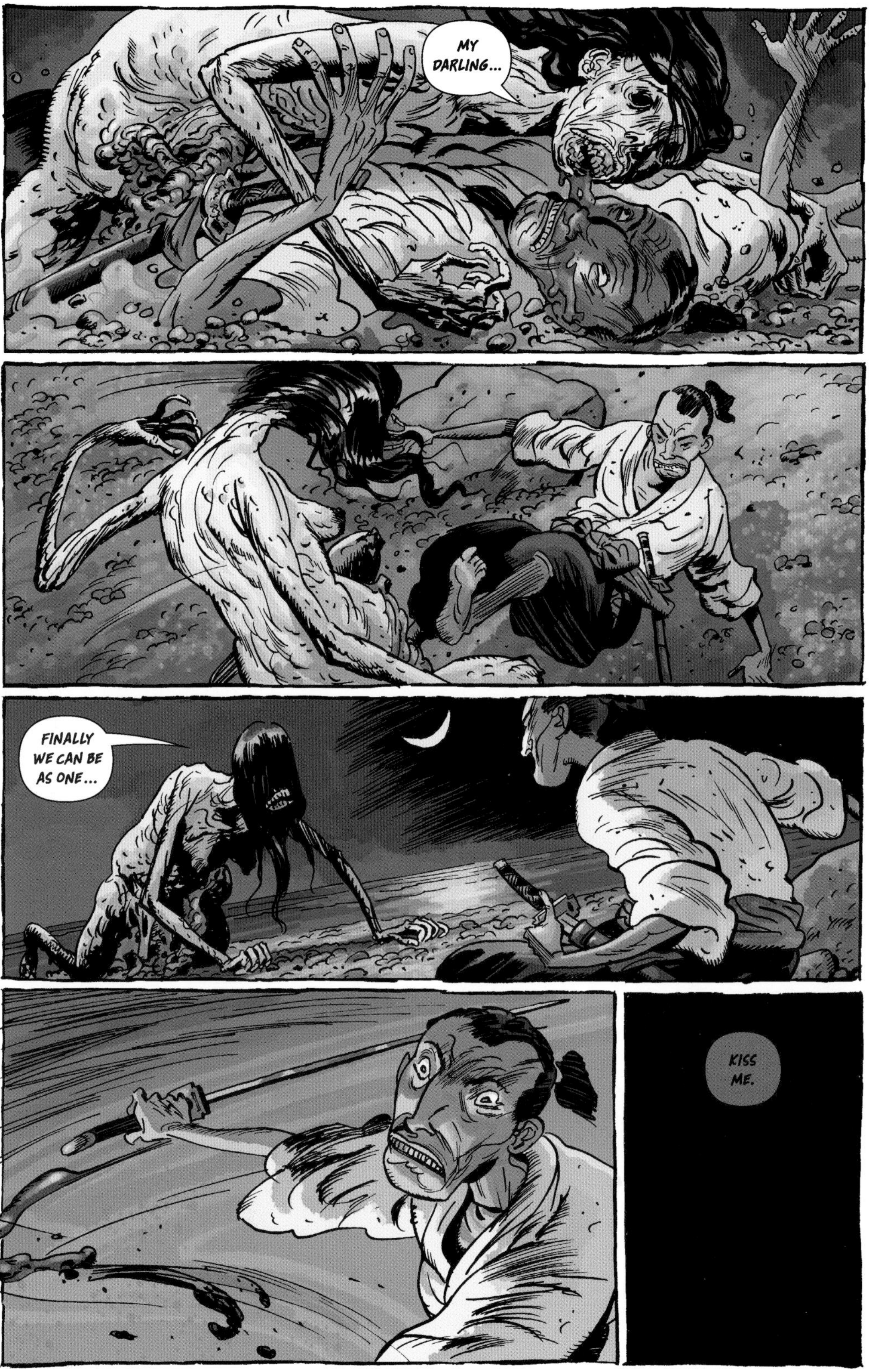
MY DARLING...
FINALLY WE CAN BE AS ONE...
KISS ME.

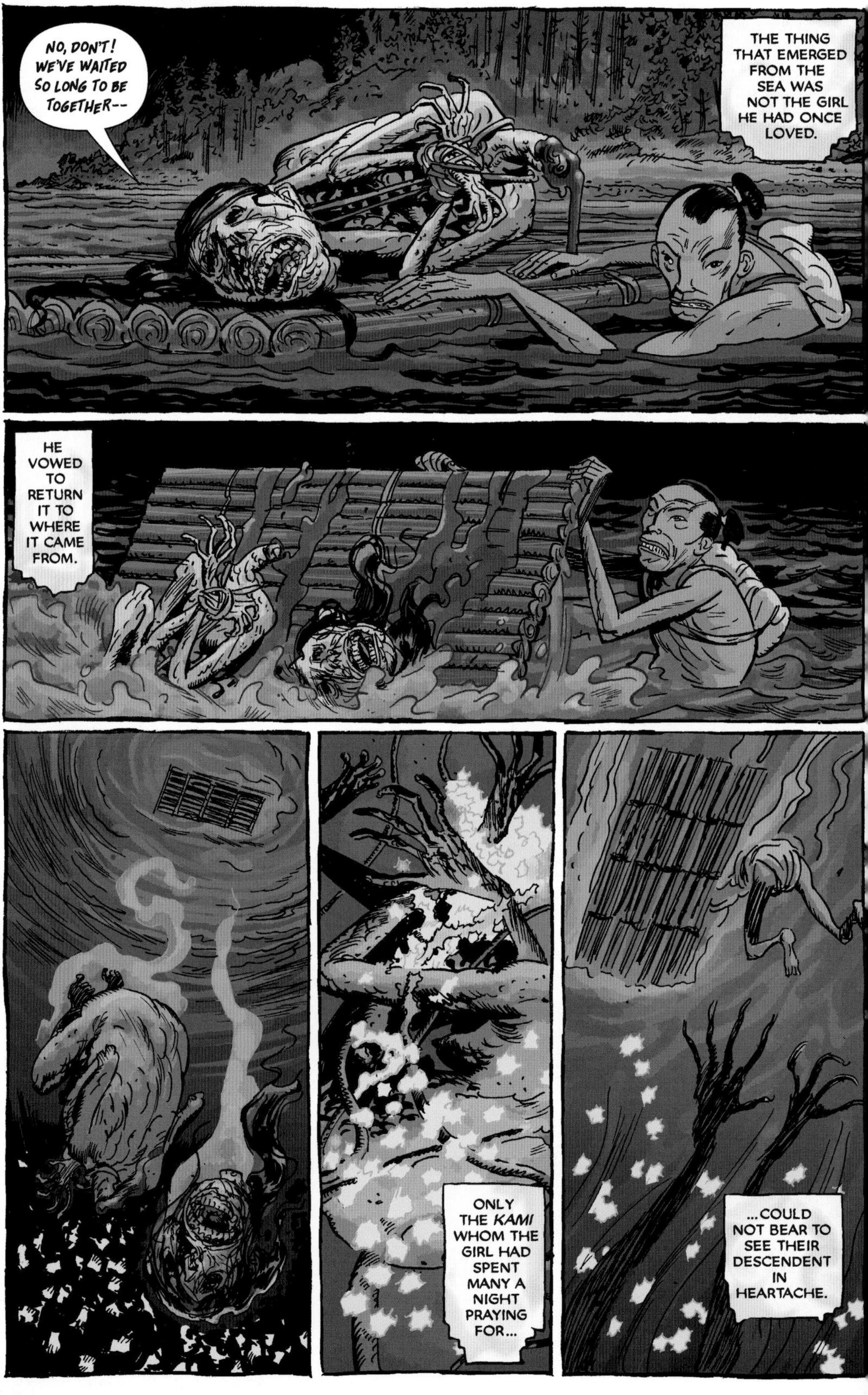
NO, DON'T! WE'VE WAITED SO LONG TO BE TOGETHER--
THE THING THAT EMERGED FROM THE SEA WAS NOT THE GIRL HE HAD ONCE LOVED.
HE VOWED TO RETURN IT TO WHERE IT CAME FROM.
ONLY THE *KAMI* WHOM THE GIRL HAD SPENT MANY A NIGHT PRAYING FOR...
...COULD NOT BEAR TO SEE THEIR DESCENDENT IN HEARTACHE.

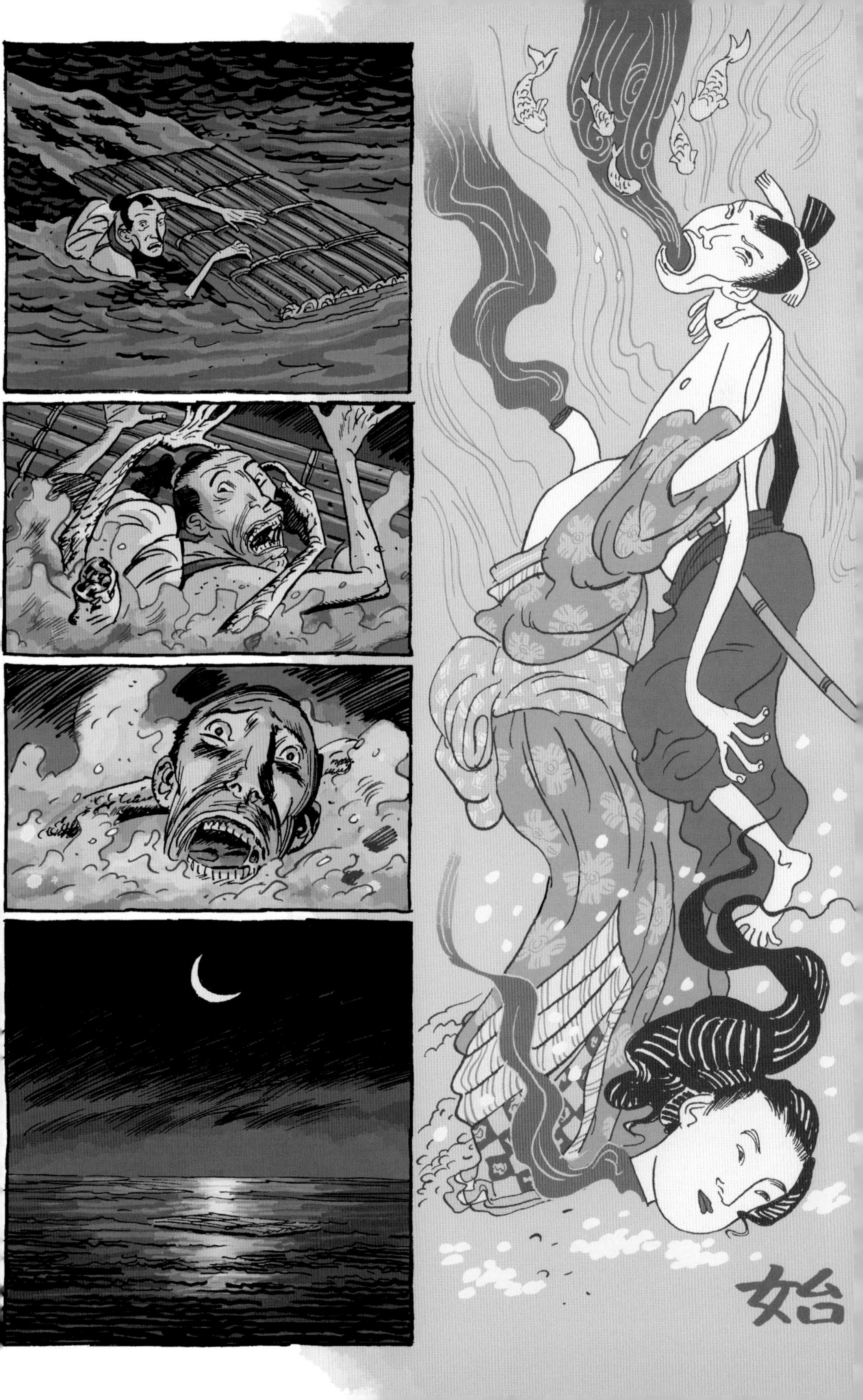
始

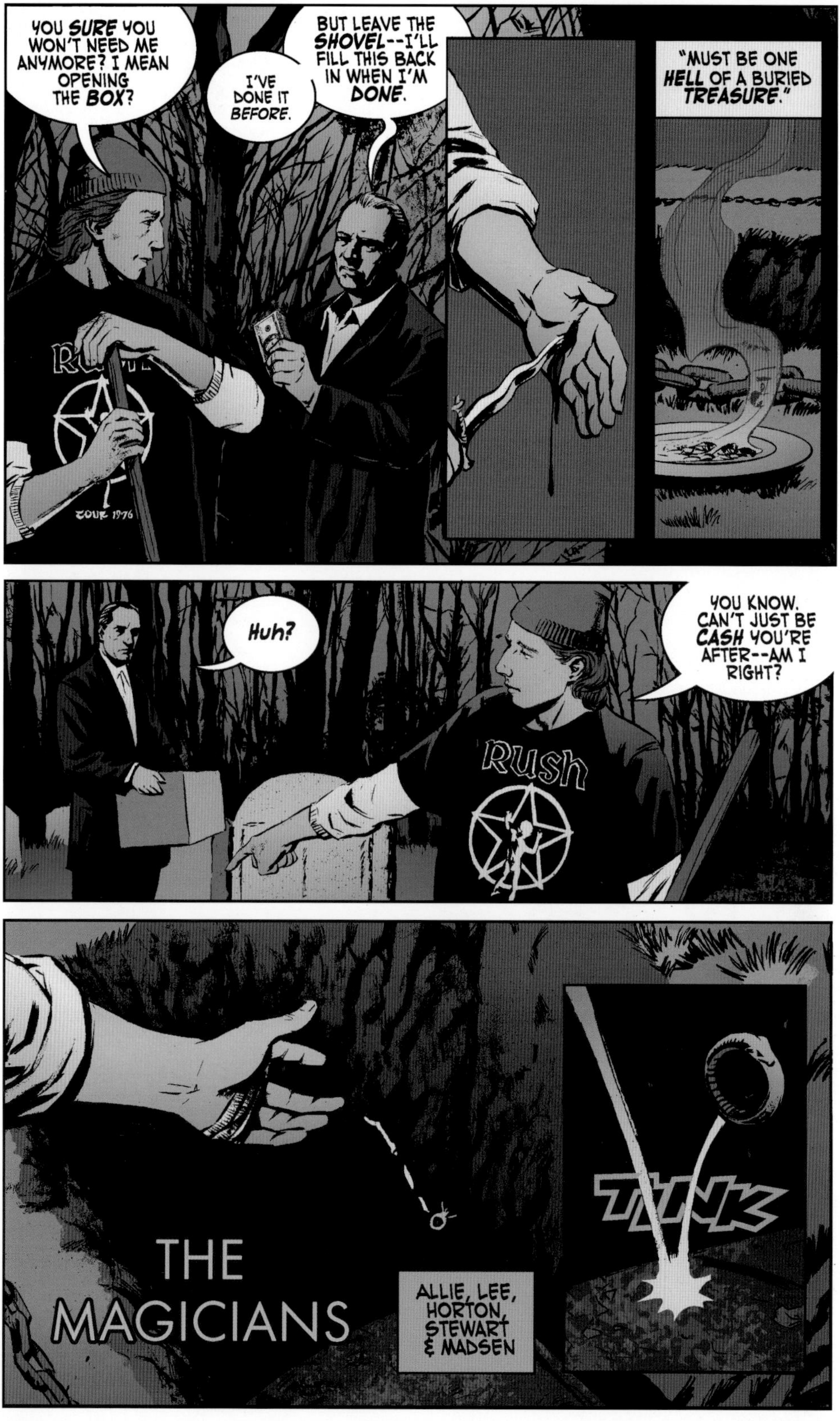
YOU SURE YOU WON'T NEED ME ANYMORE? I MEAN OPENING THE BOX?
I'VE DONE IT BEFORE.
BUT LEAVE THE SHOVEL--I'LL FILL THIS BACK IN WHEN I'M DONE.
RUSH
TOUR 1976
"MUST BE ONE HELL OF A BURIED TREASURE."
Huh?
YOU KNOW. CAN'T JUST BE CASH YOU'RE AFTER--AM I RIGHT?
RUSH
TINK
THE MAGICIANS
ALLIE, LEE, HORTON, STEWART & MADSEN

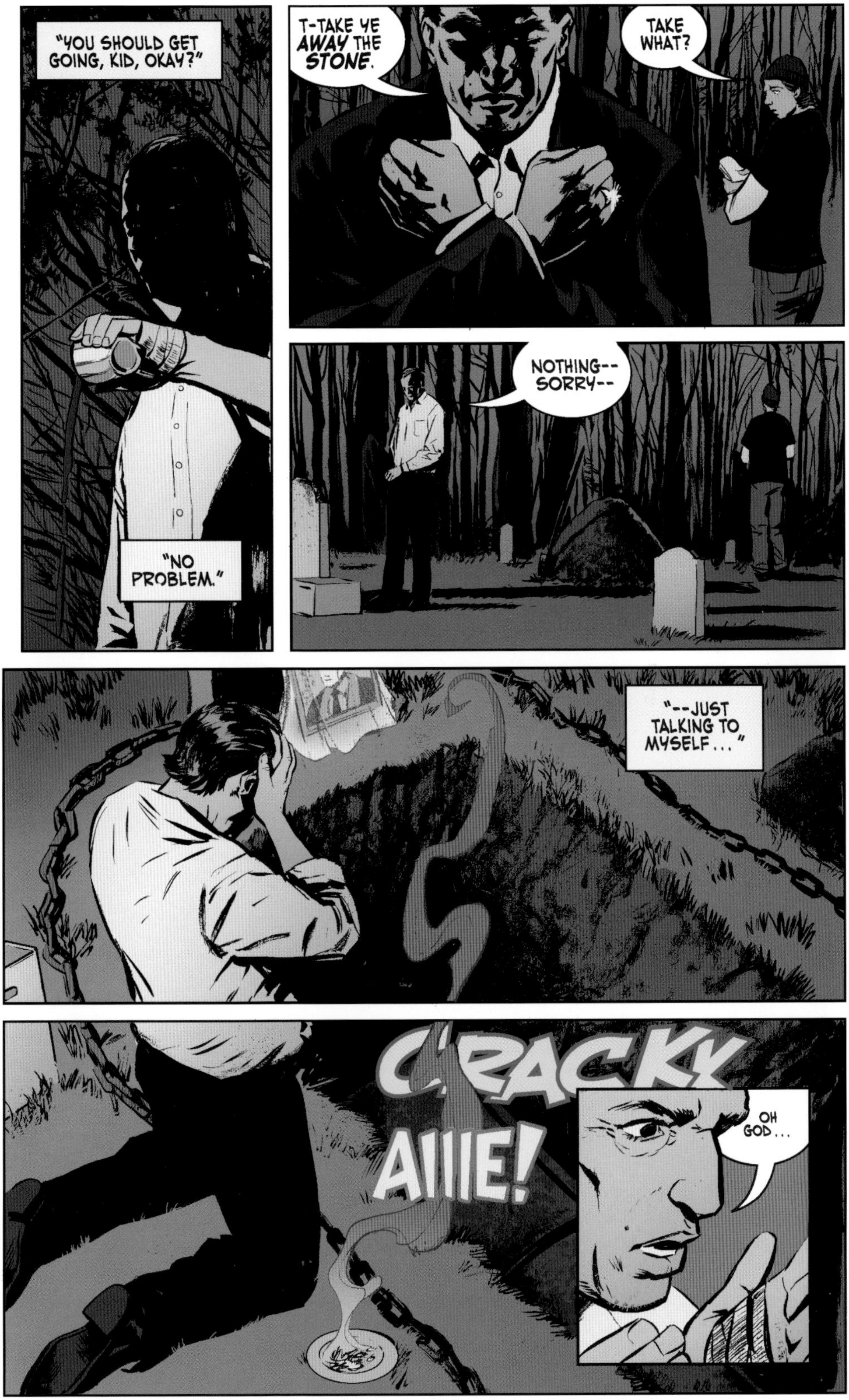
"YOU SHOULD GET GOING, KID, OKAY?"
"NO PROBLEM."
T-TAKE YE AWAY THE STONE.
TAKE WHAT?
NOTHING-- SORRY--
"--JUST TALKING TO MYSELF..."
CRACK!
AIIIE!
OH GOD...

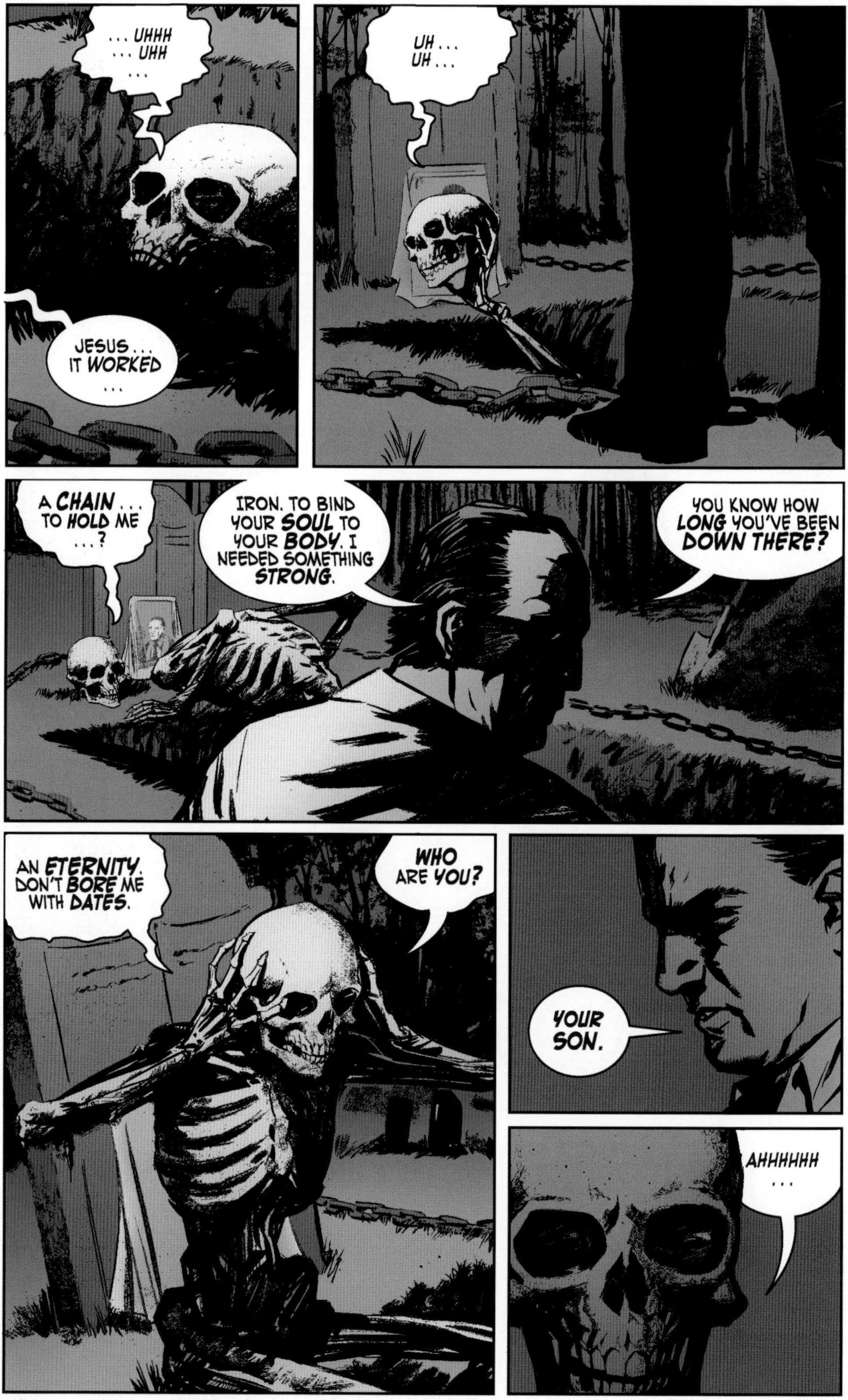
. . . UHHH . . . UHH . . .
JESUS . . . IT WORKED . . .
UH . . . UH . . .
A CHAIN . . . TO HOLD ME . . . ?
IRON. TO BIND YOUR SOUL TO YOUR BODY. I NEEDED SOMETHING STRONG.
YOU KNOW HOW LONG YOU'VE BEEN DOWN THERE?
AN ETERNITY. DON'T BORE ME WITH DATES.
WHO ARE YOU?
YOUR SON.
AHHHHHH . . .

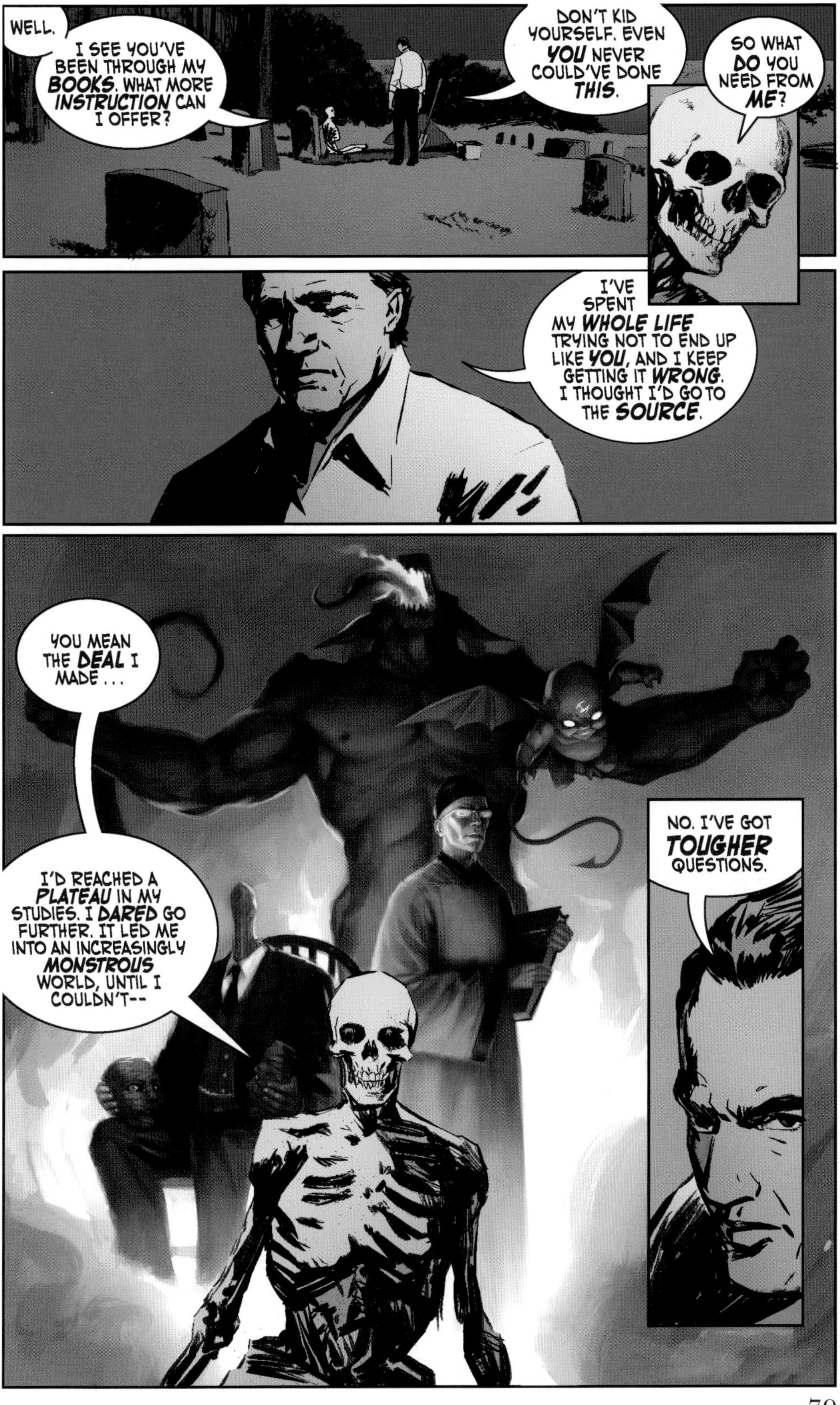
WELL.
I SEE YOU'VE BEEN THROUGH MY BOOKS. WHAT MORE INSTRUCTION CAN I OFFER?
DON'T KID YOURSELF. EVEN YOU NEVER COULD'VE DONE THIS.
SO WHAT DO YOU NEED FROM ME?
I'VE SPENT MY WHOLE LIFE TRYING NOT TO END UP LIKE YOU, AND I KEEP GETTING IT WRONG. I THOUGHT I'D GO TO THE SOURCE.
YOU MEAN THE DEAL I MADE . . .
I'D REACHED A PLATEAU IN MY STUDIES. I DARED GO FURTHER. IT LED ME INTO AN INCREASINGLY MONSTROUS WORLD, UNTIL I COULDN'T--
NO. I'VE GOT TOUGHER QUESTIONS.

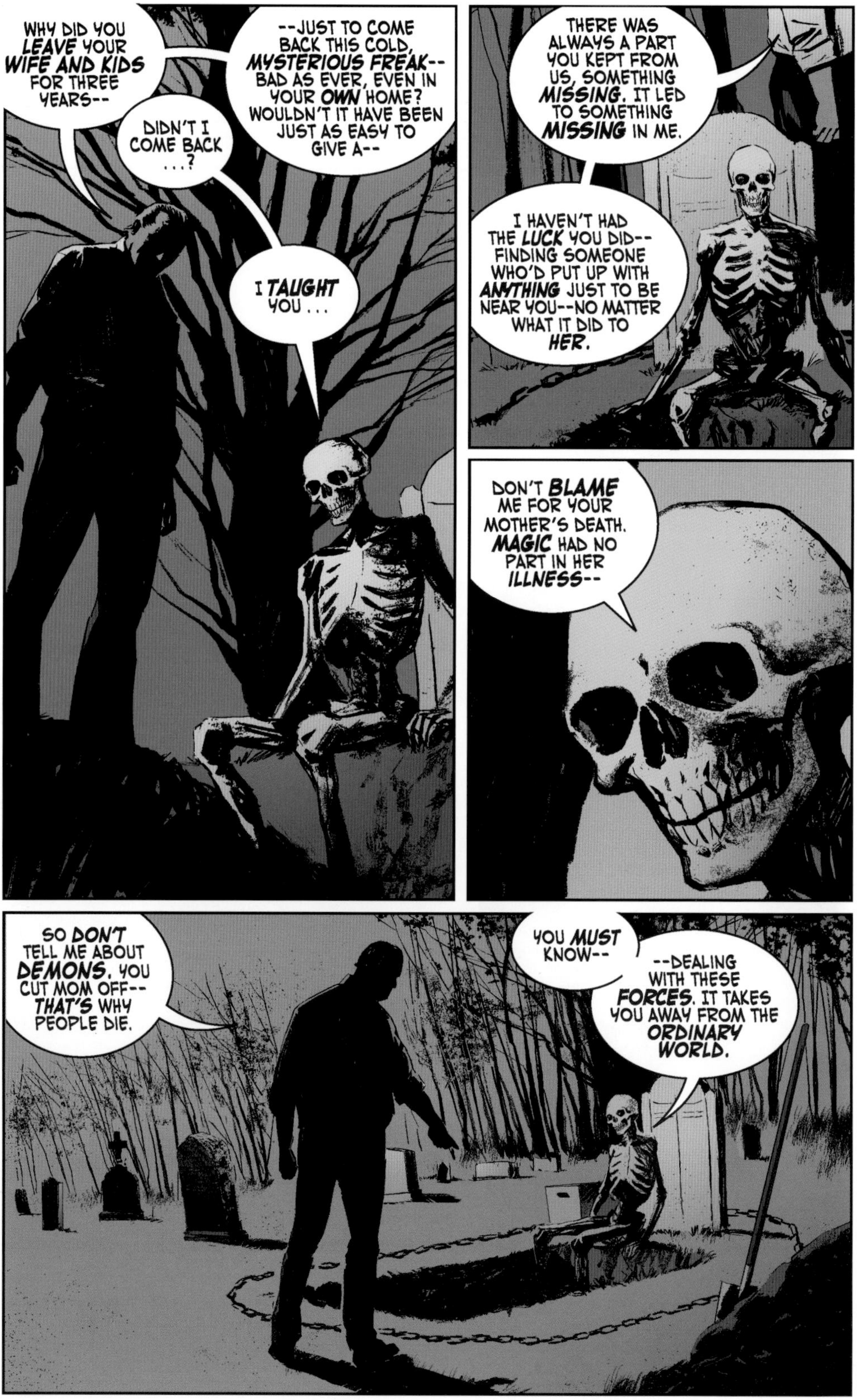
WHY DID YOU LEAVE YOUR WIFE AND KIDS FOR THREE YEARS--
--JUST TO COME BACK THIS COLD, MYSTERIOUS FREAK-- BAD AS EVER, EVEN IN YOUR OWN HOME? WOULDN'T IT HAVE BEEN JUST AS EASY TO GIVE A--
DIDN'T I COME BACK . . . ?
I TAUGHT YOU . . .
THERE WAS ALWAYS A PART YOU KEPT FROM US, SOMETHING MISSING. IT LED TO SOMETHING MISSING IN ME.
I HAVEN'T HAD THE LUCK YOU DID-- FINDING SOMEONE WHO'D PUT UP WITH ANYTHING JUST TO BE NEAR YOU--NO MATTER WHAT IT DID TO HER.
DON'T BLAME ME FOR YOUR MOTHER'S DEATH. MAGIC HAD NO PART IN HER ILLNESS--
SO DON'T TELL ME ABOUT DEMONS. YOU CUT MOM OFF-- THAT'S WHY PEOPLE DIE.
YOU MUST KNOW--
--DEALING WITH THESE FORCES. IT TAKES YOU AWAY FROM THE ORDINARY WORLD.

"WHEN I WAS IN EUROPE, *ALONE*, MY *MIND* NEARLY *BROKEN* BY THAT *CREATURE*, I HID IN A SMALL VILLAGE.

"*IT CAME*--TOLD THEM THEY HARBORED A *DAMNED* SOUL BOUND FOR *HELL*. THE SPIRIT OF THE INQUISITION WAS NOT DEAD IN THAT LAND . . .

"HE *TOYED* WITH ME, TO MAKE ME WEAK. I DIDN'T KNOW IF I WAS *MAN* OR *BEAST*.

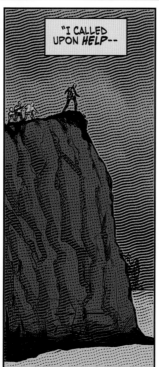

"I CALLED UPON *HELP*--

"--TO CARRY ME *AWAY*--

81

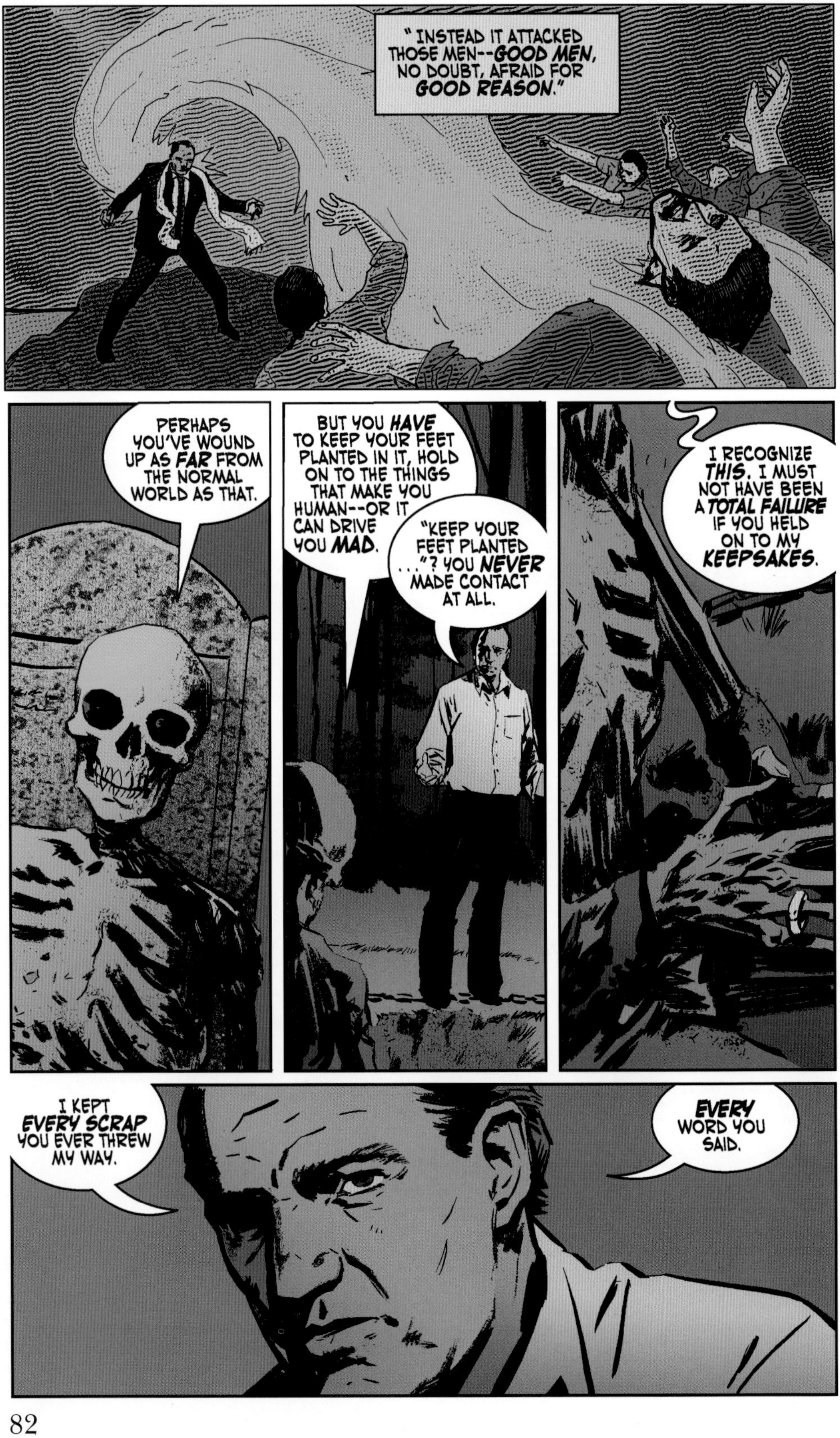
" INSTEAD IT ATTACKED THOSE MEN--GOOD MEN, NO DOUBT, AFRAID FOR GOOD REASON."
PERHAPS YOU'VE WOUND UP AS FAR FROM THE NORMAL WORLD AS THAT.
BUT YOU HAVE TO KEEP YOUR FEET PLANTED IN IT, HOLD ON TO THE THINGS THAT MAKE YOU HUMAN--OR IT CAN DRIVE YOU MAD.
"KEEP YOUR FEET PLANTED ..."? YOU NEVER MADE CONTACT AT ALL.
I RECOGNIZE THIS. I MUST NOT HAVE BEEN A TOTAL FAILURE IF YOU HELD ON TO MY KEEPSAKES.
I KEPT EVERY SCRAP YOU EVER THREW MY WAY.
EVERY WORD YOU SAID.

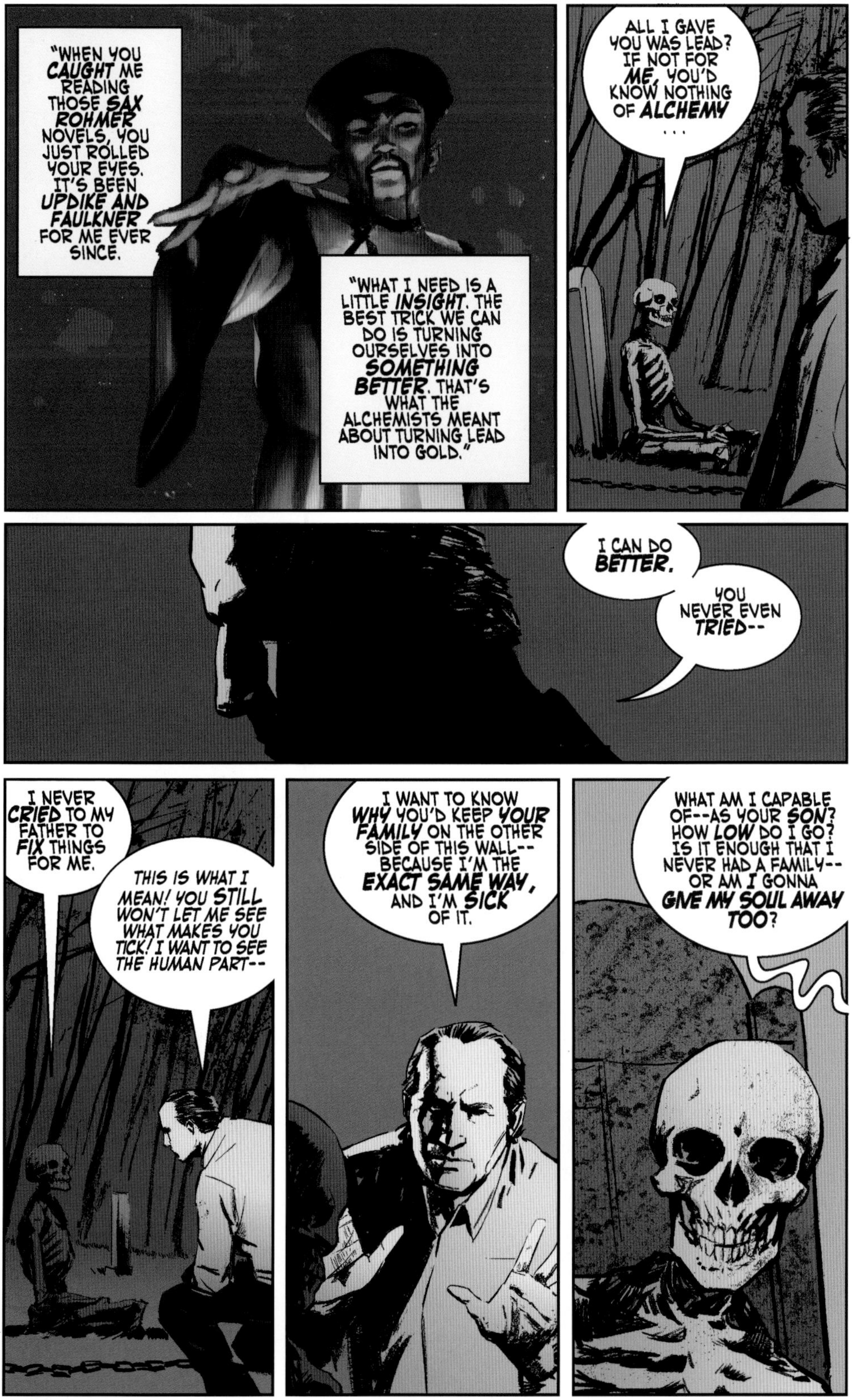
"WHEN YOU CAUGHT ME READING THOSE SAX ROHMER NOVELS, YOU JUST ROLLED YOUR EYES. IT'S BEEN UPDIKE AND FAULKNER FOR ME EVER SINCE.
"WHAT I NEED IS A LITTLE INSIGHT. THE BEST TRICK WE CAN DO IS TURNING OURSELVES INTO SOMETHING BETTER. THAT'S WHAT THE ALCHEMISTS MEANT ABOUT TURNING LEAD INTO GOLD."
ALL I GAVE YOU WAS LEAD? IF NOT FOR ME, YOU'D KNOW NOTHING OF ALCHEMY . . .
I CAN DO BETTER.
YOU NEVER EVEN TRIED--
I NEVER CRIED TO MY FATHER TO FIX THINGS FOR ME.
THIS IS WHAT I MEAN! YOU STILL WON'T LET ME SEE WHAT MAKES YOU TICK! I WANT TO SEE THE HUMAN PART--
I WANT TO KNOW WHY YOU'D KEEP YOUR FAMILY ON THE OTHER SIDE OF THIS WALL-- BECAUSE I'M THE EXACT SAME WAY, AND I'M SICK OF IT.
WHAT AM I CAPABLE OF--AS YOUR SON? HOW LOW DO I GO? IS IT ENOUGH THAT I NEVER HAD A FAMILY-- OR AM I GONNA GIVE MY SOUL AWAY TOO?

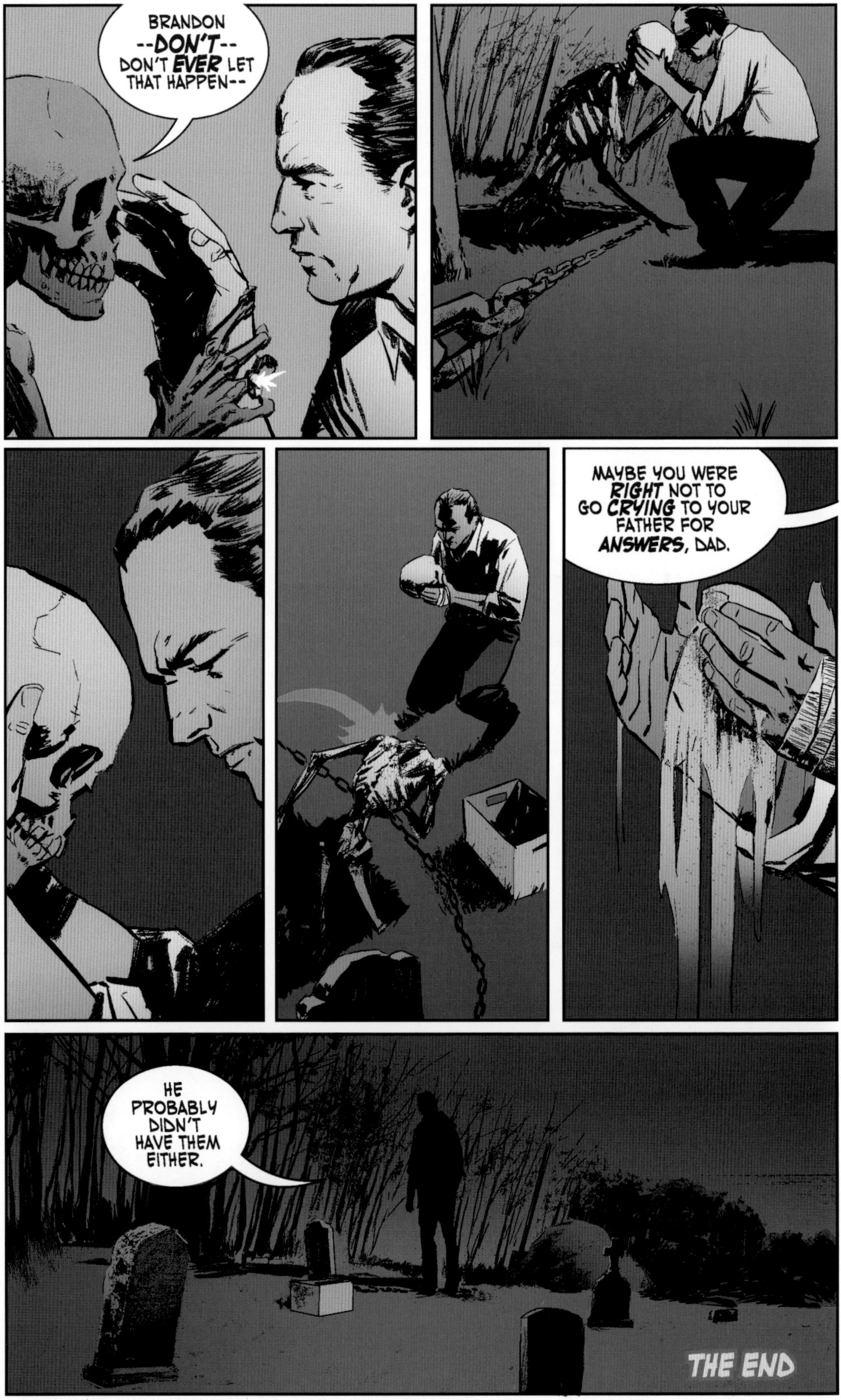
BRANDON --DON'T-- DON'T EVER LET THAT HAPPEN--
MAYBE YOU WERE RIGHT NOT TO GO CRYING TO YOUR FATHER FOR ANSWERS, DAD.
HE PROBABLY DIDN'T HAVE THEM EITHER.
THE END

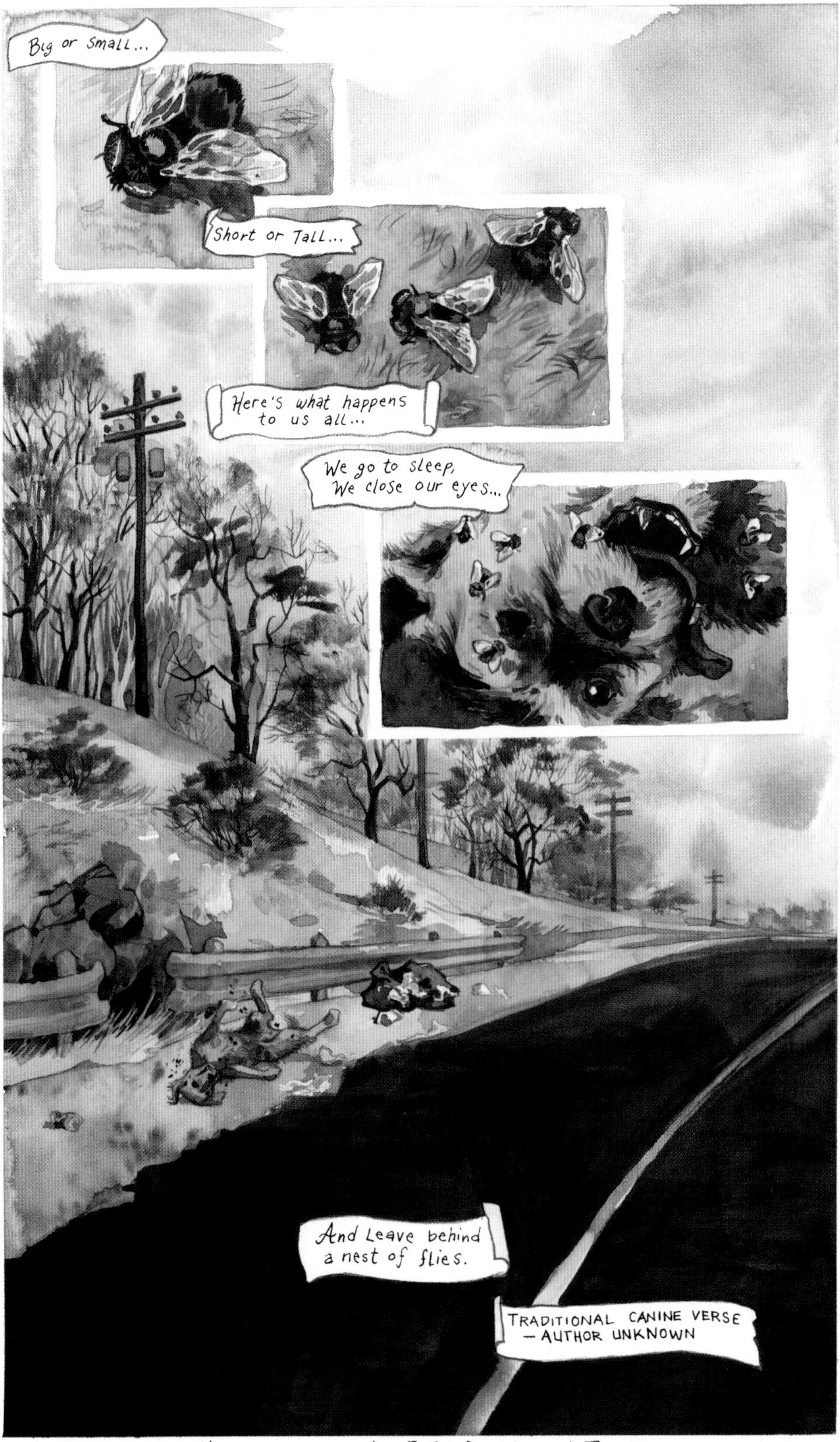
Big or small...
Short or Tall...
Here's what happens to us all...
We go to sleep, We close our eyes...
And Leave behind a nest of flies.
TRADITIONAL CANINE VERSE — AUTHOR UNKNOWN

Let Sleeping Dogs Lie by Evan Dorkin and Jill Thompson 2005

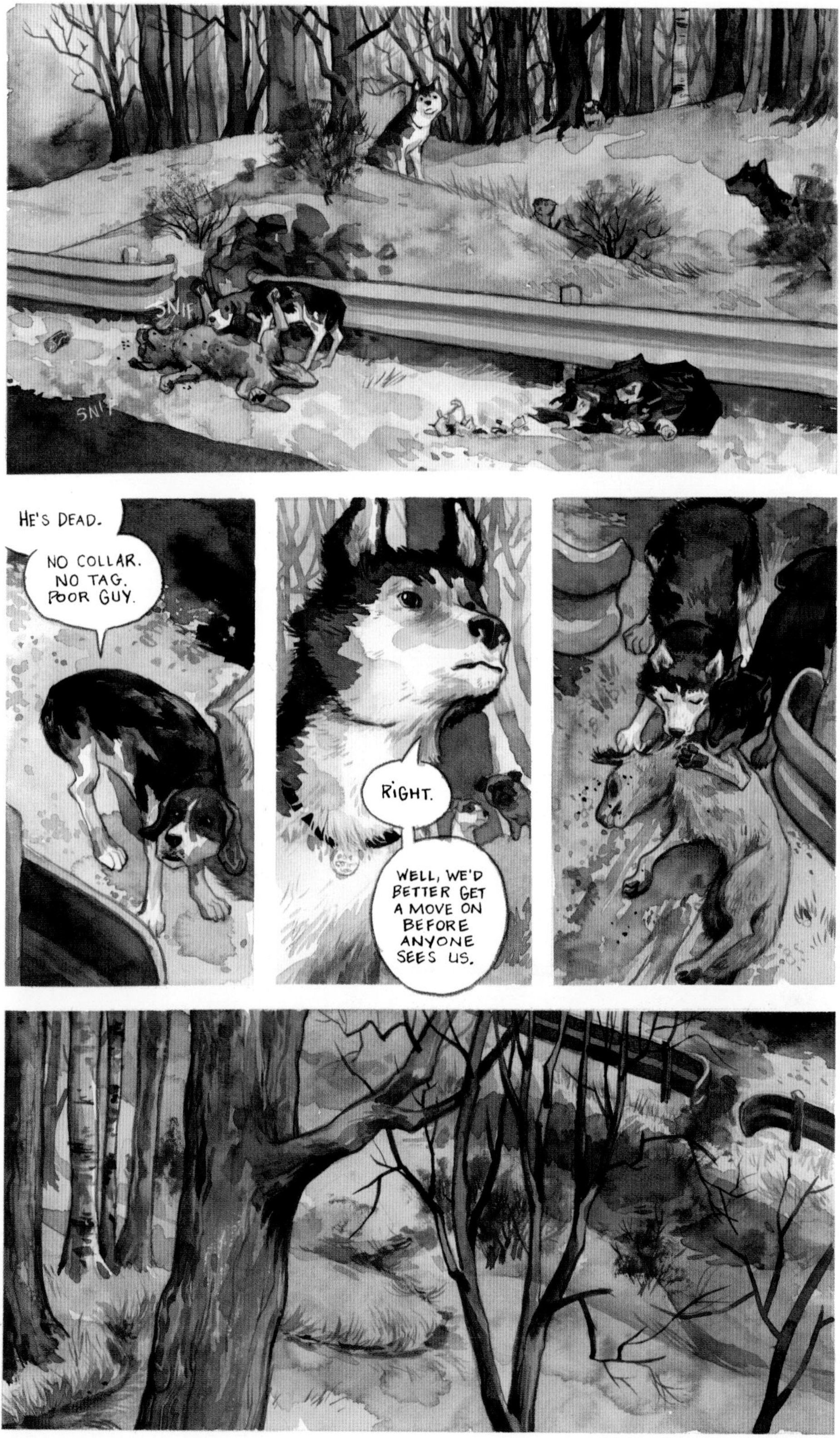
SNIF
SNIF
HE'S DEAD.
NO COLLAR. NO TAG. POOR GUY.
RIGHT.
WELL, WE'D BETTER GET A MOVE ON BEFORE ANYONE SEES US.

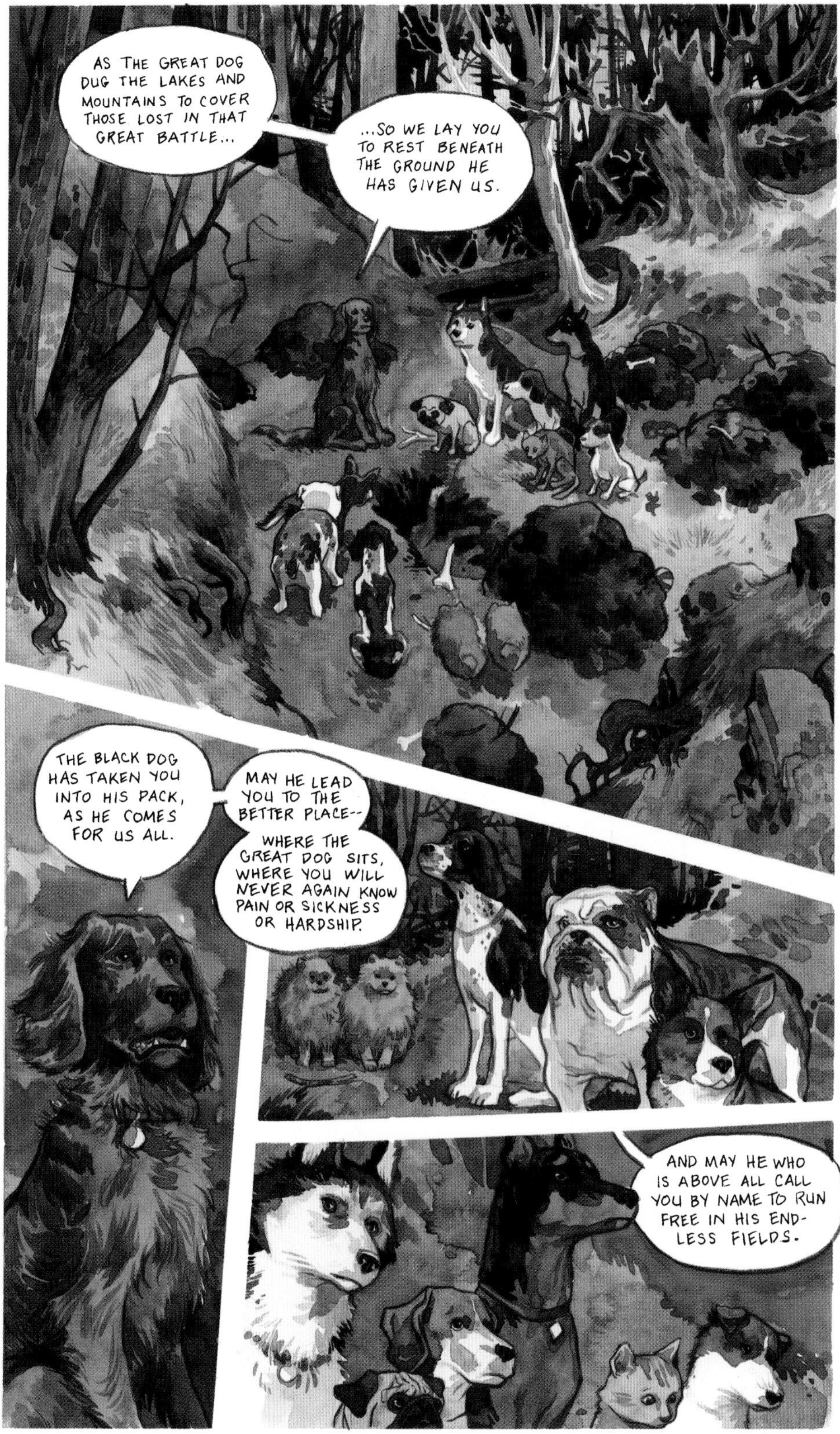
AS THE GREAT DOG DUG THE LAKES AND MOUNTAINS TO COVER THOSE LOST IN THAT GREAT BATTLE...
...SO WE LAY YOU TO REST BENEATH THE GROUND HE HAS GIVEN US.
THE BLACK DOG HAS TAKEN YOU INTO HIS PACK, AS HE COMES FOR US ALL.
MAY HE LEAD YOU TO THE BETTER PLACE--
WHERE THE GREAT DOG SITS, WHERE YOU WILL NEVER AGAIN KNOW PAIN OR SICKNESS OR HARDSHIP.
AND MAY HE WHO IS ABOVE ALL CALL YOU BY NAME TO RUN FREE IN HIS END-LESS FIELDS.

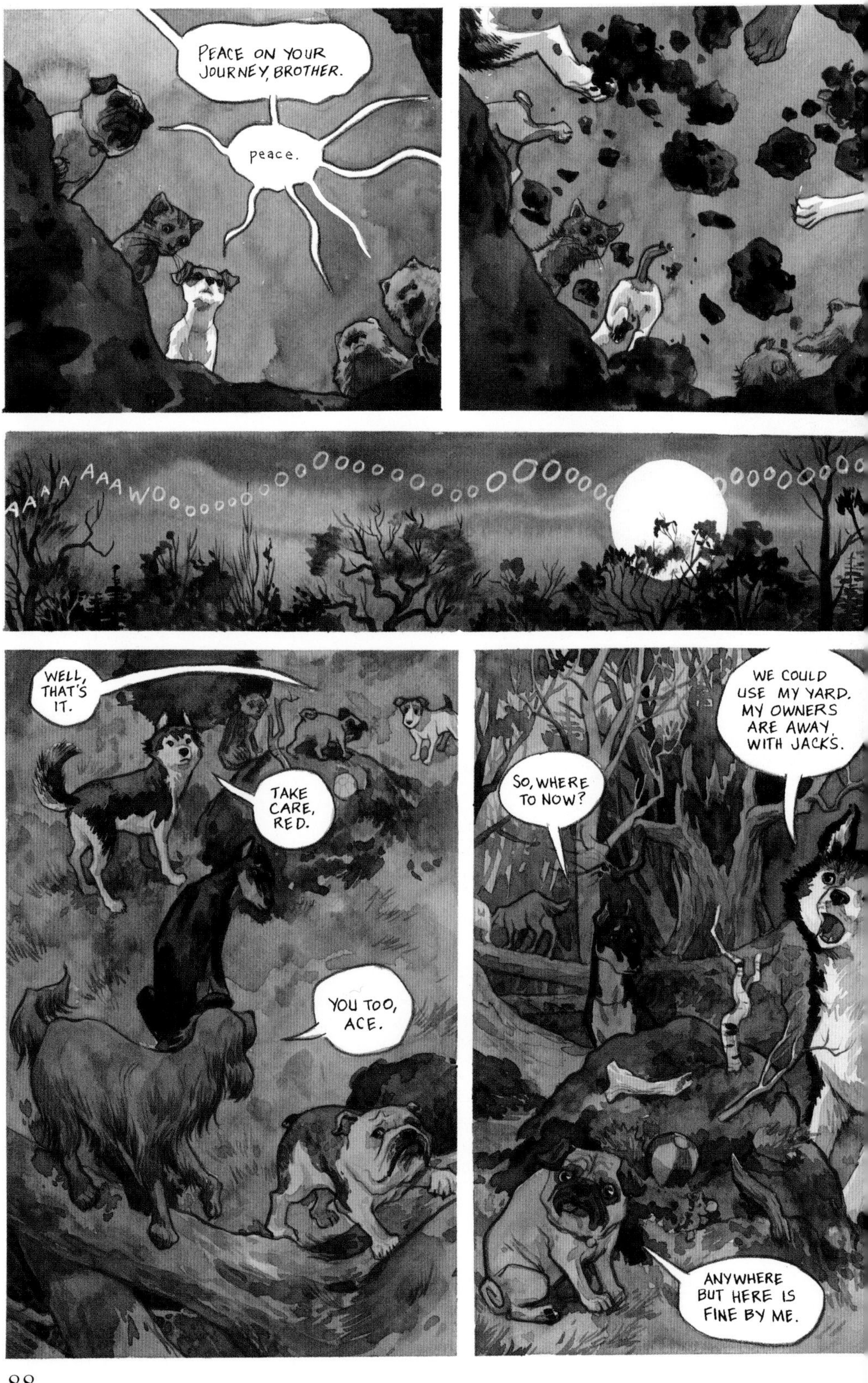
PEACE ON YOUR JOURNEY, BROTHER.
peace.
AAAAAAWOooooooooOooooooooOOOooooooOoooooo
WELL, THAT'S IT.
TAKE CARE, RED.
YOU TOO, ACE.
SO, WHERE TO NOW?
WE COULD USE MY YARD. MY OWNERS ARE AWAY WITH JACK'S.
ANYWHERE BUT HERE IS FINE BY ME.

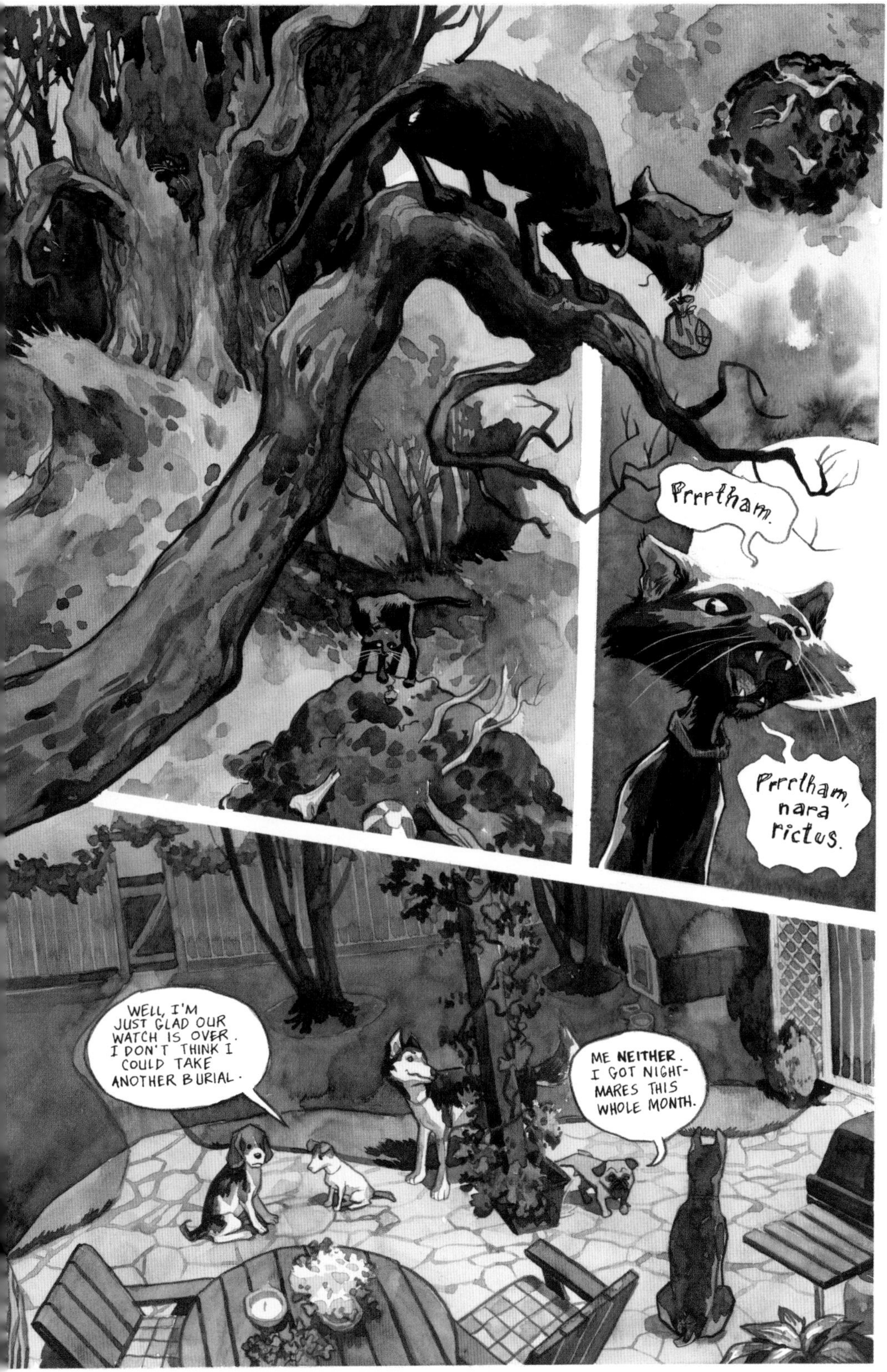
Prrrtham.
Prrrtham, nara rictus.
WELL, I'M JUST GLAD OUR WATCH IS OVER. I DON'T THINK I COULD TAKE ANOTHER BURIAL.
ME NEITHER. I GOT NIGHT-MARES THIS WHOLE MONTH.

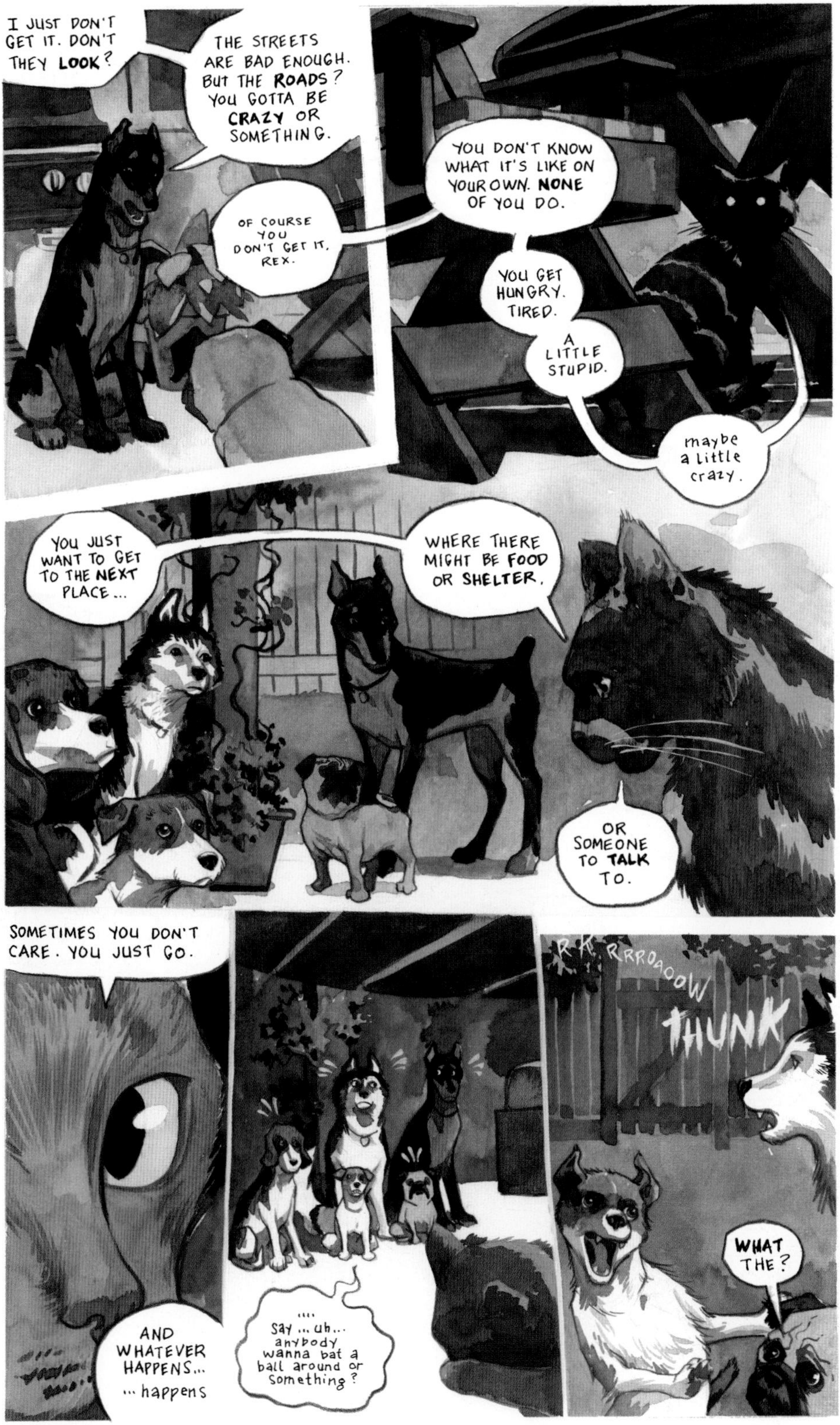

I JUST DON'T GET IT. DON'T THEY **LOOK**?
THE STREETS ARE BAD ENOUGH. BUT THE **ROADS**? YOU GOTTA BE **CRAZY** OR SOMETHING.
OF COURSE YOU DON'T GET IT, REX.
YOU DON'T KNOW WHAT IT'S LIKE ON YOUR OWN. **NONE** OF YOU DO.
YOU GET HUNGRY. TIRED.
A LITTLE STUPID.
maybe a little crazy.
YOU JUST WANT TO GET TO THE **NEXT** PLACE...
WHERE THERE MIGHT BE **FOOD** OR **SHELTER**.
OR SOMEONE TO **TALK** TO.
SOMETIMES YOU DON'T CARE. YOU JUST GO.
AND WHATEVER HAPPENS...
...happens
....
say ... uh... anybody wanna bat a ball around or something?
RRRRROAOOOW
THUNK
WHAT THE?

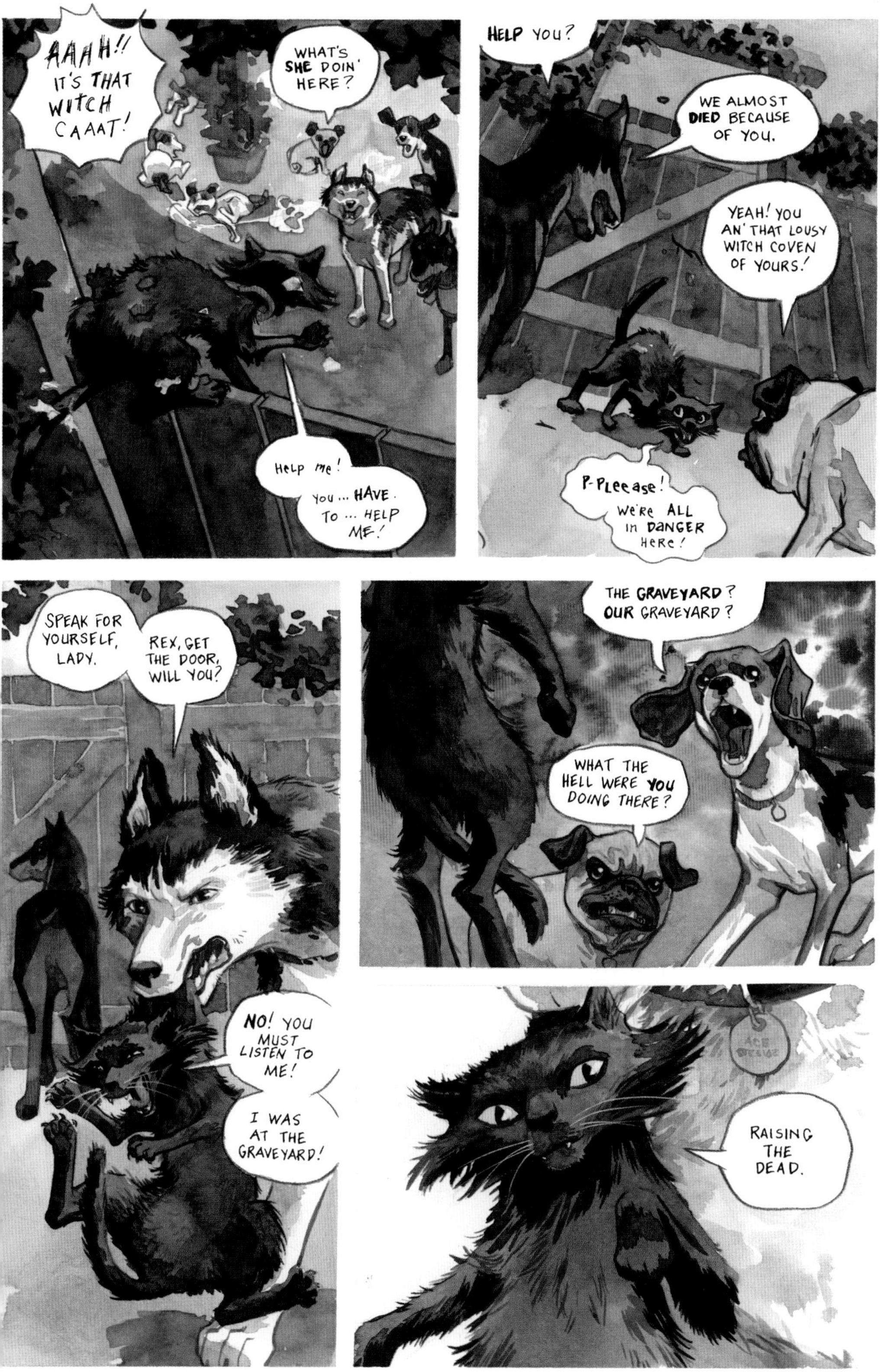
AAAH!! IT'S THAT WITCH CAAAT!
WHAT'S SHE DOIN' HERE?
Help me! You... HAVE. To... HELP ME!
HELP YOU?
WE ALMOST DIED BECAUSE OF YOU.
YEAH! YOU AN' THAT LOUSY WITCH COVEN OF YOURS!
P-Pleease! We're ALL in DANGER here!
SPEAK FOR YOURSELF, LADY.
REX, GET THE DOOR, WILL YOU?
NO! YOU MUST LISTEN TO ME!
I WAS AT THE GRAVEYARD!
THE GRAVEYARD? OUR GRAVEYARD?
WHAT THE HELL WERE YOU DOING THERE?
RAISING THE DEAD.

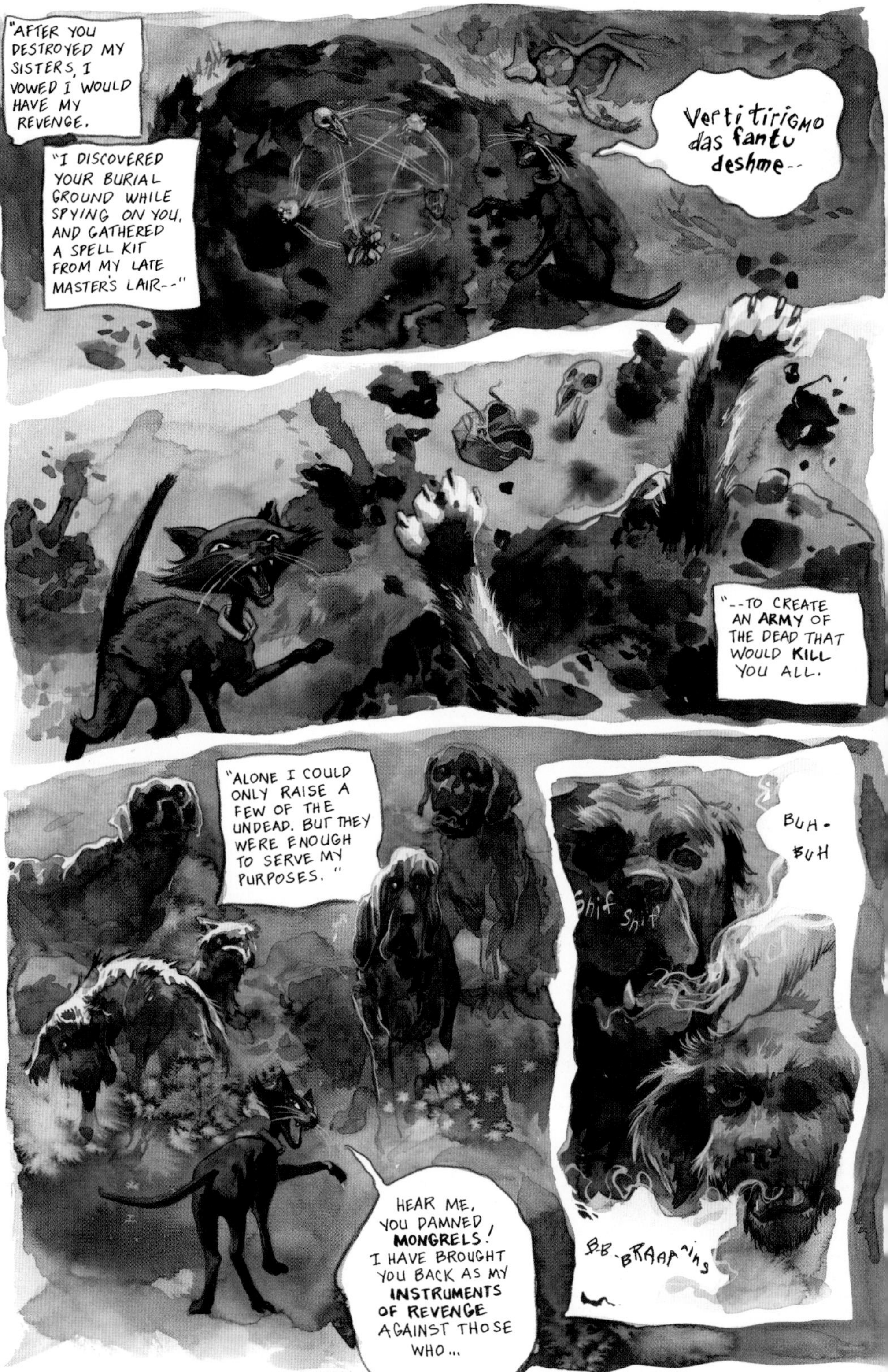
"AFTER YOU DESTROYED MY SISTERS, I VOWED I WOULD HAVE MY REVENGE.
"I DISCOVERED YOUR BURIAL GROUND WHILE SPYING ON YOU, AND GATHERED A SPELL KIT FROM MY LATE MASTER'S LAIR--"
Verti tirigmo das fantu deshme--
"--TO CREATE AN **ARMY** OF THE DEAD THAT WOULD **KILL** YOU ALL.
"ALONE I COULD ONLY RAISE A FEW OF THE UNDEAD. BUT THEY WERE ENOUGH TO SERVE MY PURPOSES."
HEAR ME, YOU DAMNED **MONGRELS**! I HAVE BROUGHT YOU BACK AS MY **INSTRUMENTS OF REVENGE** AGAINST THOSE WHO...
BUH-BUH
Shif Shif
B-B-BRAAAains

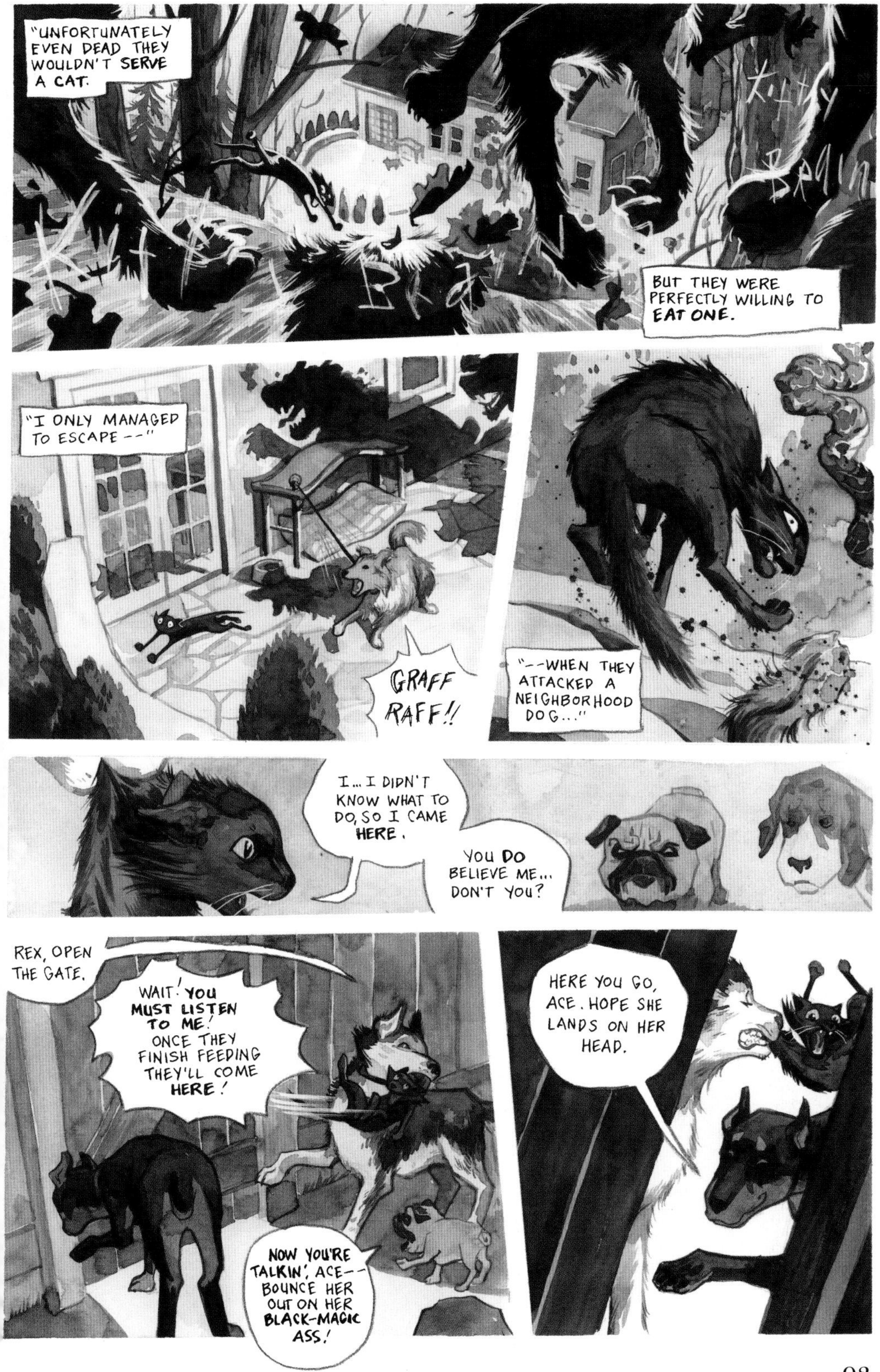
"UNFORTUNATELY EVEN DEAD THEY WOULDN'T SERVE A CAT.
BUT THEY WERE PERFECTLY WILLING TO EAT ONE.
"I ONLY MANAGED TO ESCAPE --"
GRAFF RAFF!!
"--WHEN THEY ATTACKED A NEIGHBORHOOD DOG..."
I... I DIDN'T KNOW WHAT TO DO, SO I CAME HERE.
YOU DO BELIEVE ME... DON'T YOU?
REX, OPEN THE GATE.
WAIT! YOU MUST LISTEN TO ME! ONCE THEY FINISH FEEDING THEY'LL COME HERE!
NOW YOU'RE TALKIN', ACE-- BOUNCE HER OUT ON HER BLACK-MAGIC ASS!
HERE YOU GO, ACE. HOPE SHE LANDS ON HER HEAD.

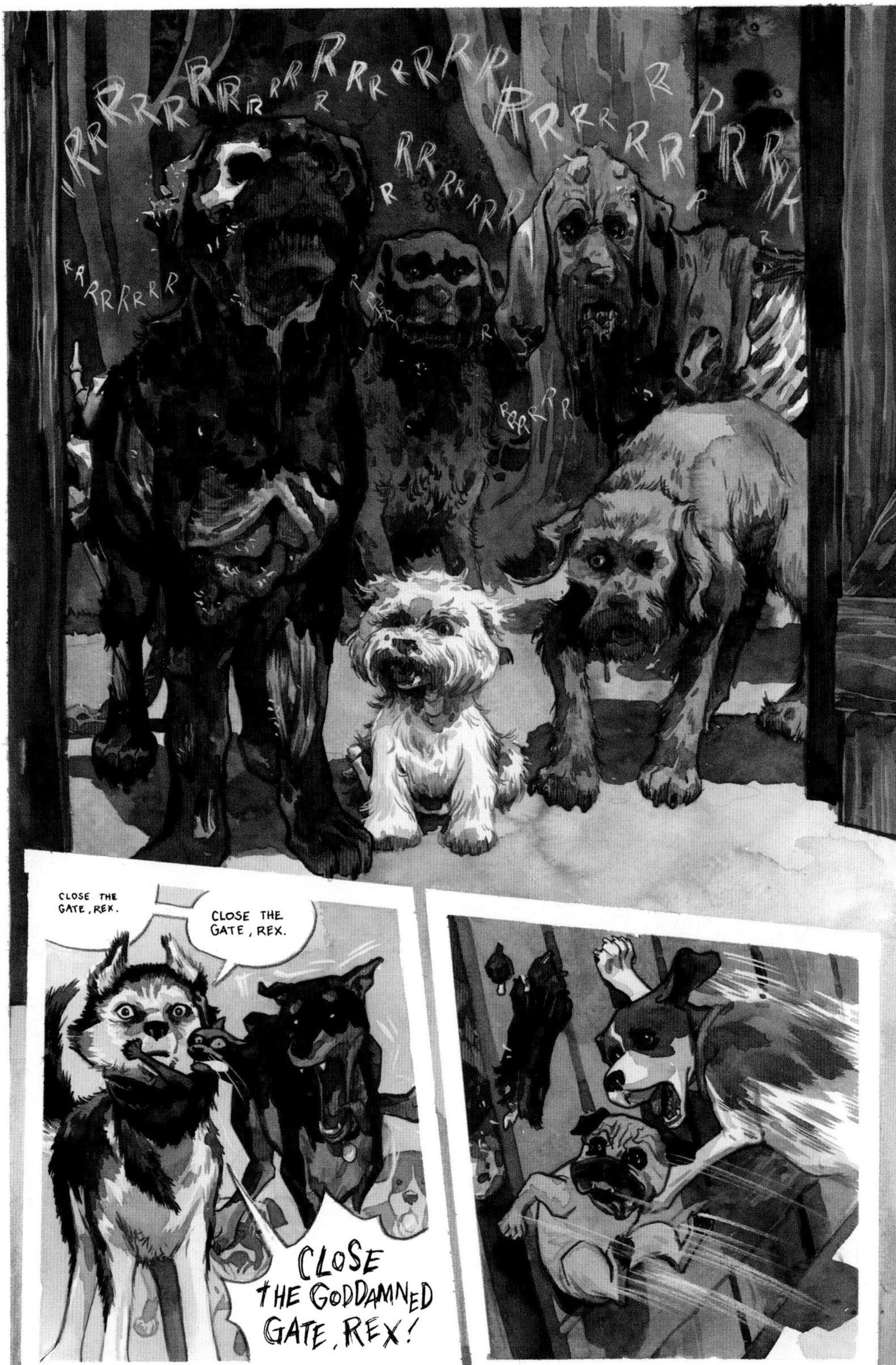
CLOSE THE GATE, REX.
CLOSE THE GATE, REX.
CLOSE THE GODDAMNED GATE, REX!

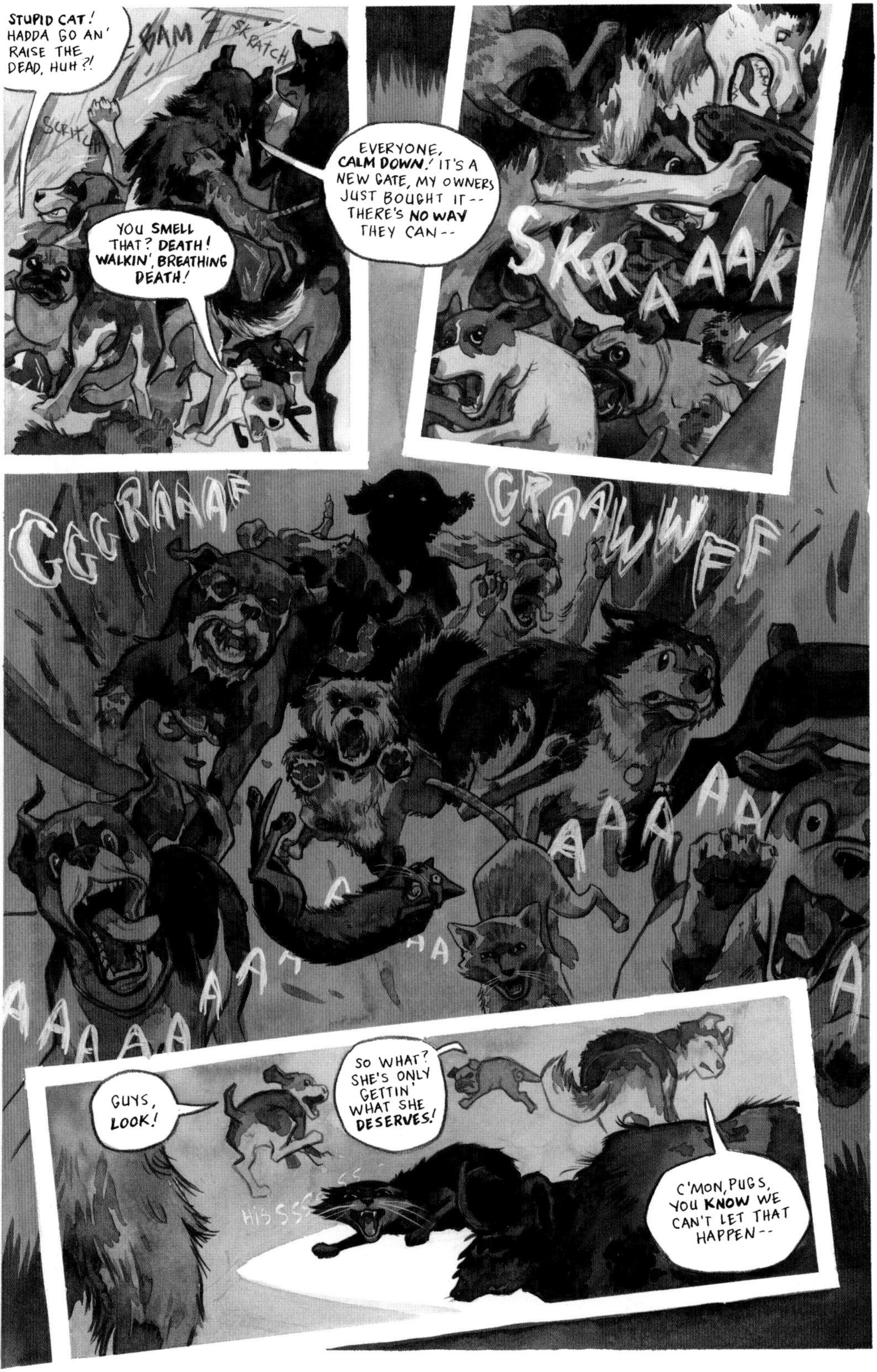
STUPID CAT! HADDA GO AN' RAISE THE DEAD, HUH?!
BAM
SKRATCH
SKRITCH
YOU SMELL THAT? DEATH! WALKIN', BREATHING DEATH!
EVERYONE, CALM DOWN! IT'S A NEW GATE, MY OWNERS JUST BOUGHT IT -- THERE'S NO WAY THEY CAN--
SKRAAAK
GGGRAAAF
GRAAWWFF
GUYS, LOOK!
SO WHAT? SHE'S ONLY GETTIN' WHAT SHE DESERVES!
HISSSS
C'MON, PUGS, YOU KNOW WE CAN'T LET THAT HAPPEN--

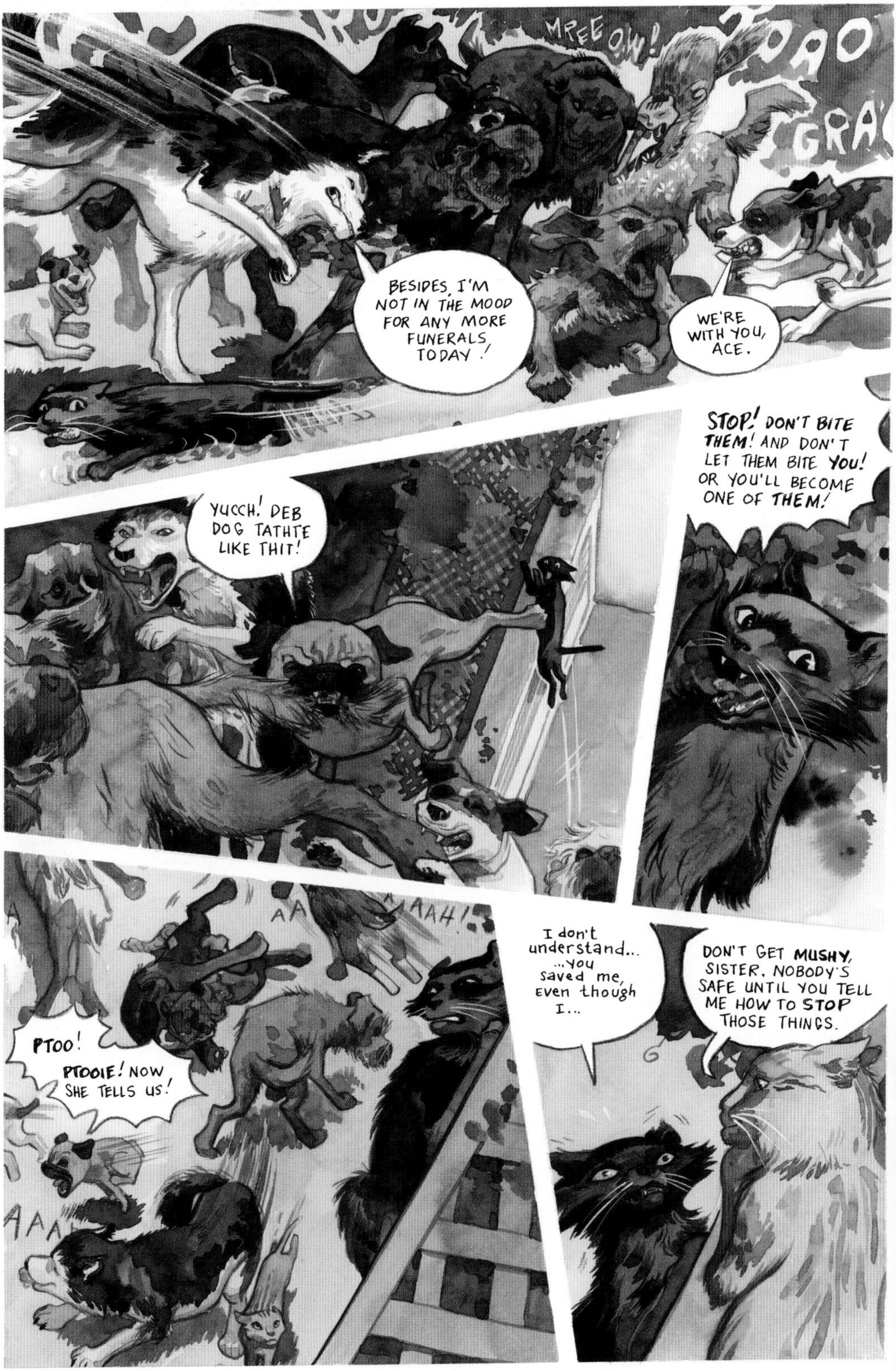
MREEOW!
BESIDES, I'M NOT IN THE MOOD FOR ANY MORE FUNERALS TODAY.
WE'RE WITH YOU, ACE.
GRA
STOP! DON'T BITE THEM! AND DON'T LET THEM BITE YOU! OR YOU'LL BECOME ONE OF THEM!
YUCCH! DEB DOG TATHTE LIKE THIT!
AAAH!
PTOO! PTOOIE! NOW SHE TELLS US!
I don't understand... ...you saved me, even though I...
DON'T GET MUSHY, SISTER. NOBODY'S SAFE UNTIL YOU TELL ME HOW TO STOP THOSE THINGS.

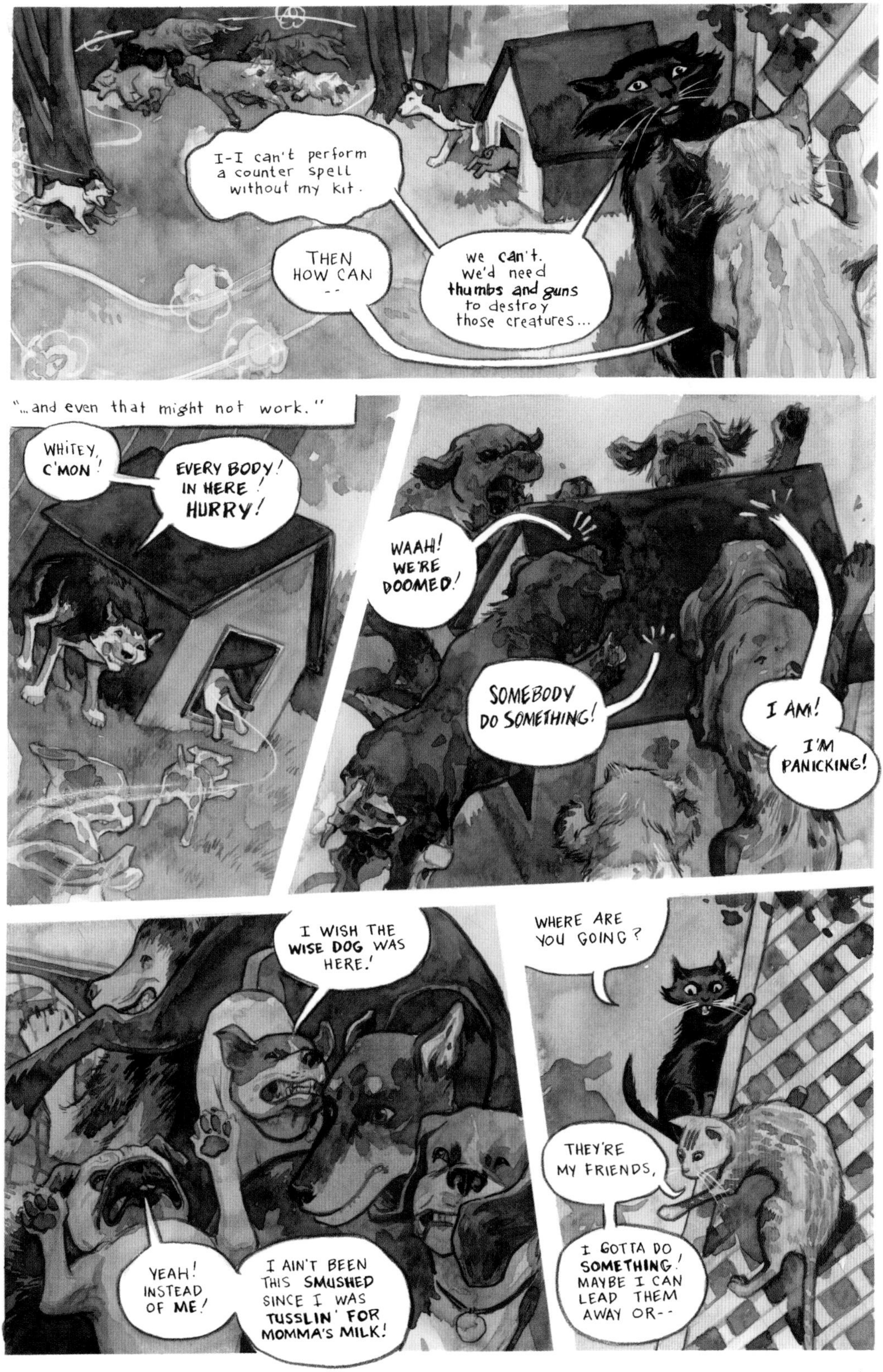
I-I can't perform a counter spell without my kit.
THEN HOW CAN --
we can't. we'd need thumbs and guns to destroy those creatures...
"...and even that might not work."
WHITEY, C'MON!
EVERY BODY! IN HERE! HURRY!
WAAH! WE'RE DOOMED!
SOMEBODY DO SOMETHING!
I AM!
I'M PANICKING!
I WISH THE WISE DOG WAS HERE!
YEAH! INSTEAD OF ME!
I AIN'T BEEN THIS SMUSHED SINCE I WAS TUSSLIN' FOR MOMMA'S MILK!
WHERE ARE YOU GOING?
THEY'RE MY FRIENDS,
I GOTTA DO SOMETHING! MAYBE I CAN LEAD THEM AWAY OR--

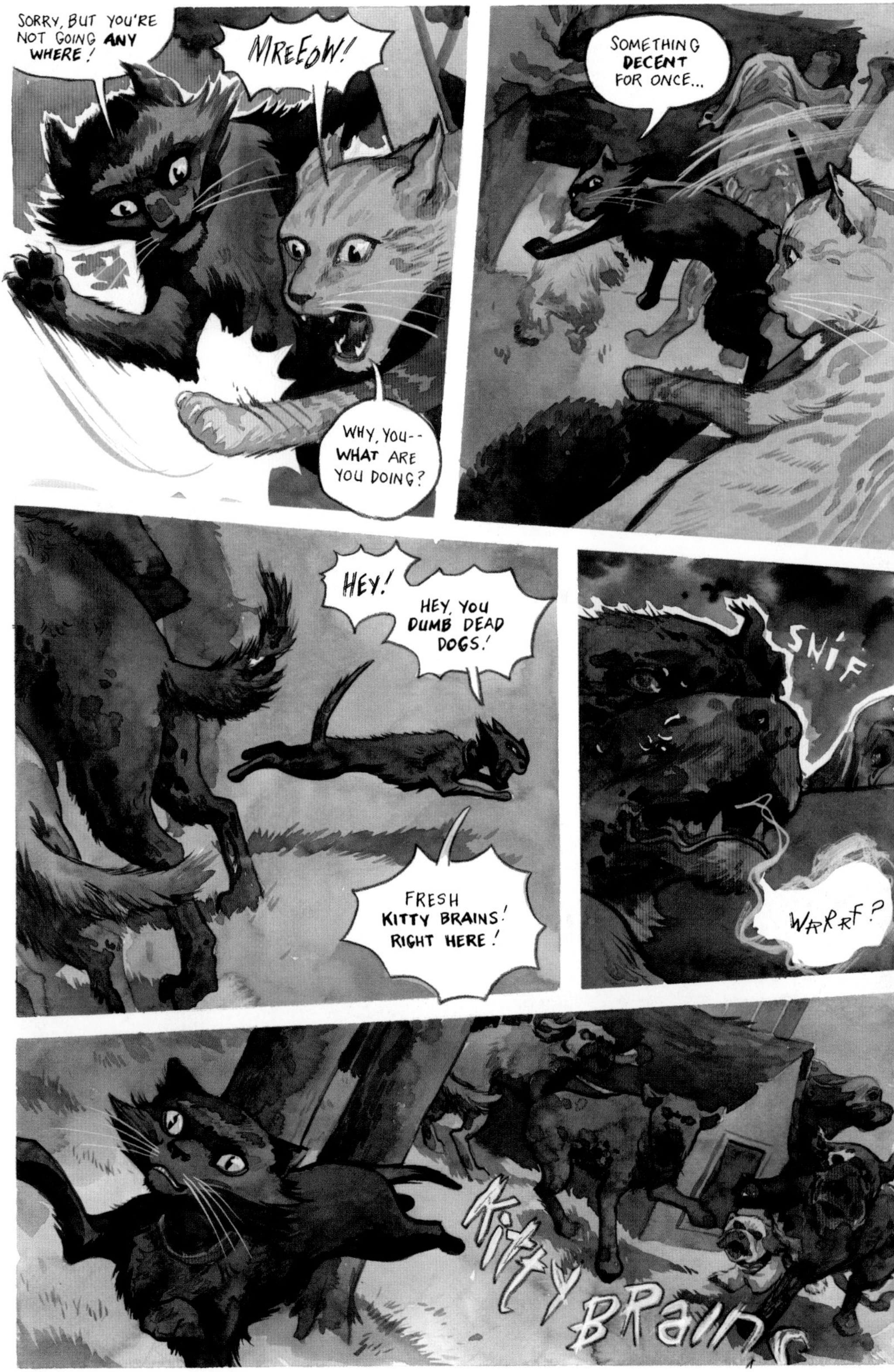
SORRY, BUT YOU'RE NOT GOING ANY WHERE!
MREEOW!
WHY, YOU-- WHAT ARE YOU DOING?
SOMETHING DECENT FOR ONCE...
HEY!
HEY, YOU DUMB DEAD DOGS!
FRESH KITTY BRAINS! RIGHT HERE!
SNIF
WARRF?
Kitty Brains

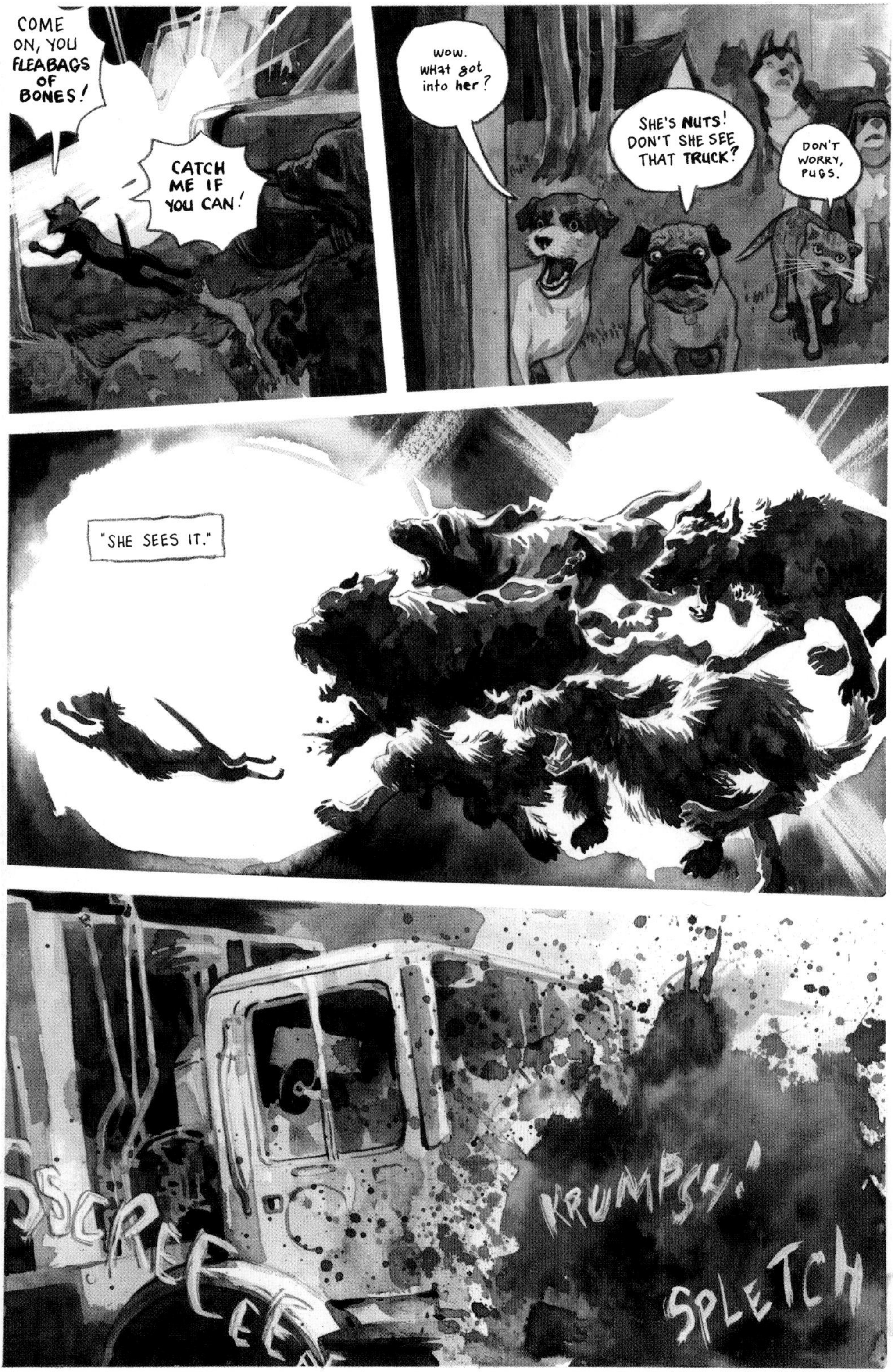
COME ON, YOU FLEABAGS OF BONES!
CATCH ME IF YOU CAN!
WOW. WHAT GOT INTO HER?
SHE'S NUTS! DON'T SHE SEE THAT TRUCK?
DON'T WORRY, PUGS.
"SHE SEES IT."
SSCREEEEE
KRUMPSH!
SPLETCH

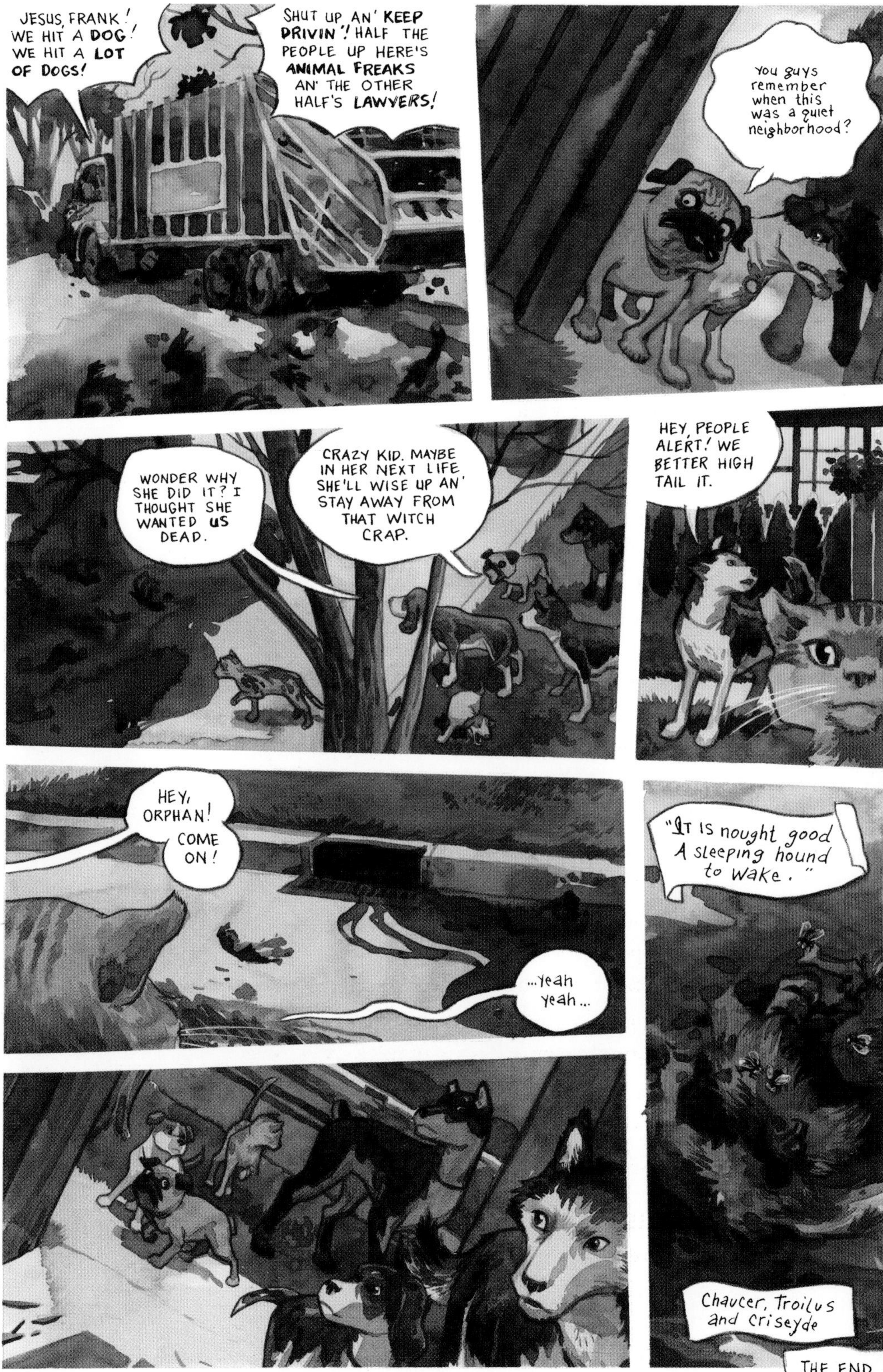
JESUS, FRANK! WE HIT A DOG! WE HIT A LOT OF DOGS!
SHUT UP AN' KEEP DRIVIN'! HALF THE PEOPLE UP HERE'S ANIMAL FREAKS AN' THE OTHER HALF'S LAWYERS!
You guys remember when this was a quiet neighborhood?
WONDER WHY SHE DID IT? I THOUGHT SHE WANTED US DEAD.
CRAZY KID. MAYBE IN HER NEXT LIFE SHE'LL WISE UP AN' STAY AWAY FROM THAT WITCH CRAP.
HEY, PEOPLE ALERT! WE BETTER HIGH TAIL IT.
HEY, ORPHAN!
COME ON!
...yeah yeah...
"It is nought good A sleeping hound to wake."
Chaucer, Troilus and Criseyde
THE END

Our Artists and Writers

KELLEY JONES has been writing and drawing comics with the blood of his victims for two hundred years. The earliest Kelley Jones sighting was in the Ozark Mountains in 1806, when settlers reported "a wild and voracious man-beast, chewing the hindquarters off the freshly killed corpse of a large bear." The horror mounted with each subsequent appearance, as did the carnage — with unsettling, horrific illustrations left at the scene of every killing. With the dawn of the 20th century, modern man made an attempt to understand Kelley Jones, the Wendigo, Sasquatch, and the other monstrous creatures of North America. Further evidence of the fabled Kelley Jones can be found in the collected editions of *The Hammer* by Dark Horse Comics and various *Batman* and *Deadman* releases from DC.

MIKE MIGNOLA is among the most highly regarded writer/artists of horror comics today, which is a unique distinction for someone whose work can be as humorous as it is frightening. He has also worked in film and television, with Francis Ford Coppola on *Bram Stoker's Dracula*, and as a production designer on *Disney's Atlantis: The Lost Empire*. He was also Visual Consultant to Guillermo del Toro on *Blade 2* and the *Hellboy* feature film. Mignola lives in New York City.

GARY GIANNI graduated from The Chicago Academy of Fine Arts in 1976. His artwork has appeared in the *Chicago Tribune*, numerous magazines, children's books, and paperbacks. Gianni debuted in the comics field in 1990 and has since been recognized with the Eisner Award for Best Short Story. He is perhaps best known for his ink drawing and oil paintings for a number of book collections including *The Savage Tales of Solomon Kane*, which is now available in an edition from Del Ray. Gianni also draws Hal Foster's classic comic strip *Prince Valiant* appearing in over 300 newspapers nationally.

Born in Texas in 1906, **ROBERT E. HOWARD** once wrote, "I was first to light a torch of literature in this part of the country, however small, frail and easily extinguished that flame may be." Although his legendary creations, Conan, Kull, Bran Mak Morn, and Solomon Kane changed the face of fantasy fiction forever, Howard felt that, "... if I ever do write anything of lasting merit it will be fiction laid in the early West." It was this interest that helped shape "Old Garfield's Heart" (1933), and much of Howard's later fiction.

TODD HERMAN was raised on a steady diet of *Noddy Adventures*, Adam West's *Batman*, and any Rankin/Bass productions he could get his hands on. He spent most of his early adult life working as a storyboard artist and designer in television stop-action animation. After uncredited assists to artists who shall now themselves remain nameless, this is his first published work in ten years.

DAVID CROUSE lives in Massachusetts with his wife, the poet Melina Draper. He has won numerous awards, including the prestigious Flannery O'Connor Award for Short Fiction. *Copy Cats*, a collection of his fiction, is available from The University of Georgia Press. This is his first work for Dark Horse.

ROGER LANGRIDGE has worked for Marvel, DC, 2000AD, Fantagraphics, and many others over the last fiteen years. His self-published comic, *Fred the Clown*, has been nominated for two Eisner Awards and one Ignatz Award, and was recently collected as a paperback by Fantagraphics Books.

BOB FINGERMAN created the critically acclaimed graphic novel, *Beg the Question* (paperback due fall 2005). He's also written several prose novels, some of which might actually see print someday. In the meantime, keep your eyes peeled for *You Deserved It*, a gruesome, full-color humor collection from Dark Horse Books, also fall 2005. For old, never-updated info, visit www.bobfingerman.com.

ERIC POWELL is a hermit who lives in the Tennessee woods with his wife Robin and his two sons Gage and Cade. After realizing he could make a living without ever having to leave his house, he opted for the comic-book industry rather than a lucrative career in the janitorial arts. He is best known for his critically acclaimed black comedy *The Goon*, published bi-monthly from Dark Horse.

PAT McEOWN has a long history with Dark Horse, including *Grendel: Warchild*, *ZombieWorld*, and *Scatterbrain*. Recently he has worked as a storyboard artist for animated series like *Batman Beyond* and *X-Men Evolution*. "The Queen of Darkness" marks his return to comics as both writer and artist. He's glad to be back.

GUY DAVIS is the Michigan-based artist of various comics including: *Sandman Mystery Theatre, The Nevermen, Fantastic Four: Unstable Molecules, Deadline,*

The Zombies that Ate the World, The Marquis, and *B.P.R.D.* For more info visit www.guydavisartworks.com.

JAMIE S. RICH is the author of the novel *Cut My Hair* and the novella *I Was Someone Dead*, published by Oni Press — where he was editor-in-chief for six years — and the forthcoming graphic novel *12 Reasons Why I Love Her*, illustrated by Christine Norrie. He lives in Portland, Oregon, with a cat who promises to eat him after he dies, so he won't become one of the walking dead.

PAUL LEE is a painter and freelance illustrator, the creator of the comics series *Lurid*, and co-creator of *The Devil's Footprints*. He works closely with Brian Horton, most notably on Dark Horse's *Buffy the Vampire Slayer* covers. He recommends fiber to promote regularity, and lives with his wife and son in Southern California.

BRIAN HORTON has been an illustrator and video-game artist for ten years. He's worked for interactive companies including Disney, Dreamworks, and Electronic Arts. Most recently he has been at The Collective, art directing *Indiana Jones and the Emperor's Tomb*. Brian moonlights in comics with his partners in crime, Scott Allie and Paul Lee, on *Buffy*, *Star Wars*, and *The Devil's Footprints*. He shares his life with his wife Susan and son Victor in Aliso Viejo, California.

SCOTT ALLIE writes and edits comics and stories for Dark Horse Comics and other publishers, including *The Devil's Footprints* with Brian Horton, Paul Lee, and Dave Stewart.

JILL THOMPSON is a renowned illustrator and the creator of the award-winning series *Scary Godmother*, which aired an animated special on the Cartoon Network in 2004. Her work has been seen in books ranging from *Classics Illustrated* and *Wonder Woman* to *Sandman*. Jill is a longtime resident of Chicago, where she lives with her husband, comic-book writer Brian Azzarello.

EVAN DORKIN is the award-winning creator of *Milk and Cheese* and *Dork* from Slave Labor Graphics, and various Marvel, Dark Horse, and DC comics. His work has appeared in *Esquire, Spin, The Onion,* and *Mad*. With Sarah Dyer, he's written for *Space Ghost Coast to Coast, Superman,* and *Batman Beyond,* and was creator of *Welcome to Eltingville,* his very own failed pilot on the Cartoon Network. He is currently late on a variety of animation, comics, and magazine deadlines.

ALSO FROM DARK HORSE COMICS!

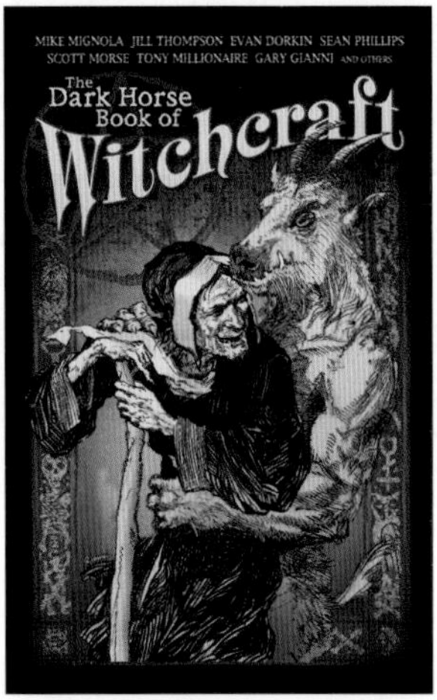
MIKE MIGNOLA JILL THOMPSON EVAN DORKIN SEAN PHILLIPS
SCOTT MORSE TONY MILLIONAIRE GARY GIANNI AND OTHERS
The Dark Horse Book of Witchcraft

THE DARK HORSE BOOK OF WITCHCRAFT

Featuring Mike Mignola, Tony Millionaire, Scott Morse, Evan Dorkin, Jill Thompson, and others; Cover by Gary Gianni

Mike Mignola's Hellboy faces the nature of monstrosity, Jill Thompson (*Scary Godmother*) and Evan Dorkin (*Hectic Planet*) return to their spectral pet adventures, and Scott Morse (*Soulwind*) presents a tale of old Salem.

Hard cover, 96 pages, Full color
$14.95, ISBN: 1-56971-935-7

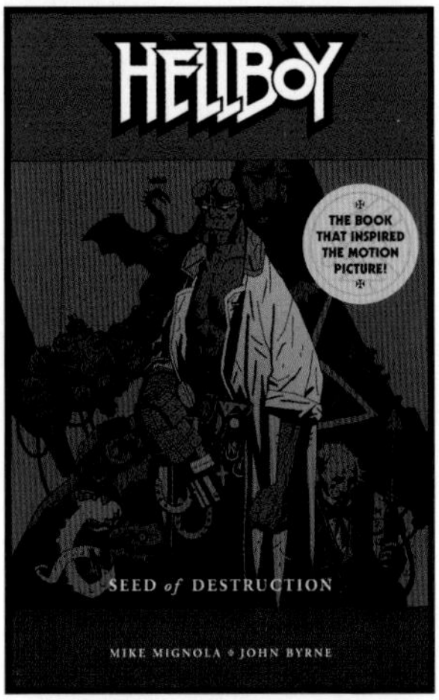
HELLBOY
THE BOOK THAT INSPIRED THE MOTION PICTURE!
SEED of DESTRUCTION
MIKE MIGNOLA • JOHN BYRNE

HELLBOY VOLUME 1: SEED OF DESTRUCTION

By Mike Mignola and John Byrne

Dark Horse presents new editions of the entire *Hellboy* line with new covers, beginning with *Seed of Destruction*. *Hellboy* is one of the most celebrated comics series in recent years. Sent to investigate a mystery with supernatural overtones, Hellboy discovers the secrets of his own origins, and his link to the Nazi occultists who promised Hitler a final solution in the form of a demonic avatar.

Soft cover, 128 pages, Full color
$17.95, ISBN: 1-59307-094-2

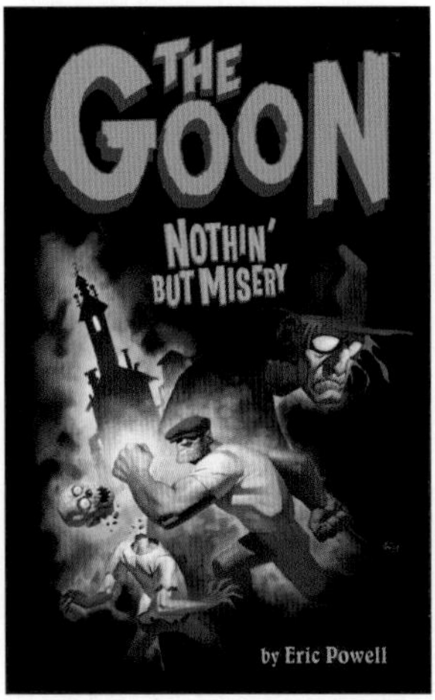
THE GOON
NOTHIN' BUT MISERY
by Eric Powell

THE GOON, VOLUME 1: NOTHIN' BUT MISERY

By Eric Powell

An insane priest is building an army of the undead, and only one man can put them in their place: the Goon. This volume collects *The Goon* issues 1-4 and *The Goon Color Special*, originally published by Albatross Exploding Funny Books; presented in full-color for the first time.

Wizard Magazine says, "Every comic should be this much fun to read!"

Soft cover, 136 pages, Full color
$15.95, ISBN: 1-56971-998-5

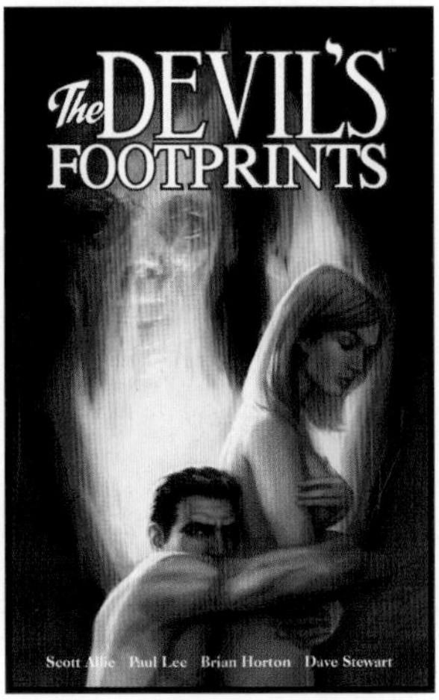
The DEVIL'S FOOTPRINTS
Scott Allie Paul Lee Brian Horton Dave Stewart

THE DEVIL'S FOOTPRINTS

By Scott Allie, Paul Lee, Brian Horton, and Dave Stewart

Brandon Waite investigates his dead father's study of witchcraft. But his desire to protect loved ones forces him to cover up his own tentative steps into the black arts, leading him to mix deception with demon conjuration, isolating himself in a terrible world where his soul hangs in the balance.

Soft Cover, 144 pages, Full color
$14.95, ISBN: 1-56971-933-0

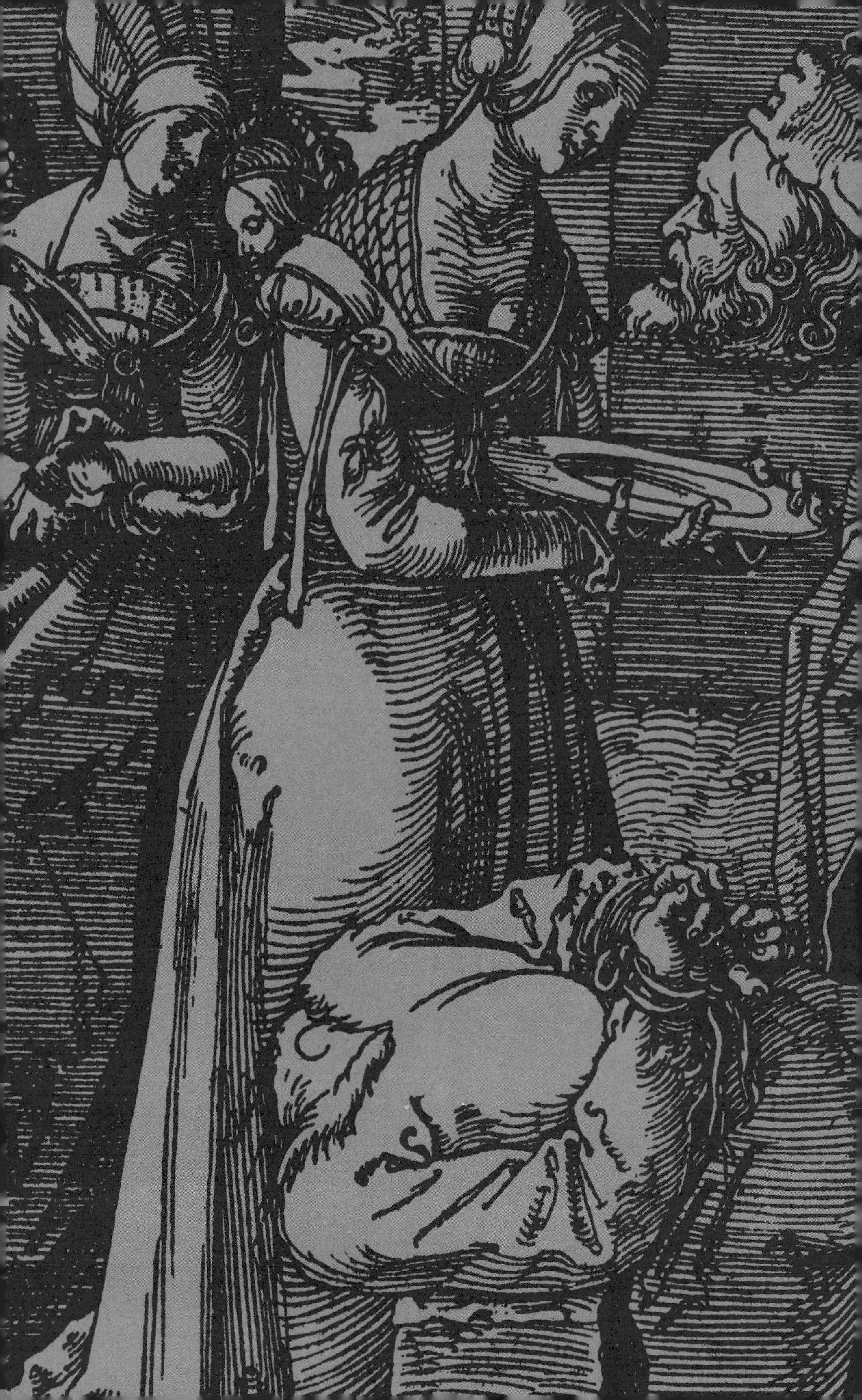